Minding the Body
Women and Literature in the Middle Ages, 800–1500
800–1500

TWAYNE'S WOMEN AND LITERATURE SERIES

Kinley E. Roby, General Editor

Minding the Body

Women and Literature in the Middle Ages, 800–1500

MONICA BRZEZINSKI POTKAY
AND
REGULA MEYER EVITT

Twayne Publishers
An Imprint of Simon & Schuster Macmillan
Prentice Hall International
London Mexico City New Delhi Singapore Sydney Toronto

Twayne Publishers
Macmillan Publishing Company
1633 Broadway
New York, New York 10019

LIBRARY OF CONGRESS CATALOGING-IN-PUBLICATION DATA

Potkay, Monica Brzezinski.
    Minding the body : women and literature in the Middle Ages,
800–1500 / Monica Brzezinski Potkay and Regula Meyer Evitt.
      p.   cm. — (Twayne's women and literature series)
    Includes bibliographical references and index.
    ISBN 0–8057–8981–2 (hardcover : alk. paper)
    1. English literature—Women authors—History and criticism.
2. English literature—Middle English, 1100–1500—History and
criticism. 3. English literature—Old English, ca. 450–1100—
History and criticism. 4. Literature, Medieval—Women authors—
History and criticism. 5. Women—Great Britain—History—Middle
Ages, 500–1500. 6. Women and literature—Great Britain—History.
7. Civilization, Medieval, in literature. 8. Body, Human, in
literature. 9. Women in literature.   I. Evitt, Regula Meyer.
II. Title.   III. Series.
PR113.P68   1997   96–36468
820.9'9287'0902—dc20   CIP

10 9 8 7 6 5 4 3 2 1

PRINTED IN THE UNITED STATES OF AMERICA

Contents

CONTENTS

General Editor's Note

Twayne's Women and Literature Series seeks to provide a critical history of British and American women writers from the Anglo-Saxon age to the modern era, to present women as the subject as well as the creators of literature, and to say something about how these dual roles have helped to shape our societies. It is often a record of struggle by women to write, to be published, and to find a sympathetic audience for their work. Each of the volumes examines the cultural influences at work shaping women's roles during a particular period and the attendant consequences for them as women and writers. The series also presents a chronological account of women's efforts to find and develop their own voices in environments frequently hostile to their being heard at all.

Acknowledgments

The authors would like to thank Professor Kinley E. Roby, the series editor, for his engaged, thoughtful, and constructive comments on our work. Three editors at Twayne—Melissa Solomon, Pauline Sultana, and Margaret Dornfeld—showed infinite patience in shepherding this book along and were always encouraging and helpful.

Monica Brzezinski Potkay wrote the introduction; chapters 1, 2, 3, 4, and 7; and portions of the epilogue. She would like to thank the National Endowment for the Humanities and the College of William & Mary for summer grants toward the research and writing of this book. Shifting to the more personal first person, I thank Roberta Rosenberg, who first encouraged me to take the project on. Theresa Coletti and Hoyt N. Duggan provided support at an early stage, and the latter, who introduced me to many of the texts discussed here, may not always be able to detect the enormity of my debt to him because of the unlikely directions I have taken his influence. Carol McAllister alerted me to resources at Swem Library and beyond. Don Monson advised me on secondary literature on the troubadours and trobairitz, and graciously gave me a prepublication look at his article on the troubadour's lady. David Morrill provided technical expertise and comic relief, and Bonnie Chandler helped in innumerable ways. My undergraduate and graduate students at William & Mary, who generously shared their insights while humoring my obsessions with certain texts and themes, were the perfect collaborators as I worked out various ideas. My graduate assistants Andrew Moran and Tacye Clarke helped with bibliographic information; Michael Blum did yeoman's work in helping to compile the bibliography and chronology. I thank Re Evitt for her appreciable contributions to my chapters, for reading my manuscripts with a sharp eye, and for her patience with my personality quirks. Most of all and always, I thank my husband, Adam Potkay. He betters Abelard as he can and does "concentrate on thoughts of Scripture or philosophy and ... put up with the constant muddle which small children bring into the home." In doing so, he made possible in both intellectual and practical terms the writing of my portion of the text. It is for Adam.

Regula Meyer Evitt wrote chapters 5, 6, 8, and 9 and parts of the epilogue. I would like to thank San Francisco State University, especially Nancy McDermid, Dean of the College of Humanities, for Professional Research and Development Stipends during the summers of 1992 and 1993; these made the initial research for this book possible. I am grateful, as well, to the National Endowment for the Humanities for supporting my participation in R. Howard Bloch's 1992 Summer Seminar, "The Old French Fabliaux and the Medieval Sense of the Comic."

I have a long-standing debt of gratitude to V. A. Kolve, Arthur Kirsch, and Eleanor Prosser for reintroducing me to medieval and Renaissance drama in my early graduate years. Kalamazoo conversations with Theresa Coletti and Sylvia Tomasch, although brief, provided considerable intellectual energy for early versions of my drama chapter. Special thanks go to Howard Bloch and my colleagues in the NEH seminar, in particular to Jan Solberg, for our "scandalous" conversations about Corpus Christi as the religious subtext for fabliaux. Faye Walker encouraged me at the outset of this project and inspired me to reread Chaucer's *Legend of Good Women*. Hoyt Duggan helped me build the foundation for my study of medieval literature. From early on his honest, tough criticism inspired my curiosity about the kinds of voices medieval women have. Heartfelt thanks go to Monica Potkay for her keen critical responses to my chapters, her organization and discipline in directing this project, and her measureless patience, both personal and professional.

I received support from colleagues at San Francisco State in countless ways. Ellen Peel and Beverly Voloshin opened my eyes to a rich trove of contemporary feminist theory. Steve Arkin, Jo Keroes, Jonathan Middlebrook, and Eric Solomon, through their administrative wizardry and sound advice, helped me carve out precious hours for research and writing from a daunting teaching schedule. John Edwards encouraged me to make the classroom the wellspring for my chapters. Elise Earthman most profoundly shares my conviction that conversations with students bring life to literature; she has proven my surest compass in exploring the Middle Ages with them.

ACKNOWLEDGMENTS

My students at San Francisco State and Stanford, both undergraduate and graduate, brought this project to life for me with their imaginative, challenging, unassuming questions. They are the invisible soul of my contributions to this book. I learned from so many but have a special debt of gratitude to those who, as seminar students and as teaching assistants, have "visited" the Middle Ages with me most frequently. For their boundary-crossing perspectives, I especially want to thank and acknowledge: Lisa Ashe, Kate Breen, Judith Baccash, Monica Bosson, James Boyd, Jyllian Boyd, Donna Bussell, Mickie Christensen, Shelly Clift, Elena Cole, Phillip Crawford, Barbara Denham, Kim Freeman, Barbara Kramer, Hilton Obenzinger, Noreen O'Connor, Lisa Phillips, Karen Poremski, Julie Prebel, Tracey Sherard, Mary Sokolowski, Jan Stirm, and Ginny Troyer.

I could not have written my part of this book without the boundless love and support of my mom and dad, Marti and Hermann Meyer. Glenn and Niklaus, husband and son, hearts of my heart, together over the last two years have taught me the considerable difference between understanding the world from without and from within. For my family.

Mary "minds the body"—integrates intellectual with physical activity—when, preparing to deliver Jesus, she reads Scripture.
East German or Bohemian missal, early fifteenth century. Bayerische Staatsbibliothek, Munich. MS Clm 14.045, fol. 41v.

Introduction

Literature and the Lives of Medieval Women

Understanding the role of medieval women within their society is a daunting task. The study of women in almost every age is confounded by a paucity of source material, since the historical record is biased toward the public and against the private sphere to which the majority of women have been relegated. The problem of limited sources is exacerbated for earlier times; manuscript culture before the mid-fifteenth-century invention of the printing press produced comparatively few documents, and many of these have not survived. The situation is particularly challenging if one wants to understand medieval women on their own terms, since texts by them are uncommon.[1] Most medieval women, like their male counterparts, were illiterate. Although among some segments of the population female literacy exceeded male, medieval convention did not consider reading and writing to go hand in hand; authorship usually was restricted to those who held social authority, particularly the university-trained male clergy. Women, furthermore, except for some nuns, were excluded from learning Latin, the lingua franca of intellectual life whose prestige conferred the greatest chance of textual preservation. The very great majority of extant texts, Latin or vernacular, literary or not, are thus male authored.[2]

Hoping to supplement the scanty documentary record, those who study medieval women have turned to literature. For the early Middle Ages, social historian David Herlihy notes, the only sources available that offer a record of women's lives are literary ones.[3] Literary texts can indeed offer a rich source of detail about medieval day-to-day reality. For example, the French poem *La Contenance des Fames*, one of a genre explicitly defining female nature, provides information about material culture by listing garments typically worn by women: mantle, tunic and overtunic, belt, neck-concealing wimple, and ornamental garland.[4] Yet as Herlihy warns, and as this introduction will detail, fictive texts need to

1

be interpreted judiciously to separate fact from fiction (xii–xiv). The veracity of many statements in *La Contenance des Fames* can be questioned, since they may have been invented to support the poem's antifeminist message: that women's mutability makes them untrustworthy. The sumptuousness of the feminine clothes described here, for example, and the number of ornaments are probably not typical but calculated for effect, since the poem adduces an extensive wardrobe as evidence of instability: A woman always wants new clothes, is forever changing the ones she has, and when fully dressed would rather be naked. Nor need the narrator's point of view be accepted as speaking for the whole Middle Ages; medievals might not necessarily view women's clothing as a sign of mutability but of social status. Indeed, this description may satirize not just female but male excesses in clothing, being inspired by sumptuary statutes designed to regulate the dress of both sexes. Furthermore, the poem's depiction of a woman's striptease in her front doorway aims to objectify her by providing a voyeuristic thrill for a male reader. Although the poem's description of women's clothing may be realistic, its definition of women's nature is more ideological than truthful.

Surprisingly, only within the last 50 years have most scholars been suspicious about the verisimilitude of medieval texts. In the nineteenth century and the first half of the twentieth, when medieval studies was established as an academic discipline, scholars regularly assumed that medieval texts mirrored their social milieu. These works, they believed, offered a simple view of contemporary life because their authors were simple—in every negative sense of that term. These critics accepted the claims of Renaissance humanists who, boasting they superseded their ancestors, invented an ignorant Middle Ages as a foil for their own brilliance. The humanists taught that the near millennium from the fall of Rome to their own generation comprised the uncivilized Dark Ages. Renaissance men were not the first to exaggerate the foibles of the past nor to gloss over their own debt to it; but they were the first to use the term "Middle Ages" and to use it as a synonym for barbarity.[5]

The humanists' self-estimate as inaugurators of cultural rebirth was accepted relatively uncritically for centuries, and their claim of breaking with the past was elaborated in the nineteenth. Jacob Burckhardt's magisterial *The Civilization of the Renaissance in Italy* (1867) codified the distinction between medieval ignorance and Renaissance knowledge when it said that the Middle Ages "lay dreaming or half awake beneath a common veil ... woven of faith, illusion, and childish prepossession."[6] More than one hundred years later, the fifth edition of the *Norton Anthology of British Literature* (replaced in 1993 by a sixth edition with entirely new introductions) taught that medieval people took "tremendous pleasure ... in all those aspects of life that children especially love," even while suffering under "the oppressive conventionality of [religious] doctrine."[7] In the Burckhardtian view, medieval people are at best playfully child-like, at worst childishly stupid, and nearly always trapped by superstition.

Viewed from the present, when historians habitually note the continuities linking the classical, medieval, and Renaissance eras as well as the breaks between them, the Burckhardtian view verges on self-parody. Yet the notion of a willfully backward Middle Ages was not challenged by professional medievalists until the late 1920s, and even then the challenge could not completely defeat the earlier theory's considerable influence.[8] Among literary critics who accepted a simple view of the Middle Ages were those who thought courtly love, as depicted in romances or troubadour lyrics, copied actual practice—that real-life lovers abased themselves before other men's wives, indulging the women's slightest, most arbitrary whims. John J. Parry, for example, introduced his 1941 translation of Andreas Capellanus's *De Amore*, a tongue-in-cheek manual depicting men's ill-fated attempts to court women, by asserting that "From [Andreas's] work we get a vivid picture of life in a medieval court like that of Troyes or Poitiers."[9] The 1960s saw a move to disprove the historicity of courtly love—John F. Benton, for example, found no evidence of courtly love at Champagne (the supposed locale of Andreas's lovers) but rather that the Middle Ages discouraged adulterous love with strict penalties, even death.[10] But Parry's statement remains in print (his is the most easily available English translation of Andreas) and continues to influence readers unexposed to other views.

Some scholars may be more sophisticated than Parry but still wrongly interpret medieval texts as mirroring history. Joan Kelly-Gadol, for example, a respected historian of the Renaissance, in 1977 noted the problematic task of reconstructing reality from literary sources yet assumed a historical basis for courtly fiction's powerful women. She contrasted the reverence accorded the feudal lady with the restraints placed on women's legal rights in the Renaissance and concluded that the modern age saw a diminishment of female self-determinacy and social power.[11] Kelly-Gadol certainly erred when she presumed that courtly texts' deference to female political authority and sexual desire necessarily carried over into the social realm. Her error, however, does not obviate her major conclusions, based on an examination of Renaissance historical and literary documents. Her arguments that the passage from medieval to Renaissance cannot be seen as purely progressive and that women's experiences do not always parallel men's articulate important caveats.

Courtly texts are not the only ones to which a simple realism or even naturalism has been misattributed. Chaucer's *Canterbury Tales*, its pilgrims drawn from all walks of life, is conventionally and justly praised as a window onto the mundanities of the fourteenth century. The text's narrator certainly invites such praise when he claims to observe objectively the social scene around him, to record the speech of his fellow pilgrims word for word.[12] But Chaucer's claim to veracity is partly ironic; it undercuts itself by naming the gospels and Plato as literary models, since these allusions suggest that Chaucer's book has a moral function and a platonic view of reality. Even the most experienced reader, however, can forget that *The Canterbury Tales* does not objectively depict Chaucer's contemporary surroundings and be trapped into accepting his fictive world as real.

The temptation is especially strong to treat Chaucer's Wife of Bath as if she were a real woman. Certainly the Wife is a vivid figure, with her red stockings, gap-teeth, and five husbands, and her Prologue compels admiration for her energetic refutation of antifeminist authorities. The old *Norton Anthology* introduces the Wife's tale with such admiration, along with appreciation for her realism. Five times the brief note praises her for being "true to life," bearing a relation to "reality itself." This tribute is not to Chaucer for creating a memorable character but to the Wife for inventing herself: She "becomes alive—wonderfully alive" (*Norton* 5th ed., 133–34n). The Wife of Bath typically excites this rare degree of suspended disbelief; many readers accept her as real. The very qualities modern readers admire in her, however, provide evidence that she originates in textuality, not reality. *The Norton Anthology*, along with its enthusiasm for the Wife's existence, noted that she is the least original of Chaucer's characters, an antifeminist cliché whose antecedents are found in classical and scriptural texts thousands of years old. The biblical book of Proverbs, for example, compiled sometime between the fifth and second centuries B.C.E. but incorporating much older Near Eastern wisdom traditions, provides analogues for the Wife's talkativeness, lust, and habit of wandering outdoors to meet young men (see Proverbs 7:10–12). The Wife tells us not so much about the instability of medieval women as about the staleness of misogynist cant.

Andreas Capellanus's courtly ladies, then, do not primarily portray women his readers encountered, nor does the Wife of Bath realistically depict a fourteenth-century English bourgeoise. Female characters in medieval texts on the whole do not so much reflect historical women as an idea of the feminine. They depict behavior or represent values the Middle Ages considered female. Medieval texts are frequently more symbolic than mimetic, and the key to their metaphoric system is often a metaphoric interpretation of the relationship of "man" to "woman": The male/female pair can represent the pairs mind/body, reason/sensuality, virtue/vice, order/chaos, God/humanity, Christian/Jew, clergy/laity, and king/country. Almost any binary hierarchy may be represented by the male/female couple. Ordinarily these hierarchies rank feminine values lower than masculine ones. Either feminine is bad and masculine good, or feminine is good and masculine better.

The inferiority that medieval culture generally imposed on femaleness, like the superiority it conferred on maleness, stems from the primary meaning attributed to the female/male pair: the relationship of body to spirit. The Middle Ages inherited from Greek culture, especially from Platonic philosophy, a deep distrust of mortal flesh, especially in contrast with the immortal soul. The corruptible body seemed to exemplify moral corruption, but the soul, sharing in God's eternal existence, participated in divinity. Since women's primary function in classical and medieval societies was motherhood (men, although fathers, were not limited to that role), they were identified with the bodily functions of conception and birth, and with the body generally. Viewed as more fleshy than men, women stood for all that the modern word *carnal* suggests: unlawful sexuality, sin, and death.

The critic chiefly responsible for drawing attention to the symbolic nature of medieval texts is D. W. Robertson Jr., whose most significant work was published in the 1950s and 1960s.[13] Robertson's methods were influential, attracting so many disciples that one could speak of a Robertsonian school. But they also provoked severe criticism, so that most literary scholars who now accept his claims do so in greatly amended form. Robertson's work was controversial because of its totalizing quality. Although he wanted to expose Burckhardt's universally simple, superstitious Middle Ages as a false construction, his own picture of an always harmonious and orthodox age of faith is just as monolithic. Robertson interpreted medieval texts virtually without exception as exhortations to love God and neighbor: "Medieval Christian poetry, and by Christian poetry I mean *all* serious poetry written by Christian authors ... is *always* allegorical when the message of charity or some corollary of it is not evident on the surface" (*Essays*, 10; emphasis added). If the text's narrative

5

does not teach the moral of love literally, then it must be read by methods that will produce the desired meaning—perhaps through irony, but more often allegorically, by assigning to literary images the meanings given them in biblical commentaries or other religious texts. Modern readers, Robertson argues, correctly interpret a medieval text only when they view it as upholding the various hierarchies symbolized by the male/female pair (*Preface*, 6–32).

For Robertson, then, "woman" is an especially important symbol because she represents those carnal forces that must be repressed. The Wife of Bath, for example, represents "femininity [as] a philosophical ... concept," "carnality with reference ... to life in general" (*Preface*, 330). For Robertson, the Wife is primarily a model of inappropriate behavior for both women and men; Chaucer does not condone her anti-antifeminist sentiments but views them with irony, as should the reader. Robertson proposed similar ironic readings of Andreas's *De Amore* and other courtly texts. No medieval author, Robertson says, as a good Christian would seriously encourage a man to serve a woman: Since any courtly lover represents reason, and any lady represents female sensuality, such an arrangement symbolizes an inverted, unacceptable hierarchy of the flesh controlling the mind. When Andreas and other medieval writers portray courtly swains loving women, they are ironically warning readers to forget about love. Their portraits of courtly couples are not exempla but satires of foolish behavior (*Preface*, 391–448; *Essays*, 257–72).

Long debate over Robertson's work has concluded that his allegorizing methodology can be used or abused. The prevailing verdict now is that Robertson was right to insist that medieval texts be read within their cultural context;[14] that much of that context was defined by the church; and that medieval writers expressed their ideas symbolically, particularly through the images of woman and man representing carnal and spiritual values. Robertson went wrong, however, when he restricted the meaning of medieval texts to an injunction to charity or other orthodox religious messages. Not all medieval authors thought alike, and clearly, from the historical evidence for frequency of heresy within the culture, some disagreed with official doctrine.

Robertson restricted the potential range of medieval texts' meanings because he limited their historical context to only the history of ideas. Believing that every medieval text was purely "a vehicle for philosophical ideas," that it located reality in "the realm of the intelligible," Robertson denied it any social dimension (*Essays*, 260 and 94). He did not recognize that texts, and the ideas in them, are shaped by the intersection of economic, political, and other social forces. Robertson, in short, failed to recognize that the values articulated in medieval texts are not so much platonic ideas as social ideologies—value systems invented to either maintain or advance the status of a given group. Most medieval texts are informed by the ideology and support the power of the dominant classes in medieval society, those represented in the top half of Robertsonian hierarchies: the clergy and the male members of the noble and knightly castes.[15] Recognizing the ideological nature of medieval texts, most critics now continue Robertson's habit of interpreting female characters as symbols, often of carnality, but unlike him emphasize that those symbols were constructed primarily by men, and often to uphold male privilege. Joan Ferrante, for example, in her pioneering book on *Women as Image in Medieval Literature* (1975), wrote that female characters represent either "philosophical and psychological problems that trouble the male world" or "[a man's] ideals, his aspirations, the values of his society."[16]

Robertson also did not acknowledge that medieval texts, if accepted as authoritative by readers, could produce the "reality" they depicted. Some readers in the later Middle Ages, for example, did not read *De Amore* ironically, as Robertson did, but quite literally, holding courts that judged lovers' violations of the Rules of Love as Andreas had described. If courtly love was not a social practice in the twelfth century, it was, in some form, by the fifteenth; monarchs even as late as Victoria held jousts and debates about love.[17] Similarly, feminine carnality may have been a medieval symbol for a philosophical attitude that could be held by men or women, but actual women were treated as if they embodied the disreputable carnal. Medieval texts, then, do picture an idea of the feminine, but an idea that held unfortunate social consequences for medieval women.

Medieval texts frequently display consciousness of both the constructed and constructing nature of feminine carnality. The Wife of Bath's Prologue is an excellent case in point. The Wife herself points out that misogynist stereotypes result not from impartial observation but from a particular point of view—often a cloistered perspective that lacks knowledge of real women: "Who painted the leon, tel me who? / By God, if wommen hadden writen stories, / As clerkes han within hir oratories, / They wolde han writen of men more wikkednesse / Than al the merk of Adam may redresse" (III (D): 692–96). The Wife, furthermore, since she fulfills misogynist stereotypes, might seem to offer living proof of their truth. But her Prologue implies that the stereotypes condition the Wife to act as she does. For example, the Wife's fifth husband, the young clerk Jankin, reads to her from his Book of Wicked Wives, a volume similar to extant collections of misogynist stories of women who kill their husbands. Angered by the book, the Wife attacks her husband—predictably, since he has just taught her that wives always physically abuse their husbands. Furthermore, in the fight over the book, Jankin hits the Wife on the ear, causing her partially to lose her hearing (III: 668). As Lee Patterson points out, although Robertsonian critics interpret the Wife's hearing impairment as a sign of her carnality—she is deaf to the spiritual meanings of the biblical texts she cites in her Prologue, hearing only their literal "carnal" meanings—that deafness and its attendant carnality are the result of violence inflicted on her by male clerical attack (*Negotiating*, 6n). Having learned the antifeminist lesson that women are always carnal by nature, Patterson argues, the Wife lives up to expectation, yet does so subversively, self-consciously enacting stereotypes to the discomfort of her largely male audience. Optimally, the female reader of the Wife's Prologue (medieval or modern), learning that the construct of woman's fleshy nature results from misogynists' stereotyping, may reject being constructed according to pattern.[18]

The Wife of Bath's Prologue is a useful reminder that medieval women were not just depicted in texts but heard or read them, and if not as authors, as an audience were involved in the production of both textual and social values. Medieval literary theory, belying Robertson's single charitable moral, often stated that a text held multiple meanings, resulting from a complex interplay among God (the source of all language), the author, the text, and the reader.[19] The reader is thus not a passive recipient for an author's message but active collaborator. Saint Augustine went so far as to claim that a book with the highest authority could produce a different valid meaning for every reader: "A reader could find re-echoed ... whatever truths he was able to apprehend."[20] A number of medieval authors welcome readers' active response by alluding to the Parable of the Sower and the Seed, in which Jesus teaches that the meaning of a text—the seed—is dependent on the type of reader—the ground—who receives it (Mark 4:1–20). Marie de France, for example, remodels the Parable to introduce a discussion of how readers supply a text's meaning "from their own wisdom."[21] Since each reader has a different store of wisdom, each will supply a different theme.

Minding the Body: Women and Literature in the Middle Ages, 800–1500 explores medieval texts' representations of women as well as women's responses to those depictions. Our focus is on England, but we have not limited texts we treat to those written in English or in Britain. English-speaking culture in the Middle Ages was greatly influenced by texts written in French, the language of the Norman upper classes, and Latin, the language of the Church and the universities. Indeed, before the fourteenth century only a minority of texts written in England were in English. Although we mainly discuss texts in the three languages of medieval England, we have not scrupled to include works written in other languages if they even at a distance influence English practice, provide an instructive contrast to it, or add to our knowledge of medieval women's literary activities.

Treating the thematically and temporally broad subject of medieval literary women in a relatively brief book necessitates that our discussion be limited in some way. We have attempted to provide a useful introduction to major concerns but do not claim to have written the "hoole book" on the topic. Again, because medieval literary theory acknowledges that readers play central roles in producing textual meaning and that such production is an individual act, we do not pretend that the interpretations we offer here are definitive. Nor do they attempt complete readings of every facet of a text but limit the focus to an examination of how a work represents women. Our notes explain when some aspect of a critical approach is controversial, and they suggest further reading. Due to considerations of space, our notes cannot always list all criticism relevant to a particular subject. We have been careful to include criticism that represents state-of-the-art methodology and older studies of especial importance, although we have favored secondary literature in English. We regret any exclusions that may have resulted from oversight. Our readings are indebted to a rich body of commentary on historical and literary women of the Middle Ages written within the last quarter century or so; readers searching for a useful overview of these studies might consult Margaret Schaus and Susan Mosher Stuard's excellent 1992 bibliographic essay.[22] Every new book catalog or journal contents page brings notice of another interesting study. Readers who wish to remain up-to-date on studies of medieval women should consult, among other publications, the *Medievalist Feminist Newsletter*, a fine source of bibliographies, reviews, and ongoing debate among those who study medieval women. It is available both in hard copy and on-line for those interested in the research prospects afforded by the Internet.

We have imagined our audience to consist primarily of those who are not specialists in medieval literature. Our aim therefore has been more to summarize current views of the roles women play in medieval literature and history than to break new ground; we hope, however, that something here will interest our medievalist colleagues. Because we imagine ourselves writing for nonspecialists, we concentrate on texts our readers might most typically encounter—those frequently taught in undergraduate classes and/or easily available in modern English translations. Although all the texts we discuss may be considered in some way canonical, the traditional canon is not the only nor perhaps the best place to learn about medieval women. Readers interested in encountering medieval literary women outside the canon will find suggestions in the epilogue.

The various chapters outline how images of women within a genre or the work of a specific author were constructed by literary and artistic conventions; religious and philosophical traditions; psychological needs; economic, ecclesiastic, political, and other social institutions; and cultural practice in general. Although the social forces constructing femininity were generally controlled by men, we believe that women did not always passively conform to manufactured images but might remodel, resist, or even reject them, thereby participating in the cultural production of femininity. Wherever possible, therefore, we have included works by women in our discussions of a genre to suggest at least one woman's point of view.

Chapter 1 concentrates on Christian texts and institutions that limited women's opportunities for learning and self-expression, and on how female writers constructed their literary authority within those limits. Religious authority, although not monolithic, often emphasized what it held to be women's inherent inferiority and their descent from sinful Eve as rationales for restricting female education. The same Christian tradition, however, provided some opportunity for women to become authors—if, for example, they modeled their behavior on that of the Virgin Mary by living chastely. Chapter 2 examines what happened when early Christianity, shaped formidably by Greek ideas, met the very different Germanic culture of the Anglo-Saxon tribes living in early medieval England. Germanic culture did not imagine female inferiority as the Greeks did; the Anglo-Saxon church therefore allowed women to assume positions of power, and Old English poems about biblical and Christian women generally show them as important contributors to spiritual and material culture.

Chapters 3, 4, and 5 concentrate on medieval traditions of courtly love, influential in England after the Norman Conquest. Chapter 3 emphasizes the Provençal court as the context for troubadour *fin'amor*; a troubadour often imagines his lady as a feminine double of his idealized self, and his quest for a refined and cultured love figures in his pursuit of virtues that will win him political favor. The political and narcissistic agenda of the courtly lyric was critiqued both by the Provençal trobairitz (female poets) and by religious poets who reinvent courtly lyric as an expression not of narcissism but of selflessness.

Troubadour courtliness is an affair of the mind, a mental construct. But medieval culture adapted its conventions to real-life situations in the genre of romance, as chapter 4 explains. Both Old French and Middle English romancers from the twelfth through the fifteenth centuries uphold the values of the feudal and chivalric establishment by constructing feminine identity socially as wife and mother, psychologically as supplement to the male psyche. These secondary roles, although made palatable to the female audience of romance by disguising them with the accoutrements of courtly love, ultimately delimit the potential for self-authorship among women in courtly culture. Chapter 5 considers how these more limited roles for women can be revoiced by a female reader-of-romance-turned-author. Writing with an emphasis on the significantly different perspective afforded her by her status as female author within an androcentric culture, Marie de France within her lais mirrors the traditional male quest of romance through female quests that explore the consequences of her culture's misogyny for both genders.

Courtly texts like those discussed in chapters 3, 4, and 5 often work to reinforce a gendered mind-body dichotomy. In contrast, the Corpus Christi cycle dramas considered in chapter 6 freely transgress those absolute gender boundaries. By focusing doubly on both the unmaking and the making (the crucifixion and the nativity) of the flesh that is spirit, the Corpus Christi plays emphasize the spiritual viability of female matter. Not only do they attribute the power of Christ's body to its feminine wounds, but they suggest that his voice derives its divine authority through its synergy of garrulous prophecy and suffering silence, both conventional misogynic tropes of female speech. Similarly, the traditional role of woman as material counterpart to male logos is turned inside out when the verbal authority conventionally assigned to male speech is rendered through the feminine, dialogic, pregnant conversation of the Virgin Mary and Elizabeth.

Many medieval genres associate women with speech—not surprising in a culture that habitually restricted their language to oral expression—even to the extent of reading women as symbols for language itself. Chapter 7 explores the use of woman as linguistic figure within the genre of dream vision. Dream texts from Boethius's *Consolation of Philosophy* through Jean de Meun's portion of the *Roman de la Rose* align female allegorical characters against real women, using the former as symbols of truthful language but the latter as icons of carnal

11

deceit. As the dream vision tradition developed, authors who wrote in the form grew self-conscious about the disparity of their texts' treatment of allegorical and real women. None, however, were as conscious of the genre's antifeminism as Christine de Pizan, who denounced Jean de Meun's misogyny in Europe's first recorded literary controversy, and then answered it by writing a dream vision, *The Book of the City of Ladies*, which privileges the speech of real women over those of female allegories.

Whether or not familiar with Christine de Pizan's work, Geoffrey Chaucer is keenly aware of the gender double standards resulting from the misogyny she decries. How to characterize his response to them is less clear. His Wife of Bath, in responding to the institutional misogyny of her culture, provides us with a fictional portrait in some senses so verisimilar that ironically she has confused for several generations of critics the demarcation between the speech of real and fictive women. The confusion is vintage Chaucer; it amplifies for us the pleasure Chaucer takes in the self-multiplying power of ventriloquism afforded him as poet—a power that Chaucer explores richly throughout his works and that he tropes with striking frequency through narratives of rape. It is a brilliant although alarming, perhaps self-implicating, strategy given the biographical fact of Chaucer's release in 1380 by Cecily Chaumpaigne from an accusation of rape. Chapter 8 examines Chaucer's interest in ventriloquism and the continuum he alerts his audience to between using voices and using bodies.

Our final chapter, a comparison of Julian of Norwich's *Showings* and *The Book of Margery Kempe*, considers how the narratives of female mystics, whether through metaphorical or carnal motherhood, name the body as the site of narratives of spiritual transcendence. The body and its experiences conjoin flesh and voice. Whether creating narratives of private revelation or public self-revelation, both Julian and Margery describe their first visions as emanating from experiences of physical suffering and relief (a life-threatening illness for Julian; severe postpartum depression for Margery). In doing so, they erase the body-mind (speech) displacement intrinsic to Chaucer's rape-ventriloquism trope.

Each chapter, besides exploring a single genre or author, also focuses on a metaphor used for a feminine role: A woman may be viewed as maternal weaver (religious texts), ornament to be treasured or traded (Old English literature), mirror of the male self (troubadour lyric), incestuous healer of male wounds (romance), paradoxically autonomous echo of the male voice (Marie de France), point of convergence for the metonymic fragmentation and metaphoric reconstitution of the social body (drama and fabliaux), visionary figure of authority (dream vision), victim of rape poetically retroped (Chaucer), or somatic site of spiritual transcendence (female mystics). We do not mean to suggest that works in a genre always use a particular metaphor or that a metaphor appears only in a given genre. Although we believed a generic organization was best for explaining the conventions of medieval literature, most conventions cross genres.

Throughout almost every genre touched on in this book is the virtually universal identification of women with the body, of men with the mind. Medieval authors, however, do not always devalue the carnal female in relation to the spiritual male. Many of the texts we examine do accept the medieval hierarchy at face value, celebrating masculine reason and decrying feminine carnality. To phrase this idea as our title does, these texts "mind" the body—that is, they define it in purely negative terms and seek to escape or at least control it. Medieval writers, however, find the problem of the carnal a recurring one; although they disdain the flesh they never succeed in repressing it. Instead they continually mind the body in the sense of contemplating its central role in human nature. The body's role, furthermore, need not be a negative one. The female body, for instance, generates new life, and women acting as real or metaphoric mothers is a theme found in almost every chapter of this book. The vitality of the flesh, furthermore, is spiritual as well as biological—Christ effected salvation through bodily suffering and by rising from death in the flesh. The human body deserves to be cherished— "minded" in the sense of looked after as vital to, even constitutive of, the social body in all its material and spiritual difference.

Medieval writers, either male or female, may give the flesh positive value. Yet women authors tend to think about the body differently than men do. Male authors are prone to separating mental functions from physical ones. Medieval women, on the other hand, do not typically divide the self into spiritual and material halves. They imagine a person as an integrated whole with the powers of both body and mind. They mind the body in this way, too, endowing it with mentality. Although there are always exceptions to generalizations, women in the Middle Ages rarely question their identification with the flesh. It is a cultural mandate they cannot escape. They do, however, reinterpret what flesh means. For a medieval woman, her body is not primarily an enemy. It is her self.

As Eve is a biblical type of the fallen woman, so Mary, the "new Eve," provides a type of the redeemed woman.
The Hours of Catherine of Cleves, Dutch, ca. 1440.
The Pierpont Morgan Library, New York. M. 917, p. 139.

CHAPTER 1

Body and Soul:
Religious Constructions of
Female Authorship

Christianity regulated everyone's behavior in the Middle Ages, yet it circumscribed women's lives more than men's. It limited women's education and prohibited them from teaching by the written or spoken word.
Still, a substantial number of medieval women achieved positions of
authority in the church and secular society; many did so through their
writing. They typically gained respect not by violating religious rule but
by availing themselves of whatever opportunities for self-expression the
ecclesiastical system left open. Medieval doctrine about women,
although often unashamedly misogynist, was not monolithic. Clerics
often praised women, especially if they served the church. Women, by
conforming to their culture's definition of feminine virtue, could carve
out for themselves identities that included that of author. Vested with the
authority of the word, they could redefine what it meant to be female in
medieval society.

Withstanding antifeminism was a formidable task for medieval
women. Christian misogyny's no-holds-barred vilifications can shock a
modern reader. The second-century theologian Tertullian, for example,
addresses his female coreligionists with strong invective in *On the
Apparel of Women*:

No one of you at all, best beloved sisters, . . . [should desire] too
ostentatious a style of dress; rather, you [should] go about in humble garb and affect meanness of appearance, walking about as Eve
mourning and repentant. . . . Do you not know that you are Eve?
The sentence of God upon this sex of yours lives on in this age; the
guilt must of necessity live on, too. You are the devil's gateway; you
are the unsealer of that forbidden tree; you are the first deserter of
the divine law; you are she who persuaded him whom the devil was
not valiant enough to attack. You destroyed so easily God's image,
man. On account of your desert—that is, death—even the Son of
God had to die.[1]

This invocation precedes Tertullian's main lecture, in which he admon-
ishes women to avoid expensive clothing, elaborate hairstyles, jewelry,
cosmetics, and dyed hair and clothing. Nothing in Tertullian's subject,
however, motivates his antifeminism. There is nothing particularly
antifemale in wishing that women dress plainly; the message had long
been aimed at Christian women. The First Letter of Peter instructs, "Let
[your adornment] not be the outward plaiting of the hair, or the wearing
of gold, or the putting on of apparel, but the hidden man of the heart in
the incorruptibility of a quiet and a meek spirit, which is rich in the sight
of God" (1 Pet. 3:3–4).[2] This writer's desire for plain dress is motivated
not by hatred but by what he considers behavior becoming to any Christian, male or female. He reasons from a Christian commonplace, that
the "exterior" human being—the physical and mortal body—is far less
important than the "interior"—the immaterial and immortal soul.
Women should not ornament the body that decays but beautify the
incorruptible spirit.[3]

Tertullian, however, employs a different logic, a misogynist one. He
argues that women do not deserve elegant clothing because it belies the
female ugliness that seethes beneath: Woman's nature is intrinsically vile
and disgusting. In Tertullian's words, women "are Eve." Eve was seduced
by the devil to eat forbidden fruit from the Tree of Knowledge. She persuaded Adam to eat the fruit, too—an act of rebellion his superior manly
virtue would not have otherwise performed. Thus Eve is responsible for
her sin and Adam's as well. She is to blame for the awful punishments—
toil, sickness, and death—with which God chastises humanity in Genesis 3.[4] Yet, Tertullian continues, Eve is not alone in her guilt. She shares
her evil nature with all her daughters, who are morally weak if not downright vicious—proud, lascivious, greedy, and deceptive. Women share
Eve's punishments, too. God, in Genesis 3, gave Eve and all women pain

16

in childbearing and made them subject to their husbands (1:1; Thelwall, 14). Christian women, Tertullian feels, despicable in nature, hardly deserve fine clothing.

Tertullian and other early Christian writers did not invent female inferiority; they inherited classical civilization's assumption that women's secondary role was natural and divinely appointed. The church fathers did, however, pass on such attitudes to the Middle Ages. Antifeminist statements like Tertullian's were repeated by more influential theologians to create one of the standard medieval views of women, that they were innately lacking in morality and hence needed to be guided by men. To emphasize misogyny is somewhat to caricature medieval religious thinking about women, since theologians were not univocal in denouncing them. They said many things about women, some more palatable to modern taste than Tertullian's jeremiad; the Pauline epistles, for example, that furnished prooftexts for Christian misogyny also maintain the equality of men and women (Gal. 3:2). Yet if a caricature is not completely faithful, it is true insofar as it emphasizes especially striking features, and the most striking characteristic of the medieval church's attitude toward women is its antifeminist strain.

Nonetheless, if that were all there was to say about medieval attitudes toward women, this would be a very short book indeed, for all female characters would be exact copies of the church fathers' criminal Eve. But not all women in medieval texts wear Eve's face. Medieval authors, male and female, drew female characters of different temperaments and of many grades of virtue and vice. They were able to create a gallery of diverse portraits because Christian teaching about women was disseminated in a metaphoric style of discourse that enabled that freedom. Doctrine could be rigidly unyielding in what it said, but it sometimes left important things unsaid or was ambiguous in its pronouncements. The church fathers' habitual use of symbolic language could be construed as ambiguous and hence open to interpretation.

Metaphoric discourse is notoriously unstable. Think about metaphors for only a little while and they start slipping away. Take the metaphor that 1 Peter uses to stand for the human soul: "the hidden man of the heart." The heart is, on the one hand, a good metaphor for the soul because, as the core of the human self, it represents its innermost essence. On the other hand, the heart is a bad metaphor for the soul because it may also stand for the soul's opposite, the flesh and its lusts: This bodily organ may stand for erotic love, the blood it pumps may represent anger. Hence when a text uses the metaphor of the heart, that metaphor may represent either the soul or the body. Or it may be an ambiguous symbol by which the author confronts readers with the difficulty of deciding where the soul stops and the body begins.

Patristic pronouncements about women, couched in symbolic language, are prone to that discourse's slipperiness and ambiguity. As later pages of this chapter will detail, particularly susceptible to interpretation, if not outright manipulation, are statements about women's intelligence, or as medievals generally term it, reason. Reason is of paramount importance for studying medieval women, both as characters in texts and creators of them, since in medieval anthropology reason is the quintessential human characteristic, the chief attribute of the soul, the faculty by which one knows divine truth. Indeed, reason can even lift humans above themselves, for, as the divine likeness in which humankind was created, it makes men and women images of God (Gen. 1:26). The Middle Ages considered this divine image to be responsible for language: The character Reason in the *Roman de la Rose* says that God her father appointed her to create names.[5] Thus, if a medieval person wished to be an author, he or she must be guided primarily by reason.

An author's need of rationality prevented most medieval women from writing, for their culture assumed that they were less reasonable than men; it accordingly gave them few opportunities to cultivate their minds or voice their opinions. Early biblical commentators believed that the creation and fall of Adam and Eve in Genesis 1–3 showed women's intellectual inferiority. The most important of these commentators is Augustine of Hippo (354–430); his commentary *On Genesis against the Manichees* states that Adam figures reason while Eve represents sensuality, a lower faculty through which the soul controls the body. The relationship between Adam and Eve, furthermore, symbolizes the proper relationship between these two faculties: "just as man ought to rule woman and ought not to allow her to rule him, ... the interior mind, like virile reason, should hold subject the soul's appetite by means of which we control the members of the body."[6]

Augustine does not say that men are rational and women sensual; he says that men *represent* reason, and women *represent* sensuality. But in metaphors the vehicle tends to color the tenor, and it was commonly accepted that men were more intelligent than women, and women more driven by their physical appetites. These gender associations were so strong that they led Gratian, whose *Decretals* (ca. 1140) formed the foundation of canon law, to state that women were not created in the rational image of God—had not Paul written that "[man] is the image and glory of God; but the woman is the glory of the man" (1 Cor. 11:7)?[7] The presumption that women are not rational underlies medieval attitudes toward all women, real or textual. It is why medievals believed women to be inferior to men and under their control. As Thomas Aquinas put it in his *Summa Theologica*, "woman is naturally subject to man, because in man the discretion of reason predominates."[8]

Because medieval women were considered of dubious mental capacity, they were forbidden to teach. The Pauline epistles were the first to use this line of argument; 1 Timothy argues that because Eve but not Adam was seduced by the serpent, women could not hold authority in the church: "I suffer not a woman to teach, nor to use authority over the man, but to be in silence" (1 Tim. 2:11–12). This Pauline ban was frequently repeated in the Middle Ages, often with some discussion of the damage Eve caused when she taught Adam. Embroidering the text of Genesis, which says nothing about her motives, medieval writers believed that Eve persuaded Adam to eat the forbidden fruit with deceptive rhetoric and spurious arguments. John Chrysostom, for example, patriarch of Constantinople (ca. 347–407), wrote that "The woman taught the man once, and made him guilty of disobedience and ruined everything."[9] Thus medieval women were sentenced to silence, and speech and writing were made male privileges.

Inasmuch as the Middle Ages assumed women's lack of literary ability, it is not surprising that few women became authors. Indeed, it is remarkable that any did. Yet a small but significant number of medieval women claimed the freedom to write. That they claimed this freedom, exercised it, and in many cases were listened to and revered by a male audience attests that the misogynistic views promulgated by the church fathers were hardly intractable but capable of a certain amount of elasticity. One reason a woman could claim the male privilege of authorship was that the Middle Ages defined the concepts of *feminine* and *masculine* as not just biological realities but habits of mind. Augustine, as we have seen, said that *woman* and *man* were symbols for the mental faculties of reason and sensuality possessed by both biological sexes. The terms then could name whichever faculty predominated in a person: "Man" could mean anyone rational, "woman" anyone driven by emotions or biological urges. If a biological woman subjected her "female" passions and body to the control of her "male" reason, she could perform functions normally reserved for men. Augustine's contemporary, Jerome, as famous for the misogyny of his antimarriage tract *Against Jovinian* as for his translation of the Bible into Latin, wrote that women could undergo a metaphoric sex change: "As long as woman is for birth and children, she is different from man as body is from soul. But when she wishes to serve Christ more than the world, then she will cease to be a woman and will be called man."[10] If it is hard to map out the precise intersection of soul and body, it is more treacherous to locate the threshold separating male from female.

A woman, then, could take up the life of the mind if she rejected her traditional duties as wife and mother to live a virginal life consecrated to prayer. The religious life offered the best opportunity for female authorship; of known medieval female writers, the majority were nuns or otherwise committed to a celibate religious life. For education in the Middle Ages was in the hands of the church, designed primarily to train clerics as administrators, pastors, or monks. Women were precluded from the first two of these roles by Paul's teaching but were permitted to live under monastic rule as men were.

In the early Middle Ages the monastery provided women the same intellectual opportunities it extended to men. The rule for monks by Benedict, founder of western monasticism (ca. 480–547), dictated they devote themselves to learning as well as prayer, since Christianity is a religion of the Book. Benedict expected monks to study the Bible and other religious texts daily, and directed that each monk be provided with a pen and tablets among other "necessary articles."[11] These Benedictine regulations were enjoined on female nuns as well as on male monks. Authors of rules specifically for women make similar provisions. Caesarius, Bishop of Arles (ca. 510–534), wrote the first rule for women, first used at the monastery headed by his sister Caesaria and later by other convents. Caesarius urged all nuns to learn to read and spend a fixed number of hours in study.[12] More than five hundred years later, the philosopher and theologian Peter Abelard (1079–1142), composing a rule for the convent of the Paraclete founded by his pupil, lover, and wife Heloise (ca. 1100–1163), urged the sisters to put all their efforts into scholarship so that they, unlike most monks, would not just mouth Latin when they prayed but understand the literal meaning and the deepest significance of the words.[13] Monastic rules of study in the earlier Middle Ages produced an impressive record of nuns' accomplishments as authors and scholars.[14] Peter the Venerable, Abbot of Cluny, for example, testified that Heloise outshone all women and most men in scholarship (*Letters*, 277).

If religious life was the main venue for female education, the duties of wife and mother in a pretechnological age provided little time for learning. One of the traditional appeals of monasticism for women was that it freed them from what could be staggering domestic burdens and a high risk of death: Before reliable contraception and modern medicine, frequent pregnancies were unavoidable and childbirth often deadly.[15] The thirteenth-century English treatise *Holy Maidenhood*, part of a small library written for female anchorites—women who served God by enclosure in a cell—advertises virginity as freedom from the "slavery" of married life. The work recounts with striking force the degradation of "filthy" sexual intercourse, the brutal demands of a swinish husband, the discomfort of pregnancy and pain of childbirth, and the nerve-racking anxiety a mother feels for her children.[16] Peter Brown argues that women of the classical world were attracted to Christian asceticism because it permitted them a measure of self-determination, releasing them from obedience to father or husband and from serving with their procreative powers family and state.[17] Medieval women, too, might seek the convent or some other form of religious life to escape the restraints of the secular world; the life of the English Christina of Markyate, who ran away from her wedding, is the classic medieval story of a woman who would rather be anchorite than wife.[18]

Life for married women in the Middle Ages could be as brutal as *Holy Maidenhood* depicts it, but we should not wholeheartedly embrace its opinions in order to romanticize the religious life. The treatise preaches to the converted, having been written for three sisters already living as anchorites. The book would not have needed to paint married life so bleakly unless it had ample attractions. A medieval woman, depending on her temperament and that of her husband, might have found life as an anchorite or nun more denigrating than marriage; the Nun of Watton, tortured by her sisters in religion because of an illicit love affair and pregnancy, was not the only woman to find the convent a harsh place.[19] Even for those with vocations, monasticism demanded self-sacrifice. A nun took vows to live chastely without personal possessions, never to leave her convent, and to obey her superiors completely. Prayer and contemplation were the chief tasks—medieval nuns were rarely the active teachers, nurses, or missionaries of today's orders.

The chance for intellectual development the convent offered, furthermore, was available to only a small minority of women. There were many fewer monasteries for women than for men—about 140 houses of religion were open to women in late medieval England, but five times as many, and larger, institutions, welcomed men.[20] Convents usually accepted only a woman of the upper classes, expecting her to pay a substantial dowry on entering as she would if she married. Poorer women could not afford dowries; if accepted by convents, they served as lay sisters, doing manual work to free nuns for prayer. Even the monasteries' support for women's intellectual endeavors declined as the Middle Ages wore on. Reform movements in the eleventh through thirteenth centuries limited female convents' self-rule by putting them under male abbots and more strictly controlling their activities. Some orders even rid themselves of their female members. One Premonstratensian canon stated that such drastic measures were necessary to save male members' souls—for "the wickedness of women is greater than all the other wickednesses of the world" (quoted by Labarge, 107). Hastening the intellectual decline in women's monastic life was the decline of monastic schools; during the thirteenth century, monasteries were replaced in importance by universities, which accepted only men. Many convents in the later Middle Ages, male or female, were mediocre establishments, and we rarely find the outstanding scholars active in earlier periods (Labarge, 98–115). Women then invented or turned to less-structured forms of religious life—as anchorites, tertiaries (lay members of orders), and beguines (members of urban communities under rules less strict than those of convents)—to support their devotional and intellectual endeavors.[21]

Women's limited opportunity for education in the Middle Ages resulted from their culture's stereotype of them as irrational and sinful. Society offered some intellectual opportunities to women who, by accepting a religious vocation, styled themselves as rational "men." But how did women react to this condemnation of their nature? Did they learn to detest their femininity? Did they come to think of themselves as metaphoric men? We can never answer these questions on behalf of most medieval women. The great majority, like their male contemporaries, were illiterate and left no record of their thoughts. Nor can we extrapolate from the female-authored texts we have. Almost all are by women born into the upper classes, possessing rights and privileges and therefore points of view their lower-order sisters did not share. Nor do these extant voices necessarily speak for all women from religious or noble backgrounds, for their authorship marks them as extraordinary. But what testimonies female medieval authors did leave suggest that they did not internalize the culture's disparagement of the feminine. Most of them do not reject their female bodies as impediments to spiritual or intellectual development, or attempt to label themselves as somehow male. Rather, they identify themselves, their reason, and their intellectual endeavors as intrinsically feminine. Women validate their femininity most often not by protesting misogyny but by manipulating the symbolic language of medieval discourse, taking advantage of the possibilities it left open for self-expression and self-empowerment.

Some evidence, at first glance, suggests that medieval women absorbed the message of female inferiority. But on closer inspection statements by women about the sinfulness of their sex turn out to be ironic parodies and hence refutations of traditional misogyny. Peter Dronke, for example, says that when the dramatist and poet Hrotsvitha of Gandersheim (ca. 935–995) describes herself as "a worthless little woman" who writes "clownish compositions," she does so with humorous self-consciousness and a vocabulary so obviously learned that it belies this abject self as a mask. Her statement that "women's understanding is held to be more retarded," when interpreted within its context—a reference to Lady Philosophy, the feminine incarnation of wisdom in the *Consolation of Philosophy*—makes it clear that Hrotsvitha does not believe it, nor does she wish her readers to.[22]

A passage by Heloise, too, might imply she believes in women's inferiority.[23] Her letter asking Abelard for a rule for the Paraclete explains that she makes this request because women, as the "weaker sex," cannot fully observe Benedictine regulations (162).[24] But the only weakness Heloise has in mind is women's lesser physical strength. All the departures she seeks from Benedictine practice—different clothing allowances, fasting requirements, and hours set aside for manual work; freedom from the obligation to house travelers; a request that the prioress who heads the convent, not her male superior, read the Gospel at services (160)—attempt to tailor the rule to the needs of women's bodies, their comparative physical frailty and desire to protect their chastity. Heloise mentions women's physical weakness, but nowhere does she disparage her sisters' mental or spiritual strength. Indeed, Heloise and her nuns hope, through their practice of the rule, to gain equality with men—to be "the equals of the rulers of the Church themselves and of the clergy who are confirmed in holy orders" (164). Heloise's letter argues that in every important way—in matters of the soul—women are no different from men. Heloise nearly quotes 1 Peter when she writes, "those who are true Christians are wholly occupied with the inner man, so that they may adorn him with virtues and purify him of vices, but they have little or no concern for the outer man" (174).[25]

Historian Caroline Walker Bynum finds that medieval women, far from disparaging their femininity or adopting male personae, describe themselves and their religious and intellectual activities in metaphors drawn from women's secular lives—they speak of themselves as lovers, wives, and mothers (*Fragmentation*, 39). Literature written for medieval women similarly describes religious life as fundamentally feminine. *Holy Maidenhood*, for example, describes the life of anchorites as marriage to God; the book urges women to repulse inadequate human suitors in favor of a far superior celestial husband (240). The metaphoric bride dedicated to a "male" God is an idea traceable to Paul, who compares a wife's submission to her husband to that of the church to Christ: "As the church is subject to Christ, so also let the wives be to their husbands in all things" (Eph. 5:24). Paul identifies Christ's bride as the corporate church (appropriately, since Latin *ecclesia* is grammatically feminine), but the metaphor could extend to its individual members, male or female. In fact, the metaphor served that purpose in medieval interpretations of the Song of Songs. This Old Testament erotic dialogue between Bridegroom and Bride was read as the love song between God and the human soul—since Christ identified himself as the Bridegroom (Mark 2:19), and the soul's Latin name, the grammatically feminine *anima*, made it a candidate for the bride.

The Cistercian Bernard of Clairvaux (1091–1153), in his influential *Sermons on the Song of Songs*, popularized the idea that anyone living under religious rule had a special status as a bride of Christ. Bernard addressed his sermons to male monks, yet the metaphor of the bride of Christ appears to have appealed more to female than to male monastics. As biological women they could better appreciate the resonances of the symbol. Although Paul used the metaphor to teach women subservience to men, it seems not to have had that effect on medieval women writers; instead it inspired them to think of men as their equals. For in this metaphorically gendered universe, all souls are female, regardless of the sex of their bodies. When medieval women do speak of their femaleness as entailing inferiority, it is the inferiority that every "female" human soul must feel in the face of a "male" God. Thus medieval women, Bynum finds, think of their femininity not as a decline from some male norm, but as the human condition (*Fragmentation*, 151–80).

The common metaphor of a human soul as the feminine *anima* offered the medieval woman not only the opportunity to define her best self as female but also to enter the world of learning usually reserved for men. For in the gendered Latin language, not only was the soul feminine, but its chief distinguishing characteristic—reason or *ratio*—was also. Medieval women writers took advantage of the grammatical gender of *ratio* and other Latin terms to imagine the mind and its operations as female. For example, although Gratian said that women were not created in the image of God, his contemporary, the polymath, musical composer, and mystic Hildegard von Bingen (1098–1179), employs Latin gender to conceive of God and divine reason as female. As Barbara Newman explains, Hildegard speaks of God manifest in the female figures *Ecclesia*, *Caritas* (Charity), *Scientia Dei* (God's Knowledge), and *Sapientia* (Wisdom)—this last drawing on the character Wisdom in the biblical books of Proverbs, Ecclesiasticus, and the Wisdom of Solomon, where she personifies God's creative intellect.[26] Hildegard's conception of a womanly divine wisdom no doubt lent her self-confidence to speak in her own voice. Other medieval writers make explicit the empowering connection between female symbols for the intellect and a positive image of women's mental abilities. Christine de Pizan, Europe's first professional woman of letters (1364–1429), says she wrote her defense of women, *The Book of the City of Ladies*, and its sequel, *The Treasury of the City of Ladies*, because of urging by the female personifications Reason, Rectitude, and Justice.[27]

If the soul and its guiding reason can be pictured as female, teaching and authorship normally restricted to medieval men could also. Male authors often describe their habits of composition through metaphors drawn from women's daily tasks and responsibilities. By appropriating these homely metaphors and stressing their literal meaning, women could claim that writing was a quintessentially female activity and thus assert their right—and even their responsibility—to put their thoughts into words.

Of all the metaphors medieval authors use to talk about composition, none is more common than motherhood. We are used to authors talking about their books as their children, but for us this is largely a dead metaphor. For medievals, the comparison between a book and a child was meaningful because they considered a text, like a human being, to comprise a body and soul. A text's "body" included the physical material of the book—actually flesh, since pages were sheepskin parchment—the words written on the page, *and* their literal meaning. This textual body contained an interior "spirit"—the meaning an author wished to communicate; Paul had urged Christians to read the Bible not literally, according to the "letter," but searching for the allegorical "spirit"—thus suggesting that this aspect is a text's soul (2 Cor. 3:6). By analogy with the habit of thinking the soul male and the body female, the spiritual meaning of a text might also be male and its literal meaning female.

Medieval authors, influenced by Paul, often described composition as taking a bookish soul and providing it a body—as taking an idea and covering it in appropriate words. Thus verbal conception becomes comparable to biological conception, for the Middle Ages accepted Aristotle's theory of procreation, that in conception a soul becomes clothed in a body. He wrote, in *The Generation of Animals,* that when a child was conceived, the father contributed its soul, and the mother the physical materials that made up its flesh.[28] Inasmuch as a mother is chiefly responsible for the physical growth and birth of the child, by analogy an author who develops and gives birth to a text is also metaphorically a mother.

Literal childbirth could be a demanding and even mortal mission for a medieval woman. But she could safely perform this traditional duty by choosing to bear metaphorical children—to conceive books instead of human bodies. By taking up verbal conception, medieval woman would be following the example of the Virgin Mary—as the mother of Jesus, Mary had conceived and given birth to the Word of God. Jesus, according to theologians, is the Word spoken by God at the beginning of creation, what the gospel of John terms the heavenly *logos* (John 1:1). This celestial Word had been lost to humanity in the Fall and could be restored only with the willing collaboration of Mary: She assented to become the mother of the Word at the angel's Annunciation (Luke 2:26–38). She clothes this immaterial Word in human flesh, enabling it to be apprehended by fallen humankind. And since God has put on human flesh, that flesh—still and always identified with the female—is no longer to be despised but respected as the dwelling of divinity (Bynum, *Fragmentation,* 205–22). In the Incarnation, feminine flesh is redeemed.

Mary, as the first woman of a new order, is often spoken of as the new Eve, and her maternal virtue undoes the crimes of that first mother.[29] Her collaborative authorship of the Word, too, atones for Eve's disobedience to God's Word in stealing the fruit of divine knowledge. The illustration at the beginning of this chapter depicts this opposition: The banner held by the angel calls Eve "authoress of sin," Mary "authoress of merit." This picture also indicates that, whereas Eve was sentenced to silence, Mary speaks. The Latin text under the miniature begins, "Lord, open my lips and let my mouth praise you"—a prayer associated with the Virgin, usually accompanying miniatures of the Annunciation in Books of Hours. Annunciation scenes generally stress Mary's involvement with the Word: As she hears the angel's spoken message, she reads a book or scroll with a biblical verse. Thus she both hears the Word and sees it;

with her mouth she assents to its power; and with her body she gives it human form.[30]

Because reading is Mary's typical activity in the visual arts, the occupation is recommended to Christian women. Eve's sin is forgiven, her daughters are no longer imprisoned in ignorance and silence but given access to the Word. Medieval women were urged to follow Mary's example by reading Scripture and other religious texts. Abelard, for example, praises Heloise for having "turned the curse of Eve into the blessing of Mary" by abandoning secular life for the study of sacred books (150). Heloise does not say that Mary's authorship of the Word encouraged her own literary efforts. But other women choose to imitate Mary's verbal conception, interpreting injunctions to follow Mary as commands not only to read texts but to write them as well. Hildegard von Bingen reports that her magisterial *Scivias* (an abbreviation of the Latin for "Know the ways of the Lord") resulted from God's command to record her mystical visions. Her description of how she received this command, Newman says, is consciously modeled on Mary's behavior in the Annunciation; like the Virgin, the mystic humbly questions whether she merits this favor and equally humbly assents to being overshadowed by divine light.[31]

A second popular metaphor for composition, and one closely related to the trope of childbirth, is weaving. Like motherhood, weaving is the production of an exterior and physical covering—not of a body for the soul, but of clothing for the body. Weaving and motherhood were considered so similar that one often served as metaphor for the other: The Carolingian Claudius of Turin speaks of the Incarnation as Mary's clothing the Word, giving it "suitable vesture" in a "veil of flesh."[32] Since weaving, like motherhood, is producing a material exterior, it too can function as a metaphor for the author's task of materially expressing an abstract idea.[33] The aptness of this figure reveals itself in the English word for a written work, *text*, from the Latin *textum*, literally something woven.

Textile production in the Middle Ages was considered women's work.[34] Women controlled the textile industry and made clothes for their families. The association of women with weaving was so close that two of our modern English words for females, *woman* and *wife*, may come from the Old English for weaver, *wifmann*. Because weaving was the emblematic profession of women, female authors sometimes choose it to stand for their literary efforts. Hrotsvitha, for example, describes composing

27

her dramas as weaving together "small patches from Philosophy's robe."[35] The poet Marie de France (ca. 1160–1215) imagines the heroine of her lai *Laustic* communicating with a lover through a piece of silk cloth embroidered with gold writing (lines 135–36). Marie's use of the weaving metaphor bespeaks its usual associations with the materiality of both literary text and carnal body, since the cloth is wrapped around the corpse of a nightingale, symbolizing the lady's actions as both poet and lover.

The metaphors of motherhood and weaving that a medieval woman uses to appropriate writing as a fundamentally female occupation have struck some modern readers as self-defeating in that they imply her role in the creation of a text is a limited one. Rather than creating something new, she claims to rearrange preexisting material.[36] The metaphor of motherhood particularly may suggest that an author's contributions are minimal. Aristotle taught that a mother's part in her child's conception is passive, that she merely receives the father's active contribution (Blamires, *Woman Defamed*, 39). If a woman chooses to use this metaphor, it might appear that she has internalized her culture's message that she, as a woman, is passive, weak, and in all ways inferior.

This denial of originality, however, would not have seemed demeaning to medieval readers. They did not expect a writer to invent a story, characters, or situations that were entirely new. Rather, authors demonstrated creativity by skillfully rearranging old materials to communicate a new theme; they put new wine in old bottles. Medieval authors, male or female, frequently stress their reception of literary materials from other authorities. The convention of referring to a past authority was so strong that it occurs even in texts that do invent something truly new. Chrétien de Troyes, for example, begins his highly original *Lancelot* by announcing that he invented nothing in it, receiving both the literal story line and its theme from the Countess of Champagne.[37]

Medieval women authors, like their male contemporaries, use formulae that claim they recycle old material. But women's use of these metaphors differs from men's. Men tend to claim that the source they reimagine is a person or a text. Women speak of God as the ultimate source of their books. Hildegard von Bingen and other mystics conceive of themselves as instruments through whom God speaks; He, not the woman He employs, is the author of the text. Even Marie de France, who writes secular love stories, begins her *Lais* by claiming a divine mandate to write: Because her knowledge and eloquence are God's gifts, she must use them (Prologue, lines 1–4).

By claiming God as the author of their texts, medieval women do not mean to erase their own contributions, but rather to add a divine sanction to their own limited human power. Their mystical texts carried a fearsome authority that enabled them to voice ideas that their contemporary audiences ordinarily would have found unpalatable—especially coming from a woman. It even permitted them to criticize and reform male-controlled institutions. Adopting the guise of a frail and humble servant could lend a woman a strong and courageous voice.

Hrotsvitha, for one, writing in her convent, demurs that she simply weaves rags torn from Lady Philosophy's dress. She seems to be obeying Tertullian's advice to Christian women: "Keep your hands busy with spinning, and stay at home" (Blamires, *Woman Defamed*, 58). And since Hrotsvitha's plays habitually praise cloistered female virginity, there seemingly is nothing in them that would rouse Tertullian's ire. But in both content and form, Hrotsvitha's creations are in no sense a silent acquiescence to male power and the values it upholds. Her dramas about female saints are eloquent defenses of women's nature, protesting that women are inherently holy. Again and again she shows female virtue triumphing over male vice, women characters outmaneuvering male oppressors—in essence, showing a world in which gender roles are, by medieval standards, upside down. By praising chastity in what is hardly a chaste style, by writing in a Latin ornamented with glittering rhetorical tropes and a vocabulary that one might even call flashy, Hrotsvitha succeeds in fashioning for herself what Tertullian would have denied her: glamorous and elegant clothing—not for herself, but for her ideas.

The figure of the English Saint Aetheldreda is surrounded by ornamental "rings"—ironically, for at her death she condemned her youthful habit of wearing jewelry as "needless vanity" (Bede, *Ecclesiastical History*, 4.19).

Benedictional of Saint Aethelwold, ca. 980.

By permission of The British Library, London. MS Add 49598, fol. 90v.

CHAPTER 2

Redeeming Ornament: Women in Old English Literature

In the middle of the fifth century, three Germanic tribes—the Angles, Saxons, and Jutes—established permanent settlements in Great Britain. The three tribes spoke dialects of a language we now call Old English. But if the English language begins with the Anglo-Saxon conquest of Britain, English literature does not. The early English did have poetry— the Roman historian Tacitus (ca. 55–120) notes that continental Germans recited "rude strains of verse"—but they had no system of writing, and their unrecorded songs are lost forever.[1] For the beginnings of English literature we look to a second conquest of Great Britain as momentous as the Germanic one: In the late seventh century, missionaries introduced Christianity and with it Latin literacy. The Anglo-Saxons adapted the Latin alphabet to the sounds of their language and used it to record legal documents, histories, religious tracts, and poetry on a wide variety of subjects.

Old English poetry, like Anglo-Saxon culture, is the product of intermixing Germanic and Christian traditions. The two cultures, however, were not always compatible. The Anglo-Saxons, for example, found Christian misogyny antithetical to their customs. Old English texts almost never assume women's mental or moral inferiority or blame them for the existence of evil in the world. Only rarely do such statements occur, and then in the writings of a clerical minority. Even these scattered comments, Christine Fell argues, largely fell on deaf ears; clerical misogyny had little practical effect on the lives of Anglo-Saxon women. As a group, they held high social status and enjoyed a great deal of self-determination. Laws guaranteed their rights to own land in their own name and to control it as they saw fit.[2]

Antifeminism was not well received by the early English perhaps because they found negative depictions of women to be counterintuitive. The Anglo-Saxon respect for women may be due to pre-Christian Germanic tradition, which reverenced women for their mental and spiritual acuity. Tacitus noted German men's tendency to be guided by feminine wisdom: "There is, in their opinion, something sacred in the female sex, and even the power of foreseeing future events. Their advice is therefore always heard; they are frequently consulted and their responses are deemed oracular" (317).[3] Although Tacitus's statement may not be completely factual—he wrote more as a moralist comparing virtuous Germans to decadent Romans than as a social anthropologist—it appears applicable to early England. The Anglo-Saxons conventionally praise the wisdom of women both fictional and historical.

One proverb in *Maxims I*, for example, tells a noblewoman to advise her husband in their joint affairs; she "must know wise counsel for both house-owners together."[4] Wisdom wears a supernatural face in *The Advent Lyrics*, where Mary prophetically explains the mysteries of faith—"what was secret, the Lord's mystery"; she interprets Scripture with divine insight (41). The English historian Bede (673–735) accords both practical and spiritual wisdom to Hild (614–80), founder of Whitby and other monasteries. Bede reports that bishops "knew [Hild] and loved her ... because of her innate wisdom and inclination to the service of God.... Her prudence was so great, that not only indifferent persons, but even kings and princes ... asked and received her advice."[5]

Whereas the picture of women in early English literature, as these examples suggest, is generally a positive one, some scholars find that the status of English women over time was damaged by Christian antifeminism.[6] These writers address the question of how Christianity influenced Germanic attitudes toward women. In this chapter I pose a rather different query, imagining the converse of this direction of influence: How did Germanic culture color Christian attitudes toward women? More precisely, how did the Anglo-Saxons' regard for femininity affect their retelling of Christian stories with female characters? When the Anglo-Saxons told traditional Christian narratives, they did not translate literally but adapted the stories to their culture. They altered these tales' depictions of women, sometimes subtly, but other times with startling unconventionality. Overall, English authors removed a misogyny foreign to their society and replaced it with a more respectful picture of women.

Some Anglo-Saxon poems revised Christian misogyny by rejecting the patristic belief that women's beauty, especially if cultivated, was reason for men to suspect them. We have noted that Tertullian's *On the Apparel of Women* preaches that women beautify themselves with cosmetics, jewelry, stylish clothing, and elaborate hairstyles out of simple cupidity; their adornments are signs of their fallen nature: "these things are all the baggage of woman in her condemned and dead state" (1.1; Thelwall, 14). Misogynists habitually connect fallen female nature and ornamentation; they do so, R. Howard Bloch concludes, to devalue women as *merely* ornamental, of secondary importance. As decorations, women are hardly necessary to the order of things in the way men are; they are supplemental, surplus, only appendages to the primary world of men.[7]

Anglo-Saxon poetry, like the church fathers, identifies women with ornament, but usually not to denigrate them. The poems typically depict beautiful women not by describing their physical features but by pointing to their jewelry or to a glow of the sort metallic jewelry casts.[8] Attractive women are described simply as "gold-adorned" or "ring-adorned"— with "ring" indicating any circular jewelry. Women are so regularly associated with rings that poets often mention both in the same breath. *Genesis A*, a retelling of the biblical book, links the two when it describes warriors as "defenders of wives and rings" (1971b, 720); the *Advent Lyrics'* Mary is a "bride adorned with rings" (292).

An Anglo-Saxon woman's jewelry is usually a sign of worth. The Anglo-Saxons admired the decorative arts, regarding them as hallmarks of civilization—not, as the church fathers did, as a falling away from it.[9] Their poetry lovingly describes the richly decorated goods that are not only products of the culture but also representations of it. In *Beowulf*, King Hrothgar of the Danes builds the hall Heorot as his realm's administrative, economic, and social center. Symbolizing the Danish nation and its wealth, Heorot is described as "the treasure-decked hall," "the gold hall of warriors, shining with plated gold."[10] Heorot is fittingly dubbed "gold hall," for there Hrothgar dispenses gold to his "thanes," the warriors who in exchange vow their loyalty. The golden objects cementing warrior society are not coins, but "rings" and "ornaments"; both terms refer not only to jewelry but to arms and armor as well, since weapons are ornamented—often "ring-adorned"—and armor is chain mail, linked rings of steel. *Ornament* and *ring* thus describe a class of objects that hold society together, representing both bonds within the warband and defenses against outsiders. Consequently, when Old English poetry associates women with beautiful rings, it places them at the center of society—not, as in patristic thinking, at its margins. *Genesis B* views Eve's beauty as proof of creation by God; the heroine of *Judith* saves people with her beauty and wisdom as well as with an ornamented sword; Queen Elene ornaments not her body but Jesus' cross, helping to establish the church. Old English poetry, however, sometimes views ornament as detrimental to women's status. The Christian martyr Juliana finds decoration lethal, and the men of *Beowulf* practice foreign diplomacy by trading women along with the rings they wear.

Genesis B (a separate composition incorporated into *Genesis A*) contests the core myth of patristic misogyny, Eve's responsibility for the fall. The poem ameliorates Eve's guilt, partly by interpreting her beauty as a sign of her divine nature. This reading starkly contrasts with the patristic view that beauty, especially women's, is created by the devil; Tertullian believed that "fictitious and elaborate beauty" "open[s] the way to temptations," having been "introduced by ... sinful devils" (*Apparel*, 2.2, 2.10; Thelwall, 19, 23). *Genesis B* acknowledges that beauty, if rated too highly, can be criminal—Satan offers his splendor as an excuse for rebellion: "He would not serve God; he said his countenance shone with light, gleaming and brightly hued" (264–66). Satan, however, loses this radiance as soon as he falls; *Genesis B* twice tells us he was beautiful only as long as he served God: "[Lucifer] formerly was the most shining of angels, the whitest in heaven, ... until [he] became too foolish" (338–40; cf. 349–51). Thus the poem discounts the patristic origin of beauty in the demonic. The fallen Satan and his minions are always ugly. When a devil tempts Adam and Eve in the form of a snake, Adam realizes he cannot be, as he claims, God's messenger: "You're not like any of His angels I've seen" (538–39). *Genesis B*, unlike Tertullian, never identifies the beautiful as intrinsically hostile to God.

Instead the poem regularly associates beauty with the divine. Eve's fairness, like Satan's prelapsarian splendor, is proof of divine origin. Before the Fall, Adam tells the snake that God "gave me this woman, this radiantly shining wife" (526–27). Eve preserves her celestial beauty after she falls; three times the poem calls postlapsarian Eve "the most shining of ladies, most radiant of women, ... the handiwork of the heavenly king" (626–28; similarly at 700–703, 821–22). Still shining, Eve bears no resemblance to fallen Satan.

Genesis B resists the church fathers' claim that female beauty has a demonic origin and also denies their argument that Eve bore greater responsibility for the Fall. The poem does assent to the patristic idea of Eve's intellectual frailty, usually adduced as the reason for her culpability: "Adam was not seduced; but the woman being seduced was in the transgression" (1 Tim 2:14). *Genesis B's* Eve, too, has a "weaker mind," "the weak thought of the woman" (590, 649)—but her dimness makes her not cause but victim of the Fall, for it leaves her prey to the devil's seduction. The temptation here differs from the Genesis promise to become "as gods" (Gen. 3:3); the English devil convinces Eve he is an angel bringing God's command to eat the formerly forbidden fruit. Should Eve not comply, God will punish her and Adam with death, and "the greatest injuries to all their children" (549–50). Eve's weak mind cannot detect the devil's lie—but it expiates her from the charge that she wantonly rebelled against God. Indeed, *Genesis B's* Eve sins from the best motives: "through a loyal spirit," she believes she serves God and the interests of her husband and children (708).

Eve's weak mind is, of course, disturbing, since it militates against the Germanic presumption of women's wisdom (Belanoff, "The Fall"). But Eve's low intelligence does not here bear the misogynist connotation it ordinarily does; Eve is emblematic not of female inferiority but of non-gendered gullibility. After Eve eats the fruit, the narrator comments, "It is a great wonder that eternal God allows many thanes seeking learning to be misled by lies" (595–98). Since *thane* normally refers only to men and since Adam is later called thane (705), weak-mindedness is not gendered as female. Indeed, Adam is no more intelligent than his wife. Alain Renoir argues that Eve's "weaker mind" in line 590 is compared not with Adam's but with the devil's; the phrase occurs within a passage on the tempter's wiles. Adam himself responds to the devil with an ignorance his speech exposes: "I do not know if you come with lies. . . . I can not understand anything of your business" (531, 533–34).[11] Adam's lack of intelligence is startling, contradicting patristic assumptions about his mental superiority. *Genesis B* even refutes 1 Timothy's statement that Adam sinned knowing what he did; here Adam—like Eve—is fooled by the devil's lies: "The thane began to change his mind, so he trusted in the promise the woman spoke to him" (705–7). The poem's weak-minded Eve may damage the Old English stereotype of wise womanhood, but its ignorant, unstable Adam does more injury to patristic certainty about male intellectual power.

A second Old English poem offers less radical revisions of scriptural commentary, yet still interprets a biblical character through the norms of Germanic culture. Tenth-century *Judith*, based on an Apocryphal text, tells of a pious Israelite widow winning a military victory for her people by killing Holofernes, leader of the invading Assyrian army. Like its source, *Judith* shows its heroine serving God with her beauty, which wins her entry to the enemy camp and distracts its general. But the Anglo-Saxon poem differs from scripture by imagining Judith's beauty, along with her wisdom, as weapons by which she fights evil. Whereas Apocryphal Judith imagines the widow accomplishing her victory through a ruse, Old English *Judith* sees its title character as a warrior faithful to her military chieftain, God—it terms her killing of Holofernes a military "battle" (123).

Judith is a conventional Anglo-Saxon heroine, wise and possessing a beauty figured as gleaming rings: She is "the fairy-bright lady wise in thought," "the wise one ornamented in gold," woman "laden with circlets, adorned with rings" (13–14, 171, 36–37). The poem derives Judith's beauty from its biblical source but largely invents her wisdom— it calls her wise nine times, although Apocryphal Judith is so praised only once, ironically by Holofernes (11:18). Old English Judith uses her wisdom and beauty as warrior's weapons to defeat Holofernes. That beauty can be a weapon is underlined by the poem's descriptions of the Israelites' blades: Judith decapitates the general with "a decorated sword" (104); the Israelite army brandishes "brightly adorned swords" (230). And when the victorious Israelites spoil the Assyrians of their weapons, the poet concludes that these objects "adorned with gold" are "a greater treasure than any man could say" (328–30). If the weapons' man-made beauty is invaluable, what is Judith's divinely wrought beauty worth? For as earthly lords give their thanes shields and swords, God gives Judith "gifts" of beauty and wisdom (1–2).

The poem casts Judith as a warrior, a role normally filled by men. Yet it does not suggest that its heroine's exploits are unusual for a woman— perhaps because the Anglo-Saxons were not wholly unfamiliar with women warriors. Tacitus reports that Germanic women accompanied their men into battle, urging them to acts of valor (*Germania*, 7); Germanic mythology had valkyries, female divinities of the battlefield.[12] Occasionally a woman might take to the battlefield as did Aethelflaed, Lady of the Mercians (early tenth century), daughter of Alfred the Great, who led troops against invading Vikings.[13] In casually treating Judith's military role, the poem revises its scriptural source, where the widow's actions violate gender expectations: The high priest tells the victorious heroine, "thou hast done manfully" (15.11). Old English *Judith*'s virtues belong to both men and women; God gave Judith courage, "as he does every earthdweller who seeks His help with wisdom and upright faith" (95–97).

Like *Judith*, the poem *Elene* by the ninth-century poet Cynewulf portrays its heroine as God's faithful warrior. Elene is based on the historical mother of Constantine the Great, Saint Helen, who in 312 traveled to the Holy Land to find Jesus' long-lost cross. In the poem this voyage is a military expedition: Elene is "the battlequeen" who commands "a troop of warriors" (254, 217). Like Judith, the queen faces her enemy armed with wisdom. Her chief weapon, though, is not beauty but language, her battlefield a flyting—a formal exchange of speeches conventional to epic poetry—with Judas, spokesman for the Jews of Jerusalem who know where the cross is. Elene's flyting with Judas is staged as the climactic battle of a war between the conflicting truth claims of Christianity and Judaism—a clash from which Elene emerges victorious.

Elene is likely to offend modern readers with its anti-Judaic sentiments. Elene especially is virulent in her treatment of the Jews, ordering Judas thrown into a cistern and starved until he converts to Christianity and reveals the cross's whereabouts. But in spite of its theme, *Elene* is not primarily about Christian attitudes toward Jews. Jews in medieval narratives are often symbolic figures, and Old English writers sometimes identify their pagan ancestors with the Jews.[14] If this is the case with *Elene*, then the poem is not about the conversion of Jews but of Anglo-Saxons. *Elene* may depict the conversion of the Anglo-Saxons to Christianity and represent through Elene and Judas two competing groups that must cooperate if the English church is to thrive. Elene as queen may represent the role of English noblewomen in the church, whereas Judas as bishop depicts the role of the clergy.

Elene stages the queen's combat with Judas very much as a confrontation between female and male forces. Elene—as the only woman in the poem—is conspicuously feminine. Her femaleness is lauded for its procreative power; the poem emphasizes the queen's maternity by introducing her as Constantine's "mother" (214). Cynewulf's vision of motherhood is like Aristotle's in that both imagine a mother providing a body for a male-produced soul. But although the Greek philosopher deemed the mother's contribution minimal, Cynewulf celebrates the crucial task of clothing the spirit in matter. He casts Elene as the mother of the church—her femininity even mirrors that of Ecclesia—who provides the material manifestation of its spiritual truth—a "male" truth that without this feminine revelation would go unknown.

Cynewulf stresses that spiritual truths are male and unknowable in his portrayal of the Jews as fathers who practice a highly spiritual yet intangible faith. Judaism is repeatedly labeled a paternal, in fact patriarchal, religion, "lore of the fathers," "what the fathers knew" (388, 398). This male creed is inscrutable; it constitutes a "mysterious word," a "secret art" (323, 522). The doctrine of Judaism is unfathomable because it worships a deity who, as transcendent spirit, is sublimely unapproachable. God is "unnameable by any man; no one can discover him on earth," Judas's father teaches (465–67).

Elene labels a spiritually minded Judaism masculine because medievals assumed that God, like every spirit, is metaphorically male. Yet Christianity posits that the Father who conceals himself in the Old Testament is revealed through his Son with the help of an earthly Mother: Jesus makes divinity manifest in the human flesh he puts on in Mary's womb. In *Elene* Christ through Mary reveals the Father: Christ is "born into the world as a child through Mary," "[God's] Son by the bright woman" (774–77, 781–82). Judaism is a religion of only patriarchs, but Christianity claims fathers and mothers; only Christian men in the poem—Jesus, Constantine, and Saint Paul (508)—have both parents.

Like Mary, Elene manifests spiritual truth. Her task is always the maternal one of revealing what before was secret and unknowable. Most importantly, she finds Christ's actual cross, a material object that appeared earlier in the poem only as a spiritual presence, a vision in Constantine's dream. Once Elene discovers the cross, she further contributes a material culture to the Christian faith. She constructs a church (1021) and then establishes the church hierarchy at Jerusalem: In a remarkable show of power, she orders the pope to appoint Judas bishop. Founding churches is suitable work for women, for this activity is described as ornamentation: Elene orders both her church and the cross "be covered with works of gold and gems, beset cunningly with the noblest precious stones" (1022–25). Adornment is traditionally the province of women, as we're reminded when Elene appears as "the war-queen bedecked with gold" (331). Christianity, however, is not an exclusively feminine faith; Cynewulf posits that the church comprises masculine and feminine elements working in concert, just as Judas and Elene work together to find the cross and establish the Jerusalem church.

Elene's picture of a woman's contribution to Christianity is possibly influenced by the important role woman played in the evangelization of the Anglo-Saxons. The first Christian "missionaries" to the English were queens like Elene, for the first kings to accept Christianity did so partly through the influence of their Christian wives. Aethelbert of Kent, who was converted in 597 by the first Roman missionary, Augustine of Canterbury, was already familiar with the religion through his queen, Bertha, a Merovingian princess. Their daughter Aethelburg moved to Northumbria in 625 upon her marriage, bringing with her Bishop Paulinus, who baptized her husband, King Edwin. Queens and noblewomen frequently donated their lands and wealth to found monasteries and build churches. In doing so they, like Elene, helped establish the material existence of the Christian church (Lucas, 31–33; Fell, 119–120). Anglo-Saxon nuns later accompanied Saint Boniface (675–755) on his evangelical mission to the continental Germans, acting as missionaries and establishing convents. They wrote letters and brief poems in Latin, and one of them, Huneburg, wrote a prose legend of Saints Willibald and Wynnebald. Along with a few other letters by English nuns, the writings of these missionaries are the only works we know by Anglo-Saxon women.[15]

In another of his poems, *Juliana*, Cynewulf describes a relation between the feminine and ornament much different from the maternal one he draws in *Elene*. The story of a fourth-century virgin martyr, the poem in many ways typifies legends of holy chastity. Juliana is betrothed to the heathen Eleusius but spurns him because her virginity belongs to Christ. Attempting to force their marriage, Eleusius tortures the saint, then imprisons her. In her dungeon a devil tempts her, but she overcomes him in a battle of wits. Pagans behead Juliana, and her soul enters heaven.

Juliana, like Judith and Elene, is described as a wise soldier: She is one of "God's warriors," and her debate with the devil is "heavy hand-to-hand combat" that she wins by her "profound thought" (17, 526, 431). But Juliana's military actions differ from those of other warrior saints in being only metaphoric; she neither wields sword nor wears armor. The purely spiritual nature of battle in *Juliana* is significant, for the poem's rejection of the carnal literal implies an overall rejection of fleshy matter. Juliana obviously denies carnality when she scorns marriage, subtly when she refuses the ornaments Eleusius tries to buy her with. The pagan "owned a horded treasure," is "a warrior prospering with gold" (22, 39). Juliana's father Africanus, too, attempts to turn the saint's mind by mentioning that Eleusius is "rich in treasure" (101–2). But the argument means nothing to Juliana: "She firmly opposed the man's love, although he possessed treasure under lock and key, countless ornaments on earth" (41–44).

Even without the rings that symbolize loveliness in Anglo-Saxon poetry, Juliana is beautiful—she "shines like the sun." Adornment, furthermore, would only deface her beauty—for in this poem golden decorations usually symbolize sin, particularly idolatry, the worship of material objects. Line 22 joins by alliteration the meaning of Eleusius's *hordgestreon* (treasure hoard) with his *haethengield* (pagan tribute); the man himself is thrice described as *"fah* with sins" (e.g., 59). *Fah* is best translated with the negative connotations of *stained*, but it can also possess the neutral meaning of *decorated*. Contrasting with Eleusius's guilty stains, Juliana is described with two adjectives, "naked" and "sinless," which seem to imply each other (187–88). But evil powers insist on besmirching Juliana's body if not her soul. When the devil commands the torturers to "[r]epay her with pain" (619), the word for "repay"—*gyldath*, which can also mean *gild*—accomplishes a neat pun connecting the scars left by torture with golden treasures. But even fire cannot deface the saint's chaste beauty: "Yet the saint stood with brightness unspotted. Neither hem nor robe, hair nor skin, body nor limb, did the fire mark" (589–92). As a virgin, Juliana must be inviolate, unscathed by sexual contact with men, the tortures they inflict, or the heathen ornaments they promise.

Unlike *Judith* and *Elene, Juliana* teaches that women achieve holiness only by rejecting the trinkets symbolizing the world, the flesh, and the devil. In this the poem agrees with Tertullian when he warned women to scorn demonic, carnal decoration. But *Juliana* does not fully agree with the patristic interpretation of deceptive ornament: Tertullian coded cupidinous ornaments feminine, Cynewulf makes them emblems of male vice. Eleusius and Africanus crave treasures, not the saint. Pointing out the male, even paternal, nature of evil, the poet makes the devil a father: The demon who tempts Juliana speaks of his father Satan three times (321, 436, 545). The poem does not vilify men—God, too, is a father (274), and Christian saints include Peter and Paul (304). But surprisingly, in light of its acceptance of many patristic values, *Juliana* does not make femininity hostile to virtue. The martyr need not be manly to become a saint.

Juliana breaks with the standard Anglo-Saxon interpretation of women's ornament as sign of power and divinity. It is not, however, the only poem to rethink the old relationship between women and rings. Gleaming jewelry brings nothing but tragedy to female characters in that most famous Old English poem, *Beowulf*. Its anonymous poet imagines the lives of his continental Germanic ancestors—the setting is the misty past, "days of yore" (1)—by focusing on the exploits of Beowulf the Geat: The hero first defends King Hrothgar and his Danes against the monster Grendel and his cave-dwelling mother, then dies protecting his own people from a fiery dragon. Like Cynewulf's *Elene*, *Beowulf* thinks of women primarily as mothers, coding ornament as sign of their maternal function. But where *Elene* celebrates motherly decoration as foundational, *Beowulf* depicts a society where mothers are devalued. Here rings worn by female Danes and Geats lead to exile and trivialize their role within Germanic society.

Elene depicted a church that needs both mothers and fathers, but in *Beowulf* the Danes and Geats construct themselves as purely paternal civilizations. We meet this all-male world at the very beginning of the poem, which supplies a brief history of the Danish royal house culminating in Hrothgar. It is a completely male history; sons are born to fathers with no mention of mothers. One woman is alluded to but not named. The poem lists children born to Hrothgar's father, Healfdane: three sons, "Heorogar, Hrothgar, and Halga the Good" (61), and one daughter. The reference to Healfdane's daughter is hopelessly garbled in the unique *Beowulf* manuscript, reading, "*elan* queen, dear bedcompanion of the lord of the Heotho-Scilfing people" (62–63). Although editors have attempted to amend *elan* to provide the name of Healfdane's daughter, Norman E. Eliason argues that the poet probably never named the Scilfing queen, since he avoids giving women's names and seems unconcerned with daughters.[16] Healfdane's daughter is only a ghostly presence in the poem, her name erased from history like those of other tribal queens whose "dear bedcompany" was necessary if son would succeed father.

The societies in *Beowulf* regularly devalue maternal bonds, imagining that in warrior civilization fathers are linked to sons directly, without the mediation of mothers. Patriarchy excludes a maternal element, for example, when Hrothgar thanks Beowulf for killing Grendel. Hrothgar notes that such an illustrious son must make his mother proud: "Whichever maiden bore a son among the races of warriors can say, if she yet lives, that the Old God was gracious to her in childbearing" (942–46). The poem omits Beowulf's mother's name, as it did Healfdane's daughter's; the omission contrasts with the 16 times we learn that Beowulf's father was Ecgtheow. The lines, furthermore, call Beowulf's mother simply that—since producing a heroic son is, for this culture, her only valuable action. Yet even this accomplishment is dismissed when Hrothgar replaces the biological mother-son bond with an artificial father-son one.

41

Hrothgar continues, "Now I wish to love you, Beowulf, best warrior, in my heart as a son; henceforth keep well the new kinship" (946–49). Beowulf accepts this new motherless filial bond; he later reminds Hrothgar of the king's vow to "stand in the place of a father" (1479).

This adoption scene's dismissal of Beowulf's mother, its lack of curiosity about whether she is alive or dead, or even who she is ("whichever maiden") models how this society regularly uses and then discards mothers to achieve the ends of men. The chief use of motherhood in *Beowulf* is the custom the poem calls "peace-weaving," where a royal woman creates a truce with a hostile nation by marrying its king; bride and groom produce children, whose joint ancestry should put an end to feuding.[17] Yet there is no really mixed blood in *Beowulf*, since its tribes consider only a father's bloodline worthy of remembrance. Take for example the marriage of a "peaceweaver" (1942), perhaps named Thryth or Modthryth (if she has a name; the manuscript is garbled here, too), to Offa, king of the Angles. In spite of her rather Medusa-like youth—she executed men who looked at her—Thryth's marriage to Offa is successful; she becomes a generous queen and produces a son. But Thryth's story ends with a brief genealogy reminding us that sons inherit no maternal history: Thryth's son Eomer is listed as related only to Offa, Offa's father, and another paternal kinsman (1960–63).

The tribal societies in *Beowulf* depend on peaceweaving as a mechanism for upholding peace. But the practice devalues women, treating them as passive objects of exchange between men. Gayle Rubin has illuminated how some societies are structured through a series of legal contracts between men, sealed when they exchange women as gifts.[18] These relationships are often between a father- and son-in-law, united through the daughter who becomes a bride—a configuration remembered today in some wedding ceremonies when the bride's father "gives her away." The patriarchal societies in *Beowulf* traffic in women—Hrothgar decides to settle a feud with the Heothobards through his daughter Freawaru (2027–29), Thryth marries Offa "because of her father's teaching" (1950)—and peaceweaving is only a glorified name for bride exchange.

The practice, furthermore, makes exiles out of women, for they must perforce leave their native lands: Danish Healfdane's daughter travels to the Scilfings, Freawaru to the Heothobards. Even Hrothgar's queen, Wealhtheow, might be an exile from her own people—Beowulf calls her "peaceweaver" (2017), and her name, which may mean *foreign slave*, suggests her alien roots and service to a people other than her own. At the end of the poem, Beowulf's nephew Wiglaf points to the peaceweaver's status as exile. Foreseeing the demise of the Geats after Beowulf's death, Wiglaf prophesies that henceforth "no maiden shall have on her neck a shining necklace, but sad in mind, bereft of gold, will walk in a foreign land" (3016–19). Wiglaf's prophecy is ironic, for *Beowulf's* women have always walked sadly in exile.

Beowulf highlights peaceweaving's objectification of women by linking their ornaments to the usual media of exchange—weapons, armor, and rings. The poem often mentions a peaceweaver's jewelry in the same breath as other tokens of male exchange. Wealhtheow, Hrothgar's queen, first appears "gold-laden" and "ring-laden" (614, 623), and she passes another precious object, a "treasure-cup" (622), in a ceremony that binds Hrothgar and his warriors. Beowulf predicts that Freawaru's peaceweaving will come to naught, because when she arrives among the Heothobards "gold-adorned" (2025), she will have as her guard a Danish warrior also adorned, with "the hard and ring-marked wealth of the Heothobards" (2037). When the Heothobards realize the Dane wears what should be their treasure, won in battle by Hrothgar and then given to his thane, they will rekindle the feud the gift of Freawaru was intended to settle. The tragic story of the Danish Hildeburh makes the strongest connection between women and ornaments as items of male exchange. Hildeburh's marriage to Finn of the Frisians fails to make lasting peace; a battle between Danes and Frisians sees the death of the queen's brother and son. Finn attempts to make peace with the Danes by offering them treasure, "rings," and "ornaments of plated gold" (1091–93). But the Danes kill Finn and take his treasure home with them—along with Hildeburh. The poet's description of the voyage home, as Gillian Overing points out, creates grammatical and thematic parallels between the treasure and the woman, each given in failed hopes of peace: "Danes carried (*feredon*) to the ship all of the king's property, whatever precious gems they could find at Finn's home. They carried (*feredon*) the noble woman on the seajourney to the Danes" (1154–58). Hildeburh is toted like an item in Finn's treasurehoard.[19]

Peaceweaving in short uses women's procreative abilities to perpetuate a culture that paradoxically denies the importance of maternal lineage. Two women in *Beowulf*, however, assert the value of their maternity, insisting that motherhood is as memorable as paternity and confers the same rights and responsibilities. One of these women is Queen Wealhtheow. She is the only female character in *Beowulf* who actually speaks; the speeches of other women in the poem are summarized in indirect discourse. Wealhtheow's two speeches significantly emphasize her motherhood (1175–87, 1216–31). Indeed, her maternal solicitude for her sons motivates her words.

Clearly Wealhtheow is troubled by Hrothgar's adoption of Beowulf; she worries the King will appoint the warrior his heir, thereby expelling Wealhtheow's sons, and hence herself, from Danish history. She advises her husband, "Leave your people and kingdom to your own kinsmen" and refers to the king's children as "*our* children." Wealhtheow insinuates her parental rights and obligations through the possessive *our*, departing from *Beowulf*'s habit of identifying sons only as fathers. The narrator underlines her claim by reporting that she then moved to stand by "*her* sons" (1180).

In that position she speaks again, after giving Beowulf two bracelets, a corselet, and a fabulous necklace. These gifts are not from Hrothgar but herself, a promise of further reward if he will serve her sons: "Advise these boys in kindness! I will remember to repay you for that.... I will grant you much treasure. Be gracious in deeds to my son!" (1219–20, 1225–27). Wealhtheow claims not only the rights of a parent but those of a lord: She gives gifts in exchange for service to herself, an action usually reserved for men. Motherhood inspires her to move from being traded to trading gifts with men. By entering the male-controlled economy of the poem as a bartering partner, she writes herself into the Danish history. This woman is not excised from the royal genealogy; *Beowulf* memorializes her.

Maternal responsibility brings a second woman, Grendel's mother, memorably into the male commerce of *Beowulf*. We know little about this monstrous woman, but that little emphasizes her interrelated roles as mother and trader. She is identified only as "Grendel's Mother" or "Grendel's Kinswoman." Like other women who are named as some man's queen, daughter, or mother, she is identified only through her relationship to a male character. But the "monster-woman" (1259) is not slighted by this familial moniker; she relishes it, for it provides her entrance—however tragically—into the poem's male business of exchange.

As Grendel's kinswoman, she is obligated to revenge his death. Law in *Beowulf* and in Anglo-Saxon society demanded a slain man's kin avenge him by killing his murderer—this was not their privilege but their responsibility. "It is better that a man avenge his friend than mourn much," Beowulf advises Hrothgar in one of the poem's most famous lines (1384–85). This maxim appears in the portion of the poem dealing with Grendel's mother. Placed here, it reminds us that vengeance is her obligation, and hers alone. Ordinarily vengeance was left to male kin, but Grendel has no other survivors to avenge him. The mother must avenge the son, and thus she enters the poem: "The avenger" is how the poem first refers to her (1256). Like Wealhtheow, she feels motherhood demands that she act on behalf of her progeny by entering into male commerce. For vengeance is a commercial exchange, one life swapped for another: When the mother exacts vengeance from one of Hrothgar's thanes, the narrator comments, "it was not a good bargain, for both sides had to pay with the lives of friends" (1306–7).

Like her son, Grendel's mother is, to be sure, a monster. But she is a monster Danish society has created. Some of the poem's critics argue that its three monsters, though attacking Germanic civilization from outside, represent the evils destroying it from within. These critics usually attach no individual significance to Grendel's mother but see her as representing the same flaw as her son.[20] I would argue that Grendel's mother represents a separate vice, whose nature depends on her female sex: She represents heroic society's diminishment of women; the damage she performs is the harm the tribe does itself when it excludes women.

For Grendel's mother occupies the same position as the other women in the poem. Jane Chance points out that the human women in *Beowulf* all appear in the section of the poem dealing with Grendel's mother. Since these female characters appear together, Chance argues, we are to compare them with one another, to contrast the human mothers' virtues with the monstrous mother's vice.[21] Chance's argument about the interrelated identities of the female characters is crucial; yet I would amend it to argue that Grendel's mother is not the antithesis of the other women in the poem but an icon of their status—she is "in the likeness of a lady" (1351). Literally this means that the mother is female, but it also suggests she is a *likeness* in the sense of a symbolic representation. For all of the human women are mothers and, as peaceweavers, exiles from their native lands. And no one is more maternal or outcast than Grendel's mother, who lives alone with her son in the boggy marshes outside civilization.

Attacking Heorot, the mother is the return of the feminine repressed—with a vengeance. Her husband-less maternal creation of Grendel is an inverted mirror for the patrilineage of *Beowulf's* Germanic tribes. The filial link between Grendel and his mother is mysterious to the Danes, for they cannot imagine a family that lacks a male parent— "they did not know about a father" (1355). The Danes call it unnatural—indeed monstrous—for a mother to give birth to a son alone. Yet they have no trouble imagining whole dynasties where fathers conceive sons without mothers. If complete matrilineage is monstrous, so too is complete patrilineage.

When *Beowulf* depicts a society making its women outcasts, it does so as part of a more general critique of the Germanic heroic code. For the author is a Christian looking back on his race's pagan past, simultaneously regretful that heroic virtue has waned and deeply sensible that heathen values are antithetical to Christianity. The code of vengeance is, from a Christian perspective, fratricide; the acquisition of gold, cupidity; and the desire for fame, pride. And using women to peaceweave marginalizes them—and demonizes them as well. For Grendel's mother, likeness of the lady outcast, is, like her son, one of the "company of devils" (756). This devilish woman is imagined in *Beowulf* as the creation of pre–Christian Germanic society. She is the result of routinely devaluing and exiling women. Thus the poet posits that making the feminine diabolic is part of the pagan past the Christian English must discard. His Anglo-Saxon audience, unlike their heathen continental ancestors, the Danes and the Geats, need to accord their women value by retaining them inside their civilization. Precisely why *Beowulf* should label traditional Germanic culture antifeminist, in contrast with all the evidence that it was not, is not clear. We know so little about *Beowulf,* including who wrote it or when, that any interpretation of the poet's intentions is guesswork. It is obvious, however, that *Beowulf,* like other Anglo-Saxon poems, refuses to incorporate into its portraits of Old English women the church fathers' devilish Eve and instead believes that women, together with men, build the foundations of society.

Narcissus would rather love his own reflection than Echo—a classical analogue for the troubadours' creation of female mirrors for their ideal selves.
Guillaume de Lorris and Jean de Meun, *Roman de la Rose*. Paris, late fourteenth century. The Bodleian Library, Oxford. MS e Mus 65, detail of fol. 12v.

CHAPTER 3

Mirror and Window: The Courtly Lady in Provençal Love Poetry and English Marian Hymns

Chapter 2 sketched portraits of women performing various roles in Old English literature: literal and metaphoric warriors, mothers and virgins, queens and missionaries. These roles compose a spectrum that, despite its breadth, excludes one feminine identity: object of a man's erotic love. Although we might expect the Middle Ages to cast women primarily as objects of male desire (even if we do not approve of the typecasting), most Old English poems are little concerned with romantic attachments.[1]

Some scholars suggest that early English poetry held small place for eros primarily because love hadn't been invented yet. They argue that love as we know it is not a natural emotion but constructed in response to medieval social forces and political ideologies.[2] Modern ideas of love do seem to have a definite historical beginning with a sentiment expressed in the eleventh-century *cansos* or love songs of the Provençal troubadours: *fin'amor* or courtly love.[3] The medieval phrase *fin'amor* points to the essential quality of the troubadours' love, its power to refine. Love confers social graces on the lover and purifies his moral character. This ennobling may occur after the lover has won his lady, for knowing the beloved (cognitively and carnally) is assumed to bring him earthly happiness and ethical perfection. But more typically the lover is perfected by wooing his beloved, for she is an elusive or even disdainful figure who must be won over by the lover's worldly accomplishments and moral worth.

Although courtly love always possesses a refining power, its less central attributes vary widely from text to text. Courtly love evolved after its birth in the eleventh century through the end of the Middle Ages over a wide geographic area, and ideology within these temporal and spatial boundaries was hardly monolithic. If courtly love is a social construct, a given poet's notion of it depends on his or her particular milieu. Courtly love is less a legal code—a list of commandments medieval lovers carried around in their pockets for easy consultation—than a fluid set of attitudes toward love that an author might adapt to a particular purpose in a particular text.

The malleable quality of courtly love will be evident throughout this chapter, which examines perspectives on courtliness within the lyric tradition. The troubadours first used the conventions of courtly love in their cansos, and the *trobairitz*—female troubadours—and English authors writing Marian hymns adapted those conventions for their own purposes. Both the trobairitz and the Marian authors, despite differing aims, criticize troubadour ideology for its narcissistic construction of the self.

If the medieval name *fin'amor* points to the refining nature of troubadour love, equally useful is the more frequent modern term "courtly love," because it reminds us that the sentiment was conceived within and reflects the values of the Provençal aristocracy.[4] The troubadours extolled their ladies in songs performed for the members of local courts. As the poet sings of his futile love, he repeatedly notes the presence of his audience, overwhelmingly young and male. He addresses them directly as his "companions" and asks them to look upon his sufferings with pity. Some scholars believe that the performance of troubadour song for a male court is the key to its essential nature, in that the performance provided for psychological interaction between masculine poet and masculine audience, an aesthetic occasion for male bonding. When the troubadour speaks in his song, he effects through his appeals to his listeners an identification with them so thorough that he in effect speaks for them and with them.

What the poet speaks is not, however, his audience's quest for love but for social prestige. His desire for a lady who recognizes his virtues symbolizes the young nobility's desire that their feudal lord recognize their worth; the troubadour's hope that he will win a place in his lady's heart voices their wish for a place of power in the court.[5] Because the lady represents courtly eminence, she is usually addressed with the male title "midons" (my lord), and the troubadour addresses her in the vocabulary of feudalism, promising to serve as her vassal.[6]

Because the troubadour speaks less for himself than for his male audience, the "I" of the lyric should not be confused with the poet who writes its words. It is an imaginary creature the poet plays at being, an idealized self embodying the shared values of court society. But within the fictional world of each lyric, this ego is aware of its constructed nature and fights against it; it longs to be not a jumble of courtly values but an authentic, self-directed whole. So the "I" continually seeks to separate itself from the male court it symbolizes. The troubadour ego has a number of interrelated strategies for protesting its independence of and superiority to the selves around it, all of them dependent on his lady—for her main function is to distinguish the ego from its look-alike fellows.

All of the lady's qualities work toward proving that the man who loves her is unique. The lady must be astoundingly alluring, inspiring the persona's bottomless desire for her. The troubadour ego insists upon the strength and depth of his desire because desire is, in one medieval tradition of psychology, the core of the self: Each person is imagined as a subject craving anything and everything that is not itself. The troubadours thus dwell on their feelings as the key to their existence, narcissistically enumerating their sufferings as they labor for their ladies' attention. "I sigh and sing.... I falter, I burn, I tremble.... I have such fear of dying": Like a hypochondriac, Cercamon (fl. 1135–45) obsesses over his pains, for they reassure him that he exists.[7]

The lover's desire for his lady is a physical appetite that longs for consummation, despite widespread modern belief that courtly love is platonic. The lover, however, insists that his passion is not lust, that it transcends mere physicality. He distances himself from lust because it threatens the integrity of his identity. For although desire may be the core of the self, it is the core of all selves. Everyone desires, and therefore desire itself cannot support the ego's claim to uniqueness. Troubadour poetry portrays the world in which lust holds sway as one lacking the concept of identity and consequently chaotic (Goldin, *Lyrics*, 6–8). Guillaume of Aquitaine (1071–1127), the first known troubadour, has a number of bawdy lyrics depicting the anticourtly world ruled not by the rules of *fin'amor* but by escalating lust—what he terms the *leis de con* (the law of cunt) [2: 10]. His comic "Song of Strictly Nothing" describes the confusion of identity that living by *con*'s laws entails. Guillaume speaks of his sexual partner as "my little friend, but I don't know who she is" (3:25). Uncertain of the woman's identity, he is downright ignorant of his own; he dwells for three stanzas on what he doesn't know about himself (II–IV). These verses repeat the words "I don't know" and "I am not"; desire alone does not lead to an integral self.

The troubadour lover, to be sure, is mesmerized by the world of relentless desire, longs to enter it because the loss of self promised by sexual climax seems a delicious prospect: The self may be necessary for survival, but maintaining it is a staggering burden. Bernart de Ventadorn (fl. 1150–80), in what may be *the* most famous troubadour canso, "Can vei la lauzeta mover" ("When I see the lark move"), describes how he envies the "melting sweetness" that makes the lark "joyfully move its wings against the light; it forgets itself, and then, having let itself go, falls" (26:1–5). Bernart wishes like the lark to forget himself in the illuminating sweetness of his lady's love. But he knows that such amnesia is fatal, for it destroys the speaking ego. As Bernart says in another song, "many times I am so lost in thought of her ... I am destroyed by my desiring" (24:9, 16). The lark who will not remember itself before it hits the ground will be dead, as will be the lover who does not remember himself before he is subsumed into the realm of desire.

Desire then both sustains the lover and annihilates him. He must paradoxically maintain a desire whose consummation will destroy him. To ensure the perpetuation of the paradox, lovers desire not a woman but the state of desire. As Bertran de Born says to his lady, "I want longing for you more than kissing and holding another" (43:67–68). Perpetual sexual frustration is the preferred state of the courtly lover. The burden of maintaining frustration is placed on the lady. In another paradox, the ideal lady must arouse desire yet thwart it. Her qualities motivate her rejection of the lover's advances. The lady may be disdainful, fickle, and unemotional. She may, however, prove receptive if her situation puts up obstacles to love's physical consummation. These obstacles may include her husband's jealousy, her desire to maintain a good reputation, her social superiority over her lover, and even her physical absence.[8] She may even reside in a foreign country and from there inspire the *amor de terra lonhdana*, "love from a far-off land," which is a favorite theme in the songs of Jaufré Rudel (mid-twelfth century). The lady keeps her distance in the troubadour lyric. She is a shadowy figure, usually silent, and described only in the most general terms. Bernard de Ventadorn's evocation of his lady as "beautiful and white, fresh and gay and soft" is as specific as any description gets (23:17).

The lady, however, cannot be so emotionally or physically removed that the lover despairs and gives up. She must encourage his attentions so that he maintains the desired state of desire. The lady must be intimate yet distant, there yet not there. Many troubadours solve the problem of the lady's simultaneous absence and presence by making the climax of the lover's quest, the supreme act of love, not the sexual act but the moment when lover and lady knowingly look in each other's eyes. Jaufré Rudel's *vida*, a fictional biography, reports that he fell in love with the Countess of Tripoli sight unseen and traveled to the Middle East "from the desire to see her." Having fulfilled that goal quite literally, he died in her arms (Goldin, *Lyrics*, 100–101). Bernart de Ventadorn obsessively remembers the single moment his lady's eyes "gave me such great honor; though a thousand people were there, they looked at where I was more than the others all around" (25:45–49). Bernart frequently uses as a *senhal*, or code name, for his lady "Mos Bels Vezers," which translates roughly as "My Beautiful Looking" (e.g., 23:43). This inelegant English phrase translates the ambiguity carried by the infinitive *vezer*, its implication that the lady both looks and is looked at.

Mutual gazing as climax lets the troubadour sustain the tension of unfulfilled desire, for it lets the lover keep his distance from the lady while affording a measure of intimacy. On the one hand, a purely visual meeting ensures some physical and psychological removal: If the lover sees the lady, his awareness of her as a separate human being lessens the danger of losing himself in her. Seeing guarantees integrity.[9] Yet it also suggests a degree of spiritual communion between lover and beloved. Courtly love borrows the visual climax from Christianity, which describes heaven as a "beatific vision" where the soul finds its greatest joy in seeing and being seen by God. Mimicking a Christian soul, Guillaume in the courtly "Mout jauzens me prenc en amar" ("Much joy prompts me to love") finds his greatest happiness "through her beautiful, pleasing regard" (8:22). He betrays the religious source for this vision when, echoing Saint Paul on the ineffability of heaven (1 Cor. 2:9), he boasts that "no man can find, no eye see, no mouth tell of" anyone more gracious than his lady (8:31–32). Courtly love often borrows the vocabulary and ritualism of Christianity to lend itself pageantry and grandeur. It does not make any direct challenge to orthodoxy—although courtly lovers and Cathar heretics shared the soil of Provence, one had little to do with the other. Some troubadours were sympathetic to the Cathars, others were fierce supporters of Rome.[10] Courtly love is not a religion. It is earthbound and earth-centered: The lover seeks happiness not with

God but with his lady, the troubadour seeks as his final reward the grace not of the heavenly but of the terrestrial court (Goldin, *Lyrics,* 122–25).

Even if the lover reaches the ecstatic vision that consummates his love, this climax is so distant in the past and has so little hope of ever being repeated that it is only a memory the lover treasures in his mind. Gace Brulé (fl. 1180–1213), one of the trouvères—northern French poets who adopted troubadour conventions—writes that "never in my life will I forget her face or look.... Neither grey eyes nor sweet look will I ever see again in my life" (16:2–4, 11–12). Gace laments the loss of his lady, yet he would rather remember her than see her or achieve any more intimate intercourse. For even seeing her propels him into the world of desire that will annihilate his being and his song: "I cannot see you," he says, for "when I see you, I am silenced; I am so conquered I do not know what to say" (16:46–48). Faced with a choice between his lady and his own voice, Gace must choose himself.

Gace willingly chooses the remembered lady of his song over the real one who silences him because poetry is his greatest good. The troubadours wrote love poems not because they were lovers but because they were poets. They expected their contemporaries to revere them not for the daintiness of their emotions but the quality of their verse. For the troubadours, the ultimate courtly virtue is speaking well: Guillaume advises an aspiring lover to above all "keep himself in court from speaking like a peasant," then points to his own verse as the epitome of courtly speech (6:6). Troubadours' songs prove their eloquence, love simply furnishes them subject matter for their song. The poets claim that their ladies, by inspiring them, are the sources of their poetic skill; Peire Vidal (fl. 1180–1205) typically says, "she gave me understanding and knowledge so that I sing courteously" (47:22–24). But the reverse is true: The troubadour's lady is not a real woman who inspires the poet's art, but a fiction, an ideal image he has created.[11]

A number of troubadours acknowledge that their ladies are artificial creatures, but none more honestly than Bertran de Born (b. 1140). In "Domna, puois de me no'us chal" ("Lady, since you do not care for me"), he laments that since his lady spurned him, he cannot "*trop* another lady to my desire" (43:8). Bertran's use of the verb *trobar* is significant: Although it means "find," it also means "create, compose" (hence the "troubadours," i.e., "composers"). In the remainder of this song, Bertran proceeds to *trobar* an ideal beloved, "to make an imaginary, composite lady" (43:19). He begs from each of a succession of women a single virtue or physical attribute that he assembles into an image "whom I desire as much as I do you" (43:62–63). Bertran's equal desire for his composite and real ladies implies that they are interchangeable, that the lady to whom he addresses this poem is as much a projection of his fantasy as the lady he cobbles together.

All ladies whom troubadours adore unite in themselves every virtue and are like Bertran's lady figures created by a poet's imagination. The fictional status of the lady is testified to by the forms she most typically takes in the poems—a work of art, a vision, a memory, or an erotic fantasy, as when Bernart de Ventadorn imagines kissing his lady so hard she wears the bruise for a month (24:39–40). As a mental construct, a troubadour's lady is a monument he erects to himself, the ideal image of his own mind. Whenever he sings her praises, he in effect sings his own, since whatever beauty and virtue she possesses has come from his imagination.

The narcissism of troubadour love reveals itself when the poets, describing the gaze they exchange with their ladies, invoke the image of a mirror. When Rigaut de Barbezieux sees his lady, he is like "the tiger who sees his noble body in a mirror" (Goldin, *Mirror*, 92n). Jaufré Rudel wants to see his lady's "beautiful eyes reflect my staff and cloak" (20:13–14). Bernart de Ventadorn, among others, addresses his lady with the *senhal* of *Miralhs*, "mirror," and confesses he has been in love "since I saw myself in you" (26:21). The lover's supreme communion with his lady, then, the moment he looks into her eyes, is simply the moment he admires himself.

The canso thus provides the lover with the ultimate proof of his existence. This confirmation is what the lyric persona always sought, for he has been unsure whether his identity is an integral self or a construct of courtly values. In the troubadour lyric he constructs a feminine persona who, as a distinct other, renders a vision of himself as self-determined and whole. His integrity hinges on the existence of the lady, her willingness to, if only for a moment, meet the lover's eyes with her own. But since the lady is just an idealized image of the lover, he can always count on her complicity.

The courtly lady, a narcissistic alter ego for the troubadour, is a decidedly misogynistic creation. In troubadour ideology, women do not exist in their own right but as fantasies engineered to celebrate the male ego. Troubadour misogyny, however, contrasts remarkably with the real situation of Provençal women, who enjoyed more self-determination and political power than women elsewhere in Europe. How is it possible to reconcile troubadour misogyny with the relatively high status of Provençal women? Some scholars note that the growing popularity of troubadour lyric around 1100 coincided with feudalism's increasing insistence that sons and not daughters inherit property. These scholars theorize that courtly love arose as a parallel attempt by the male aristocracy to contain women's power, an ideological counterpart to the political and economic constraints of feudalism.[12] Courtly love, in this view, is not so much descriptive as prescriptive, a picture of what courtly society desired in women.

Despite the antifeminist nature of the troubadour canso, some Provençal women took up its conventions. The trobairitz are of sufficient number to compose the largest group of medieval female vernacular authors. Because of the anonymity of most medieval poetry, we cannot conclude definitely how many trobairitz there were or the number of lyrics they composed. The names of 20 trobairitz have come down to us, and the work of 19 has survived, although in most cases we can attach only one poem to a name. This extant corpus dates from a relatively brief period of time, about 1170 to 1260, and consists of 23 poems, or less than 1 percent of the troubadour corpus of about 2,700 lyrics. Some experts believe that about an equal number of other poems with a female voice, sometimes in dialogue with a male speaker, were written by women.[13]

The relatively large number of trobairitz is surprising, not so much because of the misogyny of troubadour ideology, but because the canso's conventions practically forbid women to write. The troubadour lady's main function is to frustrate her lover's passion by refusing to see or speak with him. Invisible and silent, she cannot teach real women how to speak. Luckily the trobairitz had other models of female speech to emulate. The troubadours wrote poems in genres other than the canso, and these provide a range of female voices. Pierre Bec enumerates the speech-roles assigned women in male-authored poetry and argues that the trobairitz imitated these traditional voices: They express love in the chansons d'ami, sorrow when sunrise signals that their lover must depart in the alba, or suffering at the hands of a jealous husband in the song of the mal marieé; or they may simply sing as they pursue the usual tasks of female life in the chansons de toile (weaving songs).[14]

These female voices speak in an idiom different from that of troubadour lovers, and generally one less courtly. Because the trobairitz appropriate voices that eschew the more rigid conventions of the canso, some modern readers label the trobairitz more "sincere" or "authentic" than their male colleagues, believing that the trobairitz's poems communicate their authors' real thoughts and emotions (e.g., Bogin, 68–69). Although no doubt the trobairitz's lives in some way inspire their verse, and although the voices they adopt may bespeak female experience, it would be a mistake to think the trobairitz's poems offer an unmediated look at the lives of Provençal women.[15] The trobairitz are as conventional as the troubadours, but they follow a different set of conventions—one characteristic of which is, ironically, the appearance of sincerity.

The range of female voices open to the trobairitz, although based on uncourtly personae, affords them a vantage from which to critique the ideology of male courtly speech. Female voices in male-authored compositions often effect such a critique, exposing courtliness as a male fantasy and offering a less courtly view of love.[16] The troubadour Marcabru frequently uses women as debunking characters, as when he imagines a shepherdess exposing as downright lies the compliments a knightly suitor pays her. The woman, refusing to be a silent image, declares her desires. As a real woman she wants not a dreaming fop but a real man—a peasant who suits her own status (Goldin, *Lyrics*, Poem 14).

Many of the trobairitz adopt voices that, like Marcabru's shepherdess, denounce courtly love as male posturing, disclosing the aspiration for power and reputation that motivates courtly lyric. Often this disclosure occurs in a *tenson*, a dialogue with a male poet speaking as courtly lover. Isabella unmasks the troubadour Elias Cairel as a "pretender" when she compels him to admit he wrote songs about her not out of love but for "honor and profit."[17] In another tenson, the poet Lanfranc voices the courtly sentiment that a lover serves his lady best by leaving her to perform chivalric deeds; but Guillelma de Rosers deflates his aspiration for renown by maintaining that the true lover "serves his lady first" and does not abandon her to serve men (7:29). And Maria de Ventadorn accuses the troubadours of social climbing when she tells Gui d'Ussel that a lover might swear to be a lady's servant when he first woos her, but he will later seek to be her equal (9:33–40).

Since *fin'amor* brings women neither love nor power, some trobairitz refuse to play the passionless statue idolized by the troubadours. The Countess of Dia, author of four cansos, regrets her former practice of courtly love, for by denying her lover's passion she drove him away. Now determined to win him back, she imagines a future where she "holds him one evening in my bare arms" (36:10). Although the trobairitz generally distance themselves from the ideology of the troubadours, they agree that recognizing desire is the key to self-determination and self-expression. That a woman has a right to speak her desires is a frequent theme in the four songs of Castelloza. Although she confesses in one canso that her outspokenness sets a bad example for other women "because only men send messages," (31:23), in another she argues that the ban on female speech harms men inasmuch as it forces them to do all the courting. Castelloza suggests that the burden of wooing be placed on women (Poem 30). And in a third song she states that those who say "it is very unbecoming for a lady to woo a knight herself ... really don't know how to enjoy love" (29:18–19, 21).

The trobairitz's open declarations of their desires directly oppose courtliness, but sometimes the women poets effect a more subtle, indirect attack on *fin'amor*. They play along with courtly conventions to reveal that they do not work, do not lead to a narcissistic affirmation of the lover's ego. The women are able to take courtly conventions to their illogical conclusion because of a certain ambiguity in the role of mirror accorded them. The troubadours expect the lady to function as a "mirror of vanity," one that reflects their own ideal image. But like the Wicked Queen in Snow White, they often discover that mirrors may not show us what we want to see, may instead reflect our blemishes. The Middle Ages knew that one function of a mirror was to expose deficiencies in order to correct them: Augustine said that the Bible was a mirror in which you "see what you are, and if it displeases you, strive so that you will not be so."[18] The trobairitz decide to function as Augustinian mirrors of correction, revealing the deceptions in the troubadour construction of the self.

The most explicit critique of the courtly self-reflexive ego is made by Lombarda in an exchange of *coblas* (strophes) with the troubadour Barnat Arnaut d'Armagnac.[19] Barnat speaks first, converting himself into a mirror for his female partner as he says "I would like to be a Lombard for the sake of Lady Lombarda." Later he turns her into a mirror, too, addressing her with the *senhal Mirail de prez*, "Mirror of worth" (8:1, 17). Bernat's turning both himself and Lombarda into mirrors works badly as a metaphor because it wipes out any possibility of an integral self: Neither poet is real, just the reflection of another reflection. Lombarda enacts this lack of integrity in her *cobla* by agreeing to be Bernat's mirror; indeed, she makes herself not one mirror but two, one for each of his names: "I would like to have, for Bernat, the name Lady Bernada, and for Lord Arnaut be called Lady Arnauda" (8:21–22). By becoming a double mirror, she discloses to us that the troubadour self is an illusion of multiply reflected images similar to a funhouse hall of mirrors. She challenges Bernat to choose a mirror to look into: "Tell me ... the mirror

where you gaze" (8:25, 28). But faced with a choice among the two specular Lombardas and his own reflexive self, Bernat is unable to commit to
a single glass. Lombarda concludes that there is no Bernat, only "a mirror without an image," "and I do not see you, who remain silent" (8:29,
36). Lombarda thus announces that the elaborate architectonics of the
troubadour ego do not produce a self at all, merely a void.

Lurking behind the trobairitz's distrust of the mirror metaphor is their
suspicion that men and women, because of their physical differences,
can never fully reflect each other. The partial incongruity between herself and her lover is the central theme of the Countess of Dia's first song.
The Countess suggests the couple's simultaneous identity and difference
by the elegant juxtaposition of male and female forms of Provençal
adjectives. Her technique is impossible to translate into a Modern English lacking grammatical gender, but a rough approximation of a few of
her lines might be: "My friend is most *joy*ful, so I am gracious and *joy*-
ous; and since to him I am *true*, to me he must be *tru*thful" (34:3–6).
The shared meaning and etymological roots of the adjectives suggest the
shared identity of the lovers, as well as mutuality in their construction of
identities: His joy makes her joyful, her fidelity makes him faithful. But
the different suffixes of the adjectives—a difference that in Provençal
marks gender distinction—denote real and unavoidable differences
between the lovers. The lovers, as male and female, cannot be totally
alike, cannot completely mirror each other.[20]

Many trobairitz agree with the Countess that women cannot mirror
men. For this reason, the women poets do not seek confirmation of their
identity from a member of the opposite sex; the trobairitz's male friend
does not play the self-idealizing role that the lady plays for the troubadours.[21] Women poets look for an idealized self-image where it is more
likely to be found: within a member of their own sex. The corpus of
trobairitz poetry is populated with female figures whom the poets views
as empowering mirrors.

The trobairitz's reflexivity with other women can take many forms. It
may be admiration and affection. The trobairitz Azalais d'Altier sends a
verse epistle to the Lady Clara, interceding for a male suitor. Like any
troubadour looking at his mirror, Azalais states her wish to see Clara:
"You, lady, whom I wish to see more than anything else in the world"
(43:7–8). Yet Azalais is already a mirror for Clara, holding the other
woman's image inside: "I have heard so much good said of you ... that
your looks are engraved in my heart" (43:9, 12–13). When Azalais lauds
all of Clara's virtues, she praises her own. A similar mirroring exists,

though less explicitly, between Bieris de Romans and one Lady Maria. Bieris addresses Maria using the conventions of male courtly song, declaring that "in you I have my heart and my desire," "for you I very often walk around sighing" (28:14, 16). Bieris's use of erotic conventions in praise of another woman is such that some readers believe the poem a lesbian love song; one recent critic, however, argues that it is impossible to label it definitively so, since similar conventions are used when one woman, addressing another, acts as go-between for a man.[22] Regardless of whether Bieris is a lesbian, she constructs a reflexive relationship with Maria, seeing her as an ideal figure of all women, including herself: "In you ... is every virtue one might seek in a woman" (28:24).[23] Any lover would find the same womanly virtues in Maria and in Bieris.

Yet relationships between women in trobairitz poetry are not always as convivial as between these two. Often the poet competes with another woman for the love of a man. Curiously, she finds the contest with this woman empowering: That she can compete with a strong enemy confirms her own strength, that her fate depends on herself or another woman testifies to the power of women. The Countess of Dia rises to battle almost with glee when "another love takes you from me" (35:17). She is confident she can win her lover back through her own merits: "You really must recognize the most refined woman" (35:27). She then enumerates her virtues: "My worth and lineage, my beauty and even more my faithful devotion should be of some value to me" (35:29–30). The Countess values herself even if her lover does not.

Castelloza has a very different relationship with her rival, one that achieves a self-affirmation that at first appears to be self-abnegating suicide. Castelloza calls, when her lover takes up a new lady, for her own death: "I must die when I see he lives with another woman" (32:8–9). Unlike the Countess of Dia, who sings with fervent joy even when unlucky in love, Castelloza wallows in her misery. But she is not a masochist who enjoys suffering for its own sake.[24] Castelloza's masochism is conventional; she suffers and calls for death in good troubadour fashion. Although her poetry is in some ways very unconventional (she suggests that her lover and his new lady form a ménage with her, 32:19–22), Castelloza is the trobairitz who most fully writes in the traditional male idiom. Like any courtly lover, she longs for a visionary climax to her love: "Cast on me a fair look that will revive me and conquer my suffering," she pleads (32:49–50). And like any troubadour, her primary concern is her art. She desires perpetual separation from her beloved so that she will always have emotions to turn into song. "In courting I take great refreshment, when I court him in whom I have great sorrow," she confesses (29:23–24). As Peter Dronke puts it, Castelloza's "fulfillment lies far more in herself, and in her poetry, than in her man."[25]

With the exception of Castelloza, who shares the troubadours' dual absorption in self and song, the trobairitz are highly critical of the narcissism of Provençal courtly poetry. The women poets launch this criticism from a feminist standpoint: Courtliness is male egoism that both feeds on and negates feminine identity. Feminism, however, is not the only perspective from which courtliness can be critiqued. Troubadour ideology of the self is also open to attack from a religious point of view: In imagining a self-created, self-sustaining humanity, it is inherently atheistic. Because of its secular perspective, troubadour courtliness had only limited and indirect influence on Middle English literature, which is more religious than the literatures of other linguistic groups.[26] Secular poems account for less than a quarter of Middle English lyrics, and even those most influenced by the Provençal poets display this influence more in literary form than content.[27]

Courtly love did greatly influence English medieval writers, but through a religious reinterpretation. A Christian courtliness informs the Middle English poems written as prayers to the Virgin Mary. These poems, most written in the fifteenth century, give Mary the courtly qualities of the troubadour's lady. She is noble, virtuous, beautiful, and excites the speaker's desires. One Marian devotee declares that he "In her bosom desires to rest, since of all women I love her best."[28] A lyric may express its narrator's desire to serve Mary as her feudal vassal; the beautiful song "Edi beo thu (Blessed be you), Hevene Quene" tells Mary, "I cry you mercy, I am your man, in service to foot and hand" (13th: 60.22–24).

Although these poems invoke Mary as courtly lady, she functions far differently in the construction of the self than her secular predecessors. Whereas the troubadour relied on his lady to affirm himself as an integral entity, the religious poet depends on Mary to destroy his narcissistic self-reliance. The purpose of a Middle English religious lyric is often to stir its audience to repentance and devotion. It accomplishes this goal by presenting its penitent speaker as model for the audience; his first-person point of view draws in hearers or readers until it becomes their point of view, too, and they along with him declare, before the figure of Mary, their unworthiness.

The transformation of the reader's point of view is achieved in the Marian lyric through a modification of the troubadour ocular climax.

Like the troubadour lover, what the speaker of the Marian lyric—and through him the poem's reader—longs for is a glance at or from his lady. "To see my lovely lady dear" is the oft-repeated wish of "A Song of Love to the Blessed Virgin" (14th, 111:58). What the speaker sees when he looks into Mary's eyes, however, is not himself, but Mary's vision of her Son: as an infant at the Nativity, a ghastly figure suffering on the cross, or a pallid corpse in scenes reminiscent of Michelangelo's Pietà. And always the poem emphasizes the Virgin's act of looking at Jesus and the vision she sees. One poem describes Mary's search through the streets of Jerusalem for Jesus on Good Friday. Mary finds Jesus on the cross, and like any lady and her lover they gaze at each other: "I saw him hang on the cross in my sight; I looked on him and beheld him. Son, see your mother" (15th: 6:38–40).

But when poems like this emphasize Mary's act of looking at Jesus, what they seek to effect is not only a visual climax of love between Jesus and his mother, but between Jesus and the reader. We look into the poem to see Mary, but then we look through her to the Jesus she views. The Virgin's most important characteristic is her transparency, the way she disappears in front of our eyes. Like a clear pane of glass, her purity allows the light of God's grace to reach humankind. "Alighting in her, one ... shone through her seemly side ... As the sun does through the glass," says one lyric punningly.[29] Another prays, "O thou blest virgin clear, be ready always to mediate fully between God and man." The clear virgin here allows speaker and God to see each other: "Pray your Son ... to have my soul in His lovely eye," he asks (15th, 11:41–43, 60).

Mary's transparency figures her selflessness, the submission of her will to her Son's. She is a model for readers, who too must empty out their own desires in favor of the will of Jesus. If we are to take on the role of Mary, to adopt her loving glance toward Jesus, and thereby enter into the beatific vision, we must, at least for the moment, cease to be ourselves, forget if only for the moment our individual perspectives. The structures of the lyrics invite us to this self-forgetting, what Rosemary Woolf calls "an abnegation of individuality," by manipulating us to see progressively from the perspectives of the narrator and then Mary.[30] When we finally arrive at a glimpse of Christ in these poems, we do so with the awareness that the sight of God is not ours alone, but rather the communal property of these other viewers, and indeed of anyone who by reading enters into the ocular mechanisms of the poem. The lyrics thus accomplish the sense that one, even while a unique, integral individual, has worth only within the larger community of all who share the beatific vision. The Marian lyrics share the view that the self reaches its full potential only when it looks outside itself; and they agree that the self must look first toward women, and then along with them, if it is ever to escape the trap of narcissism.

*Histoire ancienne jusqu'a
César.* Paris, ca. 1375,
Vol. II, f. 199.
Oslo/London: The
Schøyen Collection,
MS. 27.

Bible Moralisé,
French, ca. 1240.
The Bodleian Library,
Oxford. MS Bodl
270b, detail of fol. 6r.

The iconography of Caesarian birth, with the child drawn through a wound in the dead
mother's side, is repeated in that of the "births" of Eve and the Church, respectively
delivered through the wounds of the male, yet maternal, Adam and Jesus.

CHAPTER 4

Love and Marriage: Women in the Family Romance

Courtly love exerted its major influence on medieval England not through troubadour lyric but through Old French romance. The genre's popularity results from the Norman Conquest of 1066. William the Conqueror systematically replaced the Anglo-Saxon aristocracy with his own Norman knights. Their political and economic bonds to William composed the feudal system—an arrangement in which all land belongs to the king, who leases it to a vassal in exchange for military service. Besides altering the political structure of England, the Norman Conquest brought immense changes to literary culture—for William's Norman knights spoke French, which displaced English as the language of the upper classes and as the prestige literary vernacular.

Among the favorite genres of the Normans was the romance, which is inherently concerned with knights and their social obligations. The typical romance features a knight who performs valorous deeds, including rescuing a lady with whom he falls in love. The central protagonist of most romances is male. Some romances feature women as main characters, but these tend to represent the feminine as it relates to and serves masculinity. A female figure in romance may, as in troubadour lyric, represent a social or psychological aspect of a man or a virtue he wishes to attain. The eponymous heroine of the French *Romance of Silence*, for example, dresses as a man to pursue a career as a jongleur, a professional performer of songs.[1] Her cross-dressing suggests she is in some fundamental way male, and *Silence* may be a meditation by its author, Heldris

64

de Cornuälle, on his role as literary creator—a role the Middle Ages often defined as feminine, as we saw in chapter 1.[2]

The hero of a romance often ends his quest by marrying the damsel he loves. Marriage, both as a social institution and locus for courtly love, is a central preoccupation of romance. Other courtly genres, like troubadour lyric, may make the courtly relationship adulterous, but French romancers reinterpreted courtesy as an aspect of married love. Their aversion to adultery may have morality behind it, but it also involves politics. Knights were a powerful group who sought to perpetuate their power through land ownership, since control of property was a medieval index of power and wealth. How much land aristocratic families controlled could depend on whom their male members married. Although a noble family originally obtained land from its feudal lord, it remained in their possession only if the family continued to exist through the birth of heirs. As medieval law developed, it stipulated that a fief could not be broken up but must be passed down intact to the eldest son (the law of primogeniture), and the so-called Salic Law precluded daughters from inheriting. Marrying one feudal lord in order to bear the next, then, was the chief role of women in aristocratic families.[3]

Many medieval romances are obsessed with marshaling their characters into familial relationships that support feudal power structures. Some critics, in light of these familial patterns, call these texts "the family romance," adopting a term Freud coined to describe children's penchant for inventing parents to replace their real ones.[4] The major theme in family romance is the perpetuation of a patriarchal bloodline. Some texts show this lineage continuing intact even in unlikely circumstances, as when a male progenitor has only daughters. In such cases, a king lacking a male heir will hope to conceive a son through his daughter, although his dynastic hopes are coded as incestuous lust. In the Middle English lai *Emaré* (c. 1450), the title princess avoids incest but ends her adventures by bearing a son who becomes her father's heir, thus preserving his line. Father/daughter incest also functions as a male fantasy of self-perpetuation in the lai *Sir Degaré* (c. 1330), which announces its theme as "love of ... great heritage."[5] The title hero's mother is raped and made pregnant by an unknown knight; fearing that people will blame her father, she hides her pregnancy and abandons her newborn son. Years later the grown Degaré returns and wins his mother in marriage by defeating his grandfather in a joust—a sign that he is a fit replacement for him indeed, as the new king is a double for the old one. Mother and son avoid marriage in the nick of time, and Degaré weds a lady whose life parallels his mother's; she is a maternal double. *Sir Degaré* conjures up the threats of both father/daughter and mother/son incest only to defuse them, while preserving both incestuous unions on a symbolic level. The result is a family tree both complex and simple, for Degaré's grandfather and mother are the only real characters—the others are mirrors for them.

Not all family romances concerned with lineage imagine it as purely male. Chrétien de Troyes's *Perceval or The Story of the Grail* fits its hero into an aristocratic lineage on both sides of his family. Perceval wishes to become a knight like his late father. The boy's success seems improbable because his mother, fearing that knighthood will bring him only death, has kept from him any knowledge of his paternal heritage or chivalry. To ensure his ignorance, she brings him up in a forest far removed from civilization. But Perceval leaves her in pursuit of knighthood. He encounters a number of tutelary figures who instruct him in chivalry as well as his genealogy—surprisingly, these mentors are his maternal uncles and cousins.

Perceval's inheriting a chivalric identity from both parents has thematic significance—his forest-dwelling mother symbolizes nature whereas his father represents civilization, and the boy learns that a knight requires gifts from both realms. But Perceval's perpetuation of his maternal line may also reflect the world in which Chrétien wrote: His patron was a powerful woman, Marie of Champagne, who inherited from her mother, Eleanor, duchess of Aquitaine and queen of England, a lineage rivaling in wealth and nobility that of her father, King Louis VII of France. In assigning Perceval an exalted maternal lineage, Chrétien acknowledges that politics and biology dictate that knights respect their heritage on both sides.

Some family romances concern not the perpetuation but the establishment of aristocratic lineage. These were often commissioned by lords who wished to buttress their power with a myth of their dynasty's magical origins. These ancestral romances are unabashed inventions, tracing the family back to a hero who marries a fairy bride. Her otherworldliness, derived from goddesses in the Celtic myths romancers used as sources, signifies that the dynasty she founds is providentially appointed to rule. The French tale of the fairy *Melusine*, for example, who every Saturday changes into a serpent from the navel down, was imagined as the origin of the house of Lusignan.[6] Melusine's story, although only a small portion of her eponymous romance—it frames stories of her sons becoming kings and princes—is by far its most compelling element. Melusine's fairy mother cursed her with her serpent form because she wreaked vengeance on her human father—he had dared view his wife in childbed, an indiscretion that miserably exiles mother and triplet daughters to the Isle of Avalon, traditional home of magical women. Melusine's story repeats her mother's, for Melusine's husband violates her command that he never see her in her serpent form, thereby perpetually turning Melusine into a serpent who bewails her lost love even while she nurses her children and guards their descendants.

Melusine, despite her serpentine attributes, is the typical bride in the "establishment of family" romance: She teaches her husband how to trick the king into granting him a large fief, thus fulfilling the main role of the bride who, whether she be fairy or human, brings a generous dowry of land that the hero rules as feudal lord. Romance thus illustrates a common fact of feudal life: Younger sons, who could not inherit wealth, had to acquire it by other means. Their best chance was in wedding the daughter of a rich but sonless lord; the daughter could inherit her father's land but not his title, which would go to her husband and then pass to his sons.

Stephen Knight argues that, by spinning plots that describe either the establishment or the perpetuation of a noble family, many romances indoctrinate their readers in feudal ideology. Women were in large part the object of such indoctrination, and romances often imagine their audiences as female. The heroine of Chaucer's *Troilus and Criseyde* listens to her niece read a romance, and the Nun's Priest swears that his Tale is as true as "the book of *Launcelot de Lake*, / That wommen holde in ful greet reverence."[8] Romances' habit of picturing their female readers reflects medieval reality: Among the upper-class laity more women than men could read, and noblewomen often acted as patrons of writers secular and religious.[9] That medieval women composed an often avid audience for romances is troubling if we modify Knight's argument to focus on romance's indoctrination of women. Romances, as feudal propaganda, teach aristocratic women to accept their lot as wives, mothers, and means of acquiring wealth. Why would women want to read texts depicting them as broodmares or meal tickets? One possibility is that they might be unaware of a text's agenda. Romancers were artful, knowing that effective propaganda conceals its aims. They present the role of feudal wife as one accruing to its heroine's benefit: It brings her prestige, honor, happiness and—above all—love of the courtly variety. Romances, to use a modern word especially appropriate here, romanticize feudal marriage, sugarcoating it with the passionate emotions of courtly love.

A given romance, however, may not have such a message at all. Whereas most medieval romances support chivalric ideology, some criticize it, and many may be open to both orthodox and heterodox interpretations. Roberta Krueger has argued that Chrétien de Troyes's *Yvain, or The Knight of the Lion*, for example, can be read as supporting or denouncing feudal marriage.[10] In *Yvain* Chrétien is candid that romanticizing socioeconomics is the business of romance, especially in a scene in which Yvain encounters a young maiden reading a romance to her wealthy family while they recline in an orchard opulently furnished with every sort of luxury.[11] Next to the orchard toil three hundred enslaved maidens whose production of textile goods provides the family's wealth. Here Chrétien suggests that the idyllic world of romance exists only for readers who ignore the real world around them—a world in which maidens are sacrificed to the financial gain of great families.

Having warned us about the romanticizing function of romance, Chrétien is not averse to some romanticization himself. *Yvain*'s main plot describes the marriage of the title knight and the widow Laudine, originally undertaken for pragmatic reasons: Laudine agrees to marry Yvain, even though she hates him, because she believes a warrior will protect her lands against King Arthur, who comes to take possession (314–15). Laudine's situation was not uncommon in the Middle Ages: A childless widow might inherit her husband's lands but thereby be considered by her feudal lord a prize to be given in remarriage to one of his political supporters (Lucas, 85–87). Chrétien emphasizes the marriage's political nature: "So now my lord Yvain is lord of her land" (322).

Yvain thus far does not romanticize feudal marriage but demystifies it, lays bare its political foundation. But the romance does not end there. Most of Yvain's story, like many romances, is not about love leading to marriage but marriage leading to love. After the wedding Yvain abandons Laudine to seek adventures that will enhance his reputation. He leaves at the instigation of his friend Gawain, who argues that marriage exists solely for the economic and social advantage of a knight; "He who has a beautiful woman as wife or sweetheart should be the better for her," he tells Yvain, and by "better" he means of greater "fame and worth" (326).

Laudine cannot accept this sort of marriage. She repudiates Yvain and brands him a "thief" (329)—literally of her heart, but implicitly of her wealth. Yvain begins a series of adventures under the *nom de guerre* of the Knight of the Lion (he is accompanied by such a beast), each adventure reprising his courtship of Laudine. In each episode Yvain serves a lady and learns that women's wealth does not serve knighthood but that knights serve women. In the end Yvain realizes that marriage demands fidelity, and he returns to Laudine, who accepts him. Chrétien comments, "now everything has turned out well, for he is loved and cherished by his lady, and she by him" (380). Seen in its totality, *Yvain* romanticizes feudal marriage, since Yvain and Laudine's union, undertaken for political reasons, ends with real devotion between the couple.

If romances' erotic relations offer a look at the complex social web of feudalism, they also open a window on the chivalric mind. For the family romance teaches its audience not only the social roles they must play but also the psychological attitudes these roles require. Romance's incest theme is often a means for such instruction, Derek Brewer argues: Plots about incest act out the anxieties maturation entails and thereby suggest how to cope with them. If romances asked their audience to identify with a hero who killed his father and narrowly avoided marrying his mother, it was because each male member of the audience would have to replace his father in the social hierarchy, assuming his responsibilities.[12]

When a romance traces the psychological maturation of its hero, his adventure often brings him to the same integrity the troubadours desired—perfect spiritual and mental wholeness. This integrity is frequently figured as male reason ruling female sensuality. As noted in chapter 1, Augustine used Adam's control of Eve to represent reason's power over sensuality. Adam and Eve indeed were an integrated pair— Genesis notes that in marriage they were "two in one flesh" (Gen. 2:24).

If the male-female hierarchy of marriage represents integrity, then the romance hero, like the troubadour lover, pursues not a lady but the mental perfection his union with her represents. The classic medieval lover completing his identity through a woman is Tristan, who cannot live without his lady, Yseut.[13] In the legend, including the version told by the Norman poet Béroul (ca. 1190) as reconstructed by Alan Fedrick,[14] Tristan's search for Yseut commences when he becomes aware he is somehow incomplete. Tristan's lack of some essential element, a void in his very self, is symbolized by a wound he receives in battle. This wound in Tristan's left breast, echoing the wound in Adam's side through which God pulled the rib he made into Eve, suggests that what Tristan lacks is a woman's love. Yseut plays Eve to Tristan's Adam, making him complete with her love while simultaneously healing his wound. Yseut's miraculous powers of healing, often attributed to romance heroines, reflects that medieval women provided medical care for their families or even larger communities in the absence or failure of trained physicians

(Labarge, 169–94). But like most motifs in romance, Yseut's healing carries significance beyond its verisimilitude.[15]

If Tristan achieves integrity through love, however, that love costs Yseut her wholeness, as is suggested in the couple's famously enigmatic love scene: The knight, by leaping into Yseut's bed to avoid leaving footprints in a film of white flour his enemies have spread on the floor, reopens his wound. Its bleeding stains the bed linen with a multivalent spot—among whose connotations is the bloodstain left after a virgin's bridal night. The stain hints that the blood is Yseut's, that in this scene she is wounded, becomes lacking: Just when Tristan achieves wholeness through Yseut, she loses it. That male integrity is achieved through female fragmentation is underlined by another valence of the blood-stained sheet: Its resemblance to the blood left by mothers in childbirth, together with a punning reference to Tristan's mother, Blanchefleur ("white flower" or "white flour"), reminds us that her physical integrity was fatally breached when she gave birth to Tristan (39). Like Yseut, Blanchefleur suffers wounding to make a man whole.[16]

The integrity Tristan effects for himself through Yseut can be only momentary, since their union defies every rule of their society: Yseut is married to Tristan's uncle Mark, king of Cornwall, making their love not only adultery but treachery and incest as well. Social forces tend to triumph in romance, and so Tristan and Yseut's love ends unhappily with their deaths. Such conflict between love and social responsibility is a favorite theme of romance, yet not all works present romantic integrity as an unrealizable ideal. Chrétien's *Lancelot, or The Knight of the Cart* is a reimagining of the Tristan and Yseut story, which considers integrity to be compatible with a knight's duties—if he achieves it through the right woman.

Chrétien's Lancelot will not be recognized by those familiar with later versions of the Arthurian legend. The knight enters as an unknown figure without a knightly reputation. His lack of fame within the romance reflects an equivalent lack in the world of the audience—for Chrétien, as far as we know, created Lancelot and the story of his adultery with Guinevere.[17] Chrétien displays his self-consciousness at creating a new Arthurian character by describing Lancelot's attainment of chivalric fame with metaphors of birth and rebirth. The birth theme becomes obvious in a scene in which the hero crosses a sharp sword that acts as a bridge. He is told that the task is impossible: "That could never happen ... anymore than a man would reenter his mother's womb and be born again"—a reference to John 3:4, where Nicodemus questions Jesus' teaching about spiritual regeneration. Lancelot's task here, however, is to give birth to himself not so much as the New Adam but as the New Knight.

Lancelot succeeds at this act of recreation. But who is the mother whose womb he must reenter? It is Guinevere. Her maternal role is suggested in the romance's prologue, where Chrétien describes his debt to his patron, Marie of Champagne. The countess, Chrétien says, "gave and delivered to him *matiere* and *san*."[18] These French words are conventional terms referring to the romance's subject matter and its sense, or thematic meaning. But Chrétien puns here, for the two words have procreational force: *Matiere* and *san* name the matter and semen that, according to Aristotle, are respectively a mother's and father's contributions to the conception of a child (Bloch, *Medieval Misogyny*, 127). Thus Chrétien depicts Marie as the giver of both the matter and semen of the romance; she is its metaphoric creator—both father and mother. As some critics have argued, Chrétien's relationship to Marie mirrors that of Lancelot to Guinevere (Krueger, *Women Reading*, 53–54). If Marie is a parent single-handedly giving birth to the text called *Lancelot*, then Guinevere, too, is such a parent, the creator of the knight with that name.

Guinevere creates Lancelot as God creates the universe: through a word. The queen gives voice to Lancelot's existence in the first scene of the romance as she is led into captivity under the evil knight Meleagant. "Ah, lover," she says, "if you knew, I don't believe you'd ever let Kay lead me even a single step away" (210). The text does not indicate whom the queen addresses, but I believe that here she is calling Lancelot into being—expressing a wish for an ideal lover who exists only to rescue her. Expressing that wish, she creates the man who fulfills it. When Lancelot does appear, fulfilling this and every other desire of Guinevere, she acts like a castrating mother. She enjoys the power she wields over the knight, resembling the troubadour's lady inventing tests to prove his love. Lancelot's abject obedience causes him to lose his knightly reputation: He becomes reviled as "the Knight of the Cart," for in searching for Guinevere he rides in such a vehicle, normally reserved for transporting the basest criminals.

Service to Guinevere costs Lancelot more than his reputation; it costs him his identity. So obsessed is he with her that "he forgot who he was; he was uncertain whether or not he truly existed; he was unable to recall his own name" (216). As a masculine appendage to Guinevere, Lancelot possesses no integral existence. His fragmented psyche is underscored with repeated images of wounds—in his side, in his hands and feet—all of them acquired in service to the queen.

Lancelot achieves wholeness with the aid of another woman, the sister of Meleagant, Lancelot's opponent, and the daughter of King Bademagu. This important character lacks a given name because she is not a full individual but the feminine entity who will enable the masculine Lancelot to achieve wholeness. She heals Lancelot after rescuing him from a tower, an enclosure that symbolizes both the womb from which he is reborn and the tomb from which he is resurrected, like Christ, as a New Man (Col. 3:10): Now the knight is "healed and healthy" (289).

Lancelot gives this young woman his heart. In shifting his affection from Guinevere to Bademagu's daughter, he declares that he no longer serves female power but rather is served by it. Guinevere, as we saw, is Lancelot's domineering mother; Bademagu's daughter is symbolically his daughter: When she heals him, she "treated him as gently as she would her own father" (289). In finding completeness through his "daughter," Lancelot follows the lead of his forefather Adam, who also found such a mate: The creation of Eve from Adam's side was envisioned by medieval artists as a birth, its iconography like that used to illustrate caesarean delivery.

Chrétien's imagining the liaison between Lancelot and Guinevere as Oedipal is entirely conventional; even the Tristan legend blends the identities of Yseut and Mother Blanchefleur. Not every romance featuring the mother/son ideal of integrity, however, accepts it unquestioningly. The English *Sir Gawain and the Green Knight* (1375–1400) reworks the motif to argue that integrity cannot be achieved through a mother nor through possession of any woman. Gawain begins the romance imagining he has the sort of integrity heroes normally seek: The coat of arms on his shield is a five-pointed star, the pentangle, which symbolizes the complex harmony of Gawain's religious, chivalric, and physical virtues, "each joined to another," "none sundred neither, / without an end."[19] This integrity Gawain owes to a maternal figure, the Virgin Mary: Her image is painted inside his shield, obverse to the pentangle. That Gawain attributes his integrity not to his biological mother but to a figure *painted* on his shield suggests that the bond with her is not real but artificial, a product of his need to believe in an integral self.

Gawain's courtliness then is directed not toward a real woman but to a fantasy about what women should be—undemanding, nurturing figures who preserve his integrity. Mary, however, takes revenge for Gawain's cavalier assumption that she exists purely to serve him. When he prays to her for refuge (737, 754), she sends him straight to Castle Hautdesert, a place ruled by two women: an ugly hag who turns out to be his maternal aunt (hence yet another mother figure), the enchantress Morgan la Fee, and the beautiful Lady of the castle whom Gawain woos. Morgan and the Lady, like Mary, have agendas that differ significantly from Gawain's. They do not exist to fulfill the knight's fantasies but have desires of their own. The poem emphasizes the Lady's repeated attempts to declare her sexual desire for Gawain. Her attempts, we learn, are in the service of Morgan, who engineered the whole plot that brought Gawain to Hautdesert.

The end of all the Lady's and Morgan's activity is to make Gawain realize that the female-dependent integrity he values is a sham. The Lady successfully tempts Gawain into telling a white lie, a small sin that breaks his integral perfection. Gawain's lack of psychic integrity is symbolized by a lack of physical integrity: The Green Knight, who serves Morgan, nicks Gawain's neck. The wound, however, needs no mistress to cure it. It heals by itself—"the hurt was whole," (2484)—suggesting that if Gawain wishes to regain integrity, he can and must do it by himself, unaided by mother or lover, real or imagined. I therefore see *Sir Gawain and the Green Knight* as a feminist rewriting of the Tristan myth, although others have interpreted it as frankly antifeminist, and with solid evidence such as Gawain's misogynist tirade (2414–28).[20]

Thomas Malory's *Le Morte D'Arthur*, like *Sir Gawain and the Green Knight*, rejects male/female integrity as a viable ideal for chivalry—but hardly because Malory respects women.[21] Malory based his *magnum opus* on many French and English sources, yet radically revised these romances' idea of integrity. The source of wholeness in the *Morte* is never a woman but rather the institution of chivalry, represented by Arthur's Round Table, large enough to seat all of his knights, "the whole number of 150."[22] Since integrity is the product of a male-to-male bond, Camelot doesn't have much use for women. Arthur sets the general tone when he remarks, after Camelot's fall, that he misses not his wife but his knights, because "queens I might have enow, but such a fellowship of good knights shall never be together" (20.9).

Malory substantially revises the motifs that romance ordinarily employs to portray women's ability to bestow wholeness. He prefers, for example, masculine to feminine healers. Lancelot cures his fellows because he is "the best knight of the world" (19.10), and the Holy Grail heals Percival (11.14) because it represents the male Christ whom chivalry ideally serves. Malory's women often fail to cure a man's wound. Even Yseut at one point cannot heal Tristram (8.35). Morgan la Fee, Arthur's sister and nemesis, celebrated in romance for her miraculous powers, fails to cure: Arthur, after his final battle with Mordred, sails with Morgan and other ladies "into the vale of Avilion to heal me of my grievous wound" (21.5). But Morgan does not succeed, and the ladies entomb a dead Arthur (21.6). In Malory's work, female enchanters like Morgan generally are wicked, using their powers to satisfy their sexual desires, thereby "destroy[ing] many a good knight" (6.3). Malory distrusted women's magic because his world did; the first half of the fifteenth century saw the beginning of the witch-hunting mania that would peak in the Renaissance; earlier medievals believed that witches were self-deluders who could not work spells.[23]

Malorean women tend to wound rather than heal, and to symbolize their ability to puncture male wholeness, they sometimes carry swords: Morgan steals her husband Uriens's sword and kills him with it. She also takes Arthur's Excalibur and throws away the scabbard that protects the king from injury (2.11, 4.13–14). A nameless damsel arrives at Camelot wearing a sword that Arthur feels "beseemeth you not" (2.1). Such an unseemly female sword is bound to wreak havoc, and the knight Balin, who draws it, not only destroys himself and his brother but also strikes the "dolorous blow" that wounds the Fisher King and initiates the Waste Land (2.2, 2.8).

Mothers do not confer integrity in Malory. They are flawed figures whose imperfections undermine male chivalry. Arthur's own mother, Igraine, is accused of treachery because she did not quash gossip about Arthur's legitimacy and thereby fomented rebellion (1.21). Arthur has besides a biological mother a spiritual one—the Lady of the Lake who gives him the sword emblematic of his power. She is accused of base acts—that "by enchantment and sorcery she hath been the destroyer of many good knights"—and is killed (2.3). Mothers are not so much the source of life but of death: Two dying brothers bemoan that "We came both out of one tomb, that is to say, one mother's belly" (2.18). Knights do well to leave such destructive mothers for the perfection chivalry confers. Chrétien's Perceval commits a grievous sin when he abandons his mother to pursue knighthood, but Malory's Percival is praised for leaving his to join the Round Table (14.2).

Malory also thinks that erotic attachment between the sexes can only harm chivalric perfection; Uther, Arthur's father, complains that love for Igraine means "that I may not be whole" (1.1). Lancelot announces that he will not take a wife or lover because both are bad for his knighthood: A wife would leave no time for tournaments and adventures, and God would punish him for an immoral love by making him lose battles (6.10). Yet Malory is stuck with the tradition that a knight is best inspired by a woman to perform valorous deeds. He therefore reimagines the courtly relationship as an asexual one: Malory maintains that lust was not a component of love in Camelot (18.25). Thus he insists, despite evidence to the contrary (19.6), that the Guenever-Lancelot affair is a nonphysical one (20.3)—Guenever favors Lancelot as a tribute to chivalry in general, and the knight expresses his love for her solely by performing "many deeds of arms" (4.1).

The ideal Malorean woman sates a knight's desire for adventure without exciting his desire for sex. Sisters, whose sole function is helping their brothers attain integrity, compose one such category of asexual women. Most prominent is Percival's sister, the only woman allowed on the Grail quest. As a dedicated virgin, she presents no sexual temptation for the questers but functions as an image of the spiritual integrity they seek (17.4). Also significant is Lynette, Sir Gareth's future sister-in-law; although she accompanies Gareth on his quest and verbally urges him on, he marries her older sister.

Sisters, however, often have minds of their own. They are not fragments of male identity but possess a separate integrity. Their independence, however, can lead to sibling rivalry. If most of the "good" women in Malory are sisters who aid their brothers, all of the "bad" women exhibit little fraternal devotion. The sword-carrying damsel who is the first cause of the Waste Land comes to Camelot because she wishes to kill her brother (2.4–5). Morgan's hatred of Arthur galls him because their relationship is especially close; he trusts her more than his wife (4.11). But Arthur's most difficult sister is Morgause, who seduces him before he is aware of their relationship and who conceives the parricide Mordred (1.19). Malory here revises another romance commonplace: Whereas many romances imagine incest as a liaison that ensures a knight's self-perpetuation, Malory depicts it as suicide. Mordred, Merlin warns Arthur, "shall destroy you and all the knights of your realm" (1.20).

Malory's place in romance tradition is rather paradoxical. On the one hand, he is untraditional, inverting the motifs romance uses to depict the social and psychological roles women play in feudal society. On the other hand, Malory is quite traditional in that he imagines women's role as assisting men to achieve integrity within the institution of knighthood. With his stark disparity between "good" and "bad" women, Malory's chivalry is more blatantly misogynist than that of earlier romancers. But its obviousness makes it easier for a female reader to resist. If the purpose of the family romance is to persuade women to accept happily their dynasty-building lot as wife and mother, then Malory fails miserably. He incites women to seek an integrity of their own.

CHAPTER 5

When Echo Speaks: Marie de France and the Poetics of Remembrance

Displaced Readers of Romance: Fictive and Historical Women

The medieval courtly genres of love lyric and romance, as we have seen, portray women as ideal beings who control men. These texts may afford their female contemporaries the semblance of esteem, yet they simultaneously construct women within their narratives as objects of male desire.[1] Even those female characters depicted in positions of some authority—cross-dressing performers, richly endowed widows, readers, storytellers, metaphoric creators, to name a few—serve as mirrors in which male protagonists search for the healing completion of their fragmented identities. The result is a conflicted portrait of women that reflects courtly society's anxieties about how to construct male identity vis-à-vis a potentially threatening female autonomy. Medieval romance and lyric respond to the presence of women in the culture by subsuming female within male identity.

As Roberta Krueger has recently observed, when medieval texts work to limit their female characters' autonomy and agency, they also seek to contain their female readers in similar ways.[2] She argues that "female characters who are initially cast in positions of power gradually lose autonomy and agency" during the course of the narrative. Members of

77

Artist painting a self-portrait from her mirror image.
Giovanni Boccaccio, *Livre des cleres et nobles femmes*. French, fifteenth century.
Bibliothèque Nationale, Paris. MS Fr. 12420, fol. 101v.

the female audience project themselves into what seems to be the privileged feminine sphere of the romance only to discover that the characters with whom they identify have been appropriated by various narrative strategies (10–11). The identities of both character and reader are "displaced" in such a scenario. Krueger emphasizes that through these various levels of displacement, romance authors construct historical women as fully as their fictional counterparts.

Although explicit historical evidence for communities of female readers may be sparse, Krueger's argument that romance authors displace their female readers rings true. Of the learned women with court connections who wrote, served as spiritual advisers, or acted as literary patrons during the twelfth century, none recorded their critical responses or those of other female members of the audience to courtly literature.[3] We do, however, have the enigmatic Marie de France, whose authorial persona provides a fascinating counterpoint to her cultural role as appropriated female reader of romance. The first woman to write in "romanz," or European vernacular, Marie may also have invented the genre of the works she is most famous for: short narrative romances that she calls "lais."[4] In the prologue to her collection of 12 lais, Marie innovatively depicts herself simultaneously as reader and author: as writing from a position of gender difference that enables her to see her culture from both without and within. Throughout her lais, Marie revises traditionally masculine conventions of romance narratives with an unusually nuanced understanding of what it is to view courtly culture from the perspective of the displaced. She holds a mirror to the misogyny of her culture and explores its consequences, private and public, for both genders. Marie offers us a glimpse of what can happen when the object of erotic desire speaks from an identity she herself has constructed.

Marie's Identities

We cannot identify with certainty any single historical figure as "Marie de France." Explicit historical evidence is scanty at best. Even the authorial title by which scholars refer to her was derived from one of her own works by an early editor.[5] Scholars more recently have used this "de France" to place Marie geographically. Glyn Burgess imagines a scenario in which Marie, born in France, composed a considerable part of her work while living in England.[6] The patrons Marie acknowledges, along with instances in which she names herself, provide a suggestive social context for reconstructing her identity. They suggest connections with prominent members of the English court. Marie dedicates her *Lais* to a "noble king,"[7] who is probably Henry II,[8] and writes her *Fables*, she tells us, "out of my love for Count William,"[9] a nobleman who has been linked with a spectrum of dynamic English "Williams" contemporary with her.[10]

Because the breadth and depth of Marie's learning reaches well beyond the bounds a noblewoman might achieve at court, scholars exploring possible historical identities for her have almost invariably considered women familiar with religious life. The rich Celtic substrata and oral traditions that her lais reveal emphasize Marie's familiarity with courtly literature, whereas scriptural allusions and devotional rhetoric underscore her clerical learning. That Marie was multilingual is self-evident from the kinds of poetic projects she undertakes. In her epilogue to the *Fables*, she relates that she has translated and versified King Alfred's Old English Aesopian fables.[11] These fables confirm for us her knowledge of Latin as well.[12] Marie's skillful use of various languages and classical sources suggests the kind of cathedral school or university education exclusively available to men—one that women could acquire only by entering a religious profession. We can surmise, then, that Marie had either exceptional private tutoring at court, that she was educated as a religious woman, or more likely, that she enjoyed some combination of these two available spheres of female education. Michael Curley suggests that if Henry II is the "noble king" to whom Marie dedicates her lais, then his half-sister, the illegitimate daughter of Geoffrey Plantagenet, count of Anjou, may be the primary historical candidate with whom we should align our literary Marie. Born in France, living in England as the abbess of Shaftesbury from 1181 to 1216, and in "close dealings with the courts of her half-brother Henry II and her nephew King John," she would have been in an excellent position to critique and compare courtly and religious experiences.[13]

Marie's Poetics of Remembrance

Most of what we know about Marie comes from her deliberate self-remembering. In a culture that envisioned the silent virgin as its epitome of female goodness, it is a delicious irony that we identify Marie's far-ranging and innovative corpus of works as her own because she explicitly claims them for herself: three times in her various prologues and epilogues. Each time Marie names herself, she emphasizes the theme of remembrance. In the epilogue of the *Fables*, after providing her readers with her name and origin, Marie adds an emphatic warning that authors who do not name themselves risk having their work appropriated by clerical copiers or, worse yet, forgotten. Similarly, in the prologue to her lai *Guigemar*, she underscores her authorial role as rememberer and charges her courtly audience to remember her words. Again in the epilogue to her third work, *Saint Patrick's Purgatory*, she names herself and reminds us of the memorial function of her work.[14] If we cannot establish her historical identity irrefutably, we can at least explore what her desire to be borne in mind might suggest.

In her authorial self-portrait in the *Prologue* to the lais, Marie is patently aware that her gender may complicate her audience's understanding of her claims to narrative authority. Because of its intriguing discussion of literary poetics, this prologue has remained an important critical focus for more than 50 years. How critics envision Marie's construction of her narrative voice within the prologue, however, has shifted dramatically. Leo Spitzer, the first to grasp its importance, is convinced that "this great teller of tales of the twelfth century is a "'clerc,' a *poeta philosophus et theologus*"[15] writing in the tradition of clerkly poets trained in the cathedral schools. However, as Stephen Nichols has more recently observed, "Spitzer's well-meaning praise [of Marie as "clerc"] constitutes an unconscious trans-sexing of Marie" that takes the focus away from the considerable lengths she goes to in the prologue, as a woman author without benefit of formal clerical education, "to spell out the nature of her knowledge and how she intends to use it" ("Working Late," 10). She contrasts her vernacular poetic enterprise in the lais with that of the clerks trained in rhetoric, exegetes writing in Latin who "gloss the letter / and supply its significance from their own wisdom" (15–16). Marie describes these scholars as a closed group whose glosses derive largely from what they understand "among themselves" (18)—quite literally from what they hear from each other.

With this description of interpretive narcissism and subtle indictment of the exegetical clerkly glossomania popular in her lifetime,[16] Marie wryly suggests that what has been missing is a woman's voice. In contrast with the human origins of clerical learning, she claims that her knowledge comes directly from God. Through a carefully crafted paraphrase of the biblical parable of the talents (Matthew 25:14–32), Marie urges that authors should manifest God's poetic gifts regardless of their gender:[17]

> Whom God has given knowledge
> and eloquence in speech
> should not herself silence it or be secretive
> but should reveal it willingly.
> When a great good is widely heard of,
> then and only then, does it bloom,
> and when that good is praised by many,
> it has spread its blossoms. (1–8)[18]

The relative pronoun with which Marie begins, "Ki"—which can be translated as either "who" or "whom"—instantly identifies her simultaneously as grammatical object and narrative subject of her prologue. Marie crafts this grammatical sense of two-way agency to suggest the doubling of self with which she characterizes her authorship. She is both God's vessel and his fleshly double, a reader and writer of his thoughts: the conduit for and cocreator of his knowledge. Her implicit comparison of herself with the Christian exemplar of the speaking vessel, the Virgin Mary, resounds doubly in its punning on their shared name. Marie's opening description of the poet as agency-endowed vessel is a dramatic allusive move that informs her poesis not only with the potency of voice usually assigned to men but also with the fecundity of body inevitably associated with women.

Marie's poetic self-mirroring is not narcissistic, however, precisely because she acknowledges that the audience must ultimately substantiate the "great good" of the words she conveys. This great good will "bloom" and "spread its blossoms," she explains, only when "widely heard of" and "praised by many" (5–8). The communal echoing she envisions calls to mind the classical speaking vessel: Echo. As Ovid explains in Book III of his *Metamorphoses*,[19] Echo diverts Juno's attention with her conversation in order to enable her companion nymphs to flee when Juno discovers them lying with Jupiter. Cursed by Juno to repeat only the last words of the many phrases she hears, Echo finds that when she falls in love, she can only express her desire for Narcissus by repeating fragments of his speech. Though an eager audience for Narcissus, Echo discovers that her responses are circumscribed by the content of his voice:

> .... He called out: "Is anybody here?" Echo answered: "Here!" Narcissus stood in astonishment, looking round in every direction ...
> Still he persisted ... , "Come here, and let us meet!" Echo
> answered: "Let us meet!" ... To make good her words she came out

of the wood and made to throw her arms round the neck she loved: but he fled from her, crying as he did so, "Away with these embraces! I would die before I would have you touch me!" Her only answer was: "I would have you touch me!" (Ovid, 84)

Yet, although her speech is echoic, her voice is clearly not empty. Echo, able only to reproduce the fragments of Narcissus's speech, manages to register the deep anguish of her desire and loss in spite of the absence of autonomous expression. Ovid closes the narrative by focusing on Echo's shame at having been scorned by Narcissus and her subsequent retreat to dwelling "in lonely caves" (84). The analogy between the displaced female reader of medieval romance and Echo is telling: Both are reduced to shadowing the voices within their respective cultural and narrative frames.

The poetic project Marie envisions in her prologue is the recuperation of Echo's shame. In exploring the potential for agency within fragmented, echoic speech, Marie suggests that we can restore the lost voices—both male and female—of her culture. In contrast to the circular interpretive activity of the clerical narcissists she initially considers as a possible literary model, Marie speculates about the possibility of "composing some good stories / and translating from Latin to Romance" (29–30). The idea of translation appeals to her because it inherently requires the literary use of an echoic voice. The verb she chooses to describe this kind of poetic activity—"s'entremetre" (32), quite literally "to place oneself between"—captures the authorial position she imagines for herself: that of imaginative conduit between her sources and her creative products. For Marie, translators, as the Old French verb "traire" implies, draw forth and reshape ideas. However, she quickly rejects more "clerkish" forms of translation because they rework ground that has already been covered: "Too many others have done it" (32). Here the process has been jaded, made pedestrian by poets who meddle too much with their sources and create translations that are, in fact, betrayals of voice (a second sense of "traire").

Rather than play the betrayer, Marie chooses a doubly redemptive poetic project: one that will restore lost Celtic voices even as it insists on the "pris" or "value" (not simply "fame") of her voice as female author within a culture in which women's voices too often go unheard. She emphasizes her role as both literary and cultural *mediatrix* in her decision to make the word flesh by writing down the previously untranscribed Breton lais she has heard. Marie explains her efforts to put the lais "into word and rhyme" (41–42) as an attempt to remember (both recall and imaginatively reconstruct) a culture whose voice was fading;[20] the lais are a tribute to those "who for remembrance made them, / the adventures they heard; / Those who first began them / and who sent them forth" (35–38).[21] Her rhetorical strategy in the prologue underscores her explicit emphasis on reembodying a lost culture by echoing its imaginative voices. Through repeated verbal doublings—what medieval rhetoricians call *recordatio*, literally a "re-hearting" of the text[22]—Marie allows us to see that repetition need not be semiotically vacuous as Echo's words may seem at first. Working with literary voices not originally her own, Echo-like Marie assembles the fragments of her culture's oral tradition, preserves them in written form, and revoices them for a new generation of audience.

Marie's artful construction of narrative déjà vu within the prologue reaches its zenith in her characterization of the "brave and courteous" king to whom she dedicates her lais. It is in the King's "heart," she emphasizes, that "all goodness takes root" (46), subtly suggesting that in his goodness he images—like prelapsarian Adam in Genesis—the "great good" (5) that constitutes the divine "knowledge / and eloquence in speech" (1–2) that Marie draws our attention to in her opening lines. She implies subtly that the King's wisdom contrasts with the obscure, narcissistic knowledge of the clerics she critiques at the outset, arguing that he, in effect, redeems male voice from narcissism by echoing God's knowledge and eloquence. She then goes on to double the echo by explaining that it is "in [her] heart [En mun quoer]" (49) that she has determined to present the lais to him: lais that are themselves the product of the knowledge and eloquence she receives from God.

If God is her poetic muse, then he is the King's political one as well, Marie implies. She emphasizes the reciprocal relationship between her poetic making and the King's wise governance by describing the potential for echoic mutual joy: "If it pleases you to receive them, / you will give me great joy; / I shall be happy forever" (51–53). Juxtaposing her own heart with the King's and hinting at their parallel divine inspiration, Marie deftly draws him into her poetics of remembrance. Clearly, the liaison of her art and his wisdom also has larger cultural implications. She invites the King to see himself mirrored in her attempts to reembody fragmented, culturally displaced voices, whether those of past Bretons or those of contemporary women.

In a startling if brief change in tone from her unusual claim to a divinely sanctioned voice in the opening lines, Marie closes her prologue with a rhetorical figure often found in the writings of women religious authors: the humility topos, a conventional literary vehicle for self-abasement. Medieval women authors from Hrotsvit of Gandersheim to Christine de Pizan characterize themselves and their works with a sequence of diminutives so extensive that when they address prospective male patrons and audiences, an ironic reading of the topos seems the only viable alternative. Marie's use of it contrasts dramatically with this strategy, however. Whereas most women authors who use the humility topos open their works with the figure, Marie establishes her own poetic agenda first, reserving her considerably abbreviated version of the figure for the last three lines of the prologue. In two tight lines addressed to the King, she says of her lais, "Do not think me presumptuous / if I dare present them to you" (54–55). Rather than accuse herself, Marie makes the King responsible for any accusation of presumption against her. In fact, the Old French ("tenez," to hold) even implies that such a thought on his part would be a type of bondage unexpected from the wise and gracious, brave, and courteous king she describes just a few lines earlier. Instead, Marie closes the prologue with a commanding request that not only draws attention to the value of her art but also firmly places her in the position of voiced subject who from experience can recommend the value of listening: "Now hear how they begin!" (56). In this prologue, a section in which male authors of romance traditionally frame the voices of their female characters or even appropriate the authority of their female patrons (Krueger, 4–7), Marie defines a new feminine poetics of remembrance that embodies her voice and establishes textual ownership. Echo speaks.

Romance from the Space of the Displaced

Marie fuels her poetic projects with a synthesis of clerkly or religious learning and courtly experience. She explores in myriad ways how her clerical tools might apply to the matter of popular culture. And although Marie develops an authorial identity that accommodates these different influences, she chooses the vernacular as her foremost vehicle for social communication.[23] In the *Prologue* to the *Lais*, we see hints in her allusions to Priscian of her interest in the work of medieval grammarians and rhetoricians. Marie's repeated references in the *Lais* to Breton sources and to Breton and Anglo-Saxon doublings for Anglo-Norman words similarly suggest a scholarly, linguistic interest in etymological transgressions of semiotic boundaries. Her playful attention to language points us in the direction of her larger critical fascination with intertextual influences and intercultural dynamics. Precisely this charged interest in the tension created by overlapping written and oral cultures in her own lifetime and her resulting curiosity about the transgressive defines Marie's work.[24] As Nichols suggests, Marie "breaches a cultural line of demarcation between learned and popular culture," between masculine and feminine domains of literary production, which ultimately defines a new space between the two ("Working Late," 16), what I refer to below as the "space of the displaced." It is a space Marie uses to explore a spectrum of gender-variegated responses to her culture's central gender fiction: that of male superiority and female inferiority.

Although both the *Fables* and *Saint Patrick's Purgatory* provide intriguing literary topographies of this new space of gender inquiry, the *Lais* offer a particularly revealing mirror of twelfth-century attempts to restructure the gender system.[25] In these short narrative romances, Marie interweaves her oral Breton materials with classical sources, Arthurian legend, and contemporary theological controversy. We will look specifically at three lais in which Marie reexplores traditional romance topographies from her doubled cultural status as author-subject/woman-object, from her perspective as autonomous Echo. *Guigemar*, *Lanval*, and *Yonec* offer a spectrum of Celtic otherworld journeys through which Marie critiques, even explodes, the gender double standards inherent in the *fin'amor* prized by her own courtly culture.

The gender hierarchy that Marie sets out to reconsider in her lais is a paradigm firmly grounded in patristic readings of the creation story narrated in Genesis 2. Here Adam is made first, and Eve subsequently (after God has created and Adam has named all the beasts of the earth) is made from a fragment of Adam's own body, from his rib. Patristic commentaries interpret this to mean that she is created not in the image of God as Adam is, but in the image of man: Eve becomes Adam's echo. This patristic authorization of man's chronological and ontological superiority to woman becomes a culturally accepted norm by the twelfth century—a given that we have already seen Marie calling into question through her playful reworking of the Narcissus-Echo myth in her prologue to the lais.

Ecclesiastical displacement of women and the resulting social displacements create a sexual identity crisis in the twelfth century that Jo Ann McNamara perceptively suggests has as its root the desire for a unified male identity, forever lost to Adam and his descendants after the creation of Eve.[26] The resulting "crisis of masculine identity," McNamara argues,

> was resolved by biology's reaffirmation of the fearfulness of women.
> The debate on the creation of Eve reestablished correct gender
> relationships.... The dialogue that redefined the natures of men
> and women and the construction of a public sphere that belonged
> to men alone had many repercussions. On one level, it defined
> men as people and blotted out the humanity of women. But the
> price was the loss of male humanity itself at the institutional level
> and the transformation of masculinity into a brutal caricature at the
> level where men intersected with women. (22)

In her lais, Marie responds to this doubly destructive polarization of the
sexes by critiquing both her culture's construction of a public-private
dichotomy between male and female roles and the essentialized perception of male superiority that such a dichotomy reinforces.

Marie addresses the gender anxieties that result from the double myth
of female inferiority and unified male identity through gender-compli-
cated "other world" quests in three lais. She explores a spectrum of transgressive gender behaviors—narcissism in *Guigemar*, hermaphroditism in
Lanval, and morphic exchange in *Yonec*—to achieve her ends. In each,
she revises traditional androcentric romance quest structure to address
both the social inequities for women in her courtly culture and the
related burden of expectation that accompanies a quest for male per-
fectibility. A key feature of these narratives is that the literal journey to
the "other world" invariably doubles as a psychological quest through
which the protagonist, usually male, learns something about his own
identity that will allow him to restore harmony to the community he
returns to. Marie doubles this quest structure in all three lais to offer her
audience the opportunity to imagine a woman's experience of the quest
and to explore the gender inequities of her culture from not only a male
but also a female perspective.

Guigemar: Echoing the Quest

Guigemar opens with a hallmark of the traditional quest narrative—a
portrait of the superlative male protagonist—but Marie begins, almost
immediately, to reshape the conventional gender cues for the *aventure*
she tells. She describes Guigemar as the most handsome man in the
kingdom whose devoted parents place him well at court (39–48);
unequaled in battle, he is championed by the king and desired by

women everywhere (59–64). However, he is, if anything, too perfect: so quintessentially and publicly masculine in his heroic feats that he has no desire to explore something as private and stereotypically feminizing as love (57–58). It is his unnatural imbalance of public and private, of masculine and feminine desire, Marie suggests, that Guigemar needs to redress in order to escape the narcissism of his self-sufficient pride.

While visiting his family one day, Guigemar goes on a hunt (often an allegory for pursuit of love in the Middle Ages) that turns into an encounter with the marvelous in which Guigemar confronts his ambivalence about heterosexual desire. With his bow Guigemar shoots a strangely androgynous white hind. Antlered like a male deer but accompanied by a fawn and gendered feminine by Marie, the hind subsumes male and female within a single identity. The hind's self-contained procreative powers prove emblematic of the self-sufficiency Guigemar desires for himself; the wound he gives her, however, suggests that the incipient narcissism of such a desire will leave him particularly vulnerable. In fact, the hind's wound becomes Guigemar's. The arrow he shoots rebounds with such force that it goes through Guigemar's thigh and into the flank of his horse (87–99). Traditionally, the thigh wound in romance is a euphemism for an emasculating injury and must be redressed through some superhuman effort to reestablish the protagonist's "maleness." Here, however, Marie uses this wound not to insinuate Guigemar's loss of masculinity, but to emphasize his pressing need to experience more actively the realm of feminine suffering. Marie implies that it is Guigemar's excessive preference for the public, homosocial world of the court with its focus on knightly valor through aggressive martial conduct that injures him, leaves him out of balance: if not literally sexually impotent, then certainly without a measured understanding of the continuum between desire for the feminine and desire for the masculine.

The white hind suggestively evokes Christ: not necessarily a masculine, triumphant Christ, but rather the wounded, suffering, feminized Christ of the crucifixion.[27] Its curse initiates for Guigemar a quest explicitly designed to engage him in the female suffering that he has previously ignored:

> Neither herb nor root,
> neither physician nor potion,
> will cure you
> of that wound in your thigh,

> until a woman heals you,
> one who will suffer, out of love for you,
> pain and grief
> such as no woman ever suffered before.
> And out of love for her, you'll suffer as much. (110–18)

Marie's use of the word *plaie* for wound (113) is remarkably resonant. *Plaie* and its homophones, gendered both masculine and feminine, echo throughout the lai. In addition to its significance as bleeding wound, *plaie* is also Marie's word for the bandage Guigemar initially makes out of his shirt to stanch his wound (139–40). As an extension of the literal wound, Marie uses the noun later to depict the self-inflicted metaphorical wound Guigemar experiences when he discovers the woman whose love for him will heal him (379–84). She varies, in turn, this metaphoric usage when she employs one of its homophones—"plait"—for the love talk he exchanges with this lady (525). In this form it signifies as well the emblematic knots the lovers exchange, in anticipation of their eventual parting, to pledge their continued mutual love and fidelity (557–76). Punning on its root sense of "fold," Marie pleats the term repeatedly as a way of suggesting that the continuity between the masculine and feminine experience of quest is bivalent suffering.

In his quest to the other world, Guigemar of course discovers the woman who will suffer for him "as no woman ever suffered before" (117) and quickly finds himself healed through their mutual love. Eventually, however, the lady's husband discovers the lovers in her bedchamber. Although he doesn't believe Guigemar's strange explanatory narrative of his quest, he nevertheless releases him without punishment to return to his own world (611–16), imprisoning his wife instead. She endures "bad days, worse nights"—indescribable "pain," "suffering," "anguish," and "grief" (Marie quadruples the nouns for emphasis) in a dark marble tower for "two years and more" (660–65)—until she discovers the door to her prison unlocked and escapes. On the shore near her prison, she finds the magic boat that initially brought Guigemar to her, and in a journey that explicitly mirrors Guigemar's own in reverse, is transported to Brittany.

I emphasize the quality of reversal here because the circumstances of Guigemar's quest are strikingly different from the unnamed woman's. Guigemar leaves a world in which he has considerable public status and approval, finds both physical and emotional healing in a world reminiscent of but an improvement over his own, and returns to friends who rejoice and honor him (637–50). Although his experience of "other worldly" love personally chastens him, leaves him "sad and distracted" (644) and hoping for a reunion with his beloved, it nevertheless restores him to his community in the most conventional way. In contrast, when we first hear of the unnamed woman who eventually becomes Guigemar's lover, her husband's jealousy literally contains her. He keeps her locked up and under guard, immured in a tower with a walled garden, with the company of just one serving woman. He even covers the walls of her bedchamber with paintings that depict Venus in various guises of love to project his own erotic fantasies into her last refuge of privacy. Simultaneously isolated from a larger social community but refused the privacy that such isolation might afford, she is a woman utterly displaced. What proves to be a healing world for Guigemar is simultaneously a nightmarish existence for the woman he falls in love with.

Marie intensifies the irony of this double standard with her framing of the lady's fate after she comes to port in Brittany at the castle of Meriaduc, Guigemar's feudal lord. Although initially Meriaduc sees to it that she is richly dressed and well cared for, when she rejects his pleas of love, drawing attention instead to the knotted belt she wears in remembrance of her love for Guigemar, he angrily cuts the laces of her tunic and tries to open the belt. Failing in his own attempted assault, he summons all the knights in his region to try their luck, emphatically underscoring his ownership and commodification of the lady with this scenario of repeated attempts at rape (721–44). The lady's quest simply moves her from a private, isolated, domestic prison to a publicly accessible one. Her "other world" is a place in which her initial suffering is magnified, not healed.

Marie, of course, reunites the lovers and concludes the lai with Guigemar's rescue of the lady, but not without a series of ironic narrative twists that encourage us to explore more deeply the implications of female suffering for both genders. Although Guigemar ultimately comes to his lady's aid, it is not because he hears of her distress but because he is pressed into service in one of Meriaduc's wars. In fact, when he encounters the lady at Meriaduc's court, he initially questions his own recognition of her and agrees to Meriaduc's command that she publicly untie his knotted shirt. Here Marie adds yet another telling irony to underscore the gender double standard in this courtly culture. Guigemar has to send a servant to retrieve the shirt. Unlike the lady, who wears her knot perpetually (much like a chastity belt), Guigemar can take his on and off as he desires. Her belt may, indeed, bear witness to Guigemar that she has preserved her physical integrity, but Marie uses it subtly to draw attention to the value her culture places on virginity and chastity as measures of desirability. The woman's value both to Guigemar and to Meriaduc is her inaccessibility and signifies, finally, her status as a commodity of love.[28] Marie uses Guigemar's verbal exchange with the lady at this moment to juxtapose their diametrically opposed experiences of the quest: "My beautiful one," he said, "what a lucky adventure / that I've found you like this! / Who brought you here?" (822–24). She, in turn, tells him "about the grief, / the great pains, the monotony / of the prison where she was held captive, / and everything that had happened to her— / how she escaped . . . ." (825–29). Guigemar, who tellingly asks who brought his love to Meriaduc's court, sees the adventure as the happy conclusion to his own search. The unnamed lady, quick to counterbalance his joy at the reunion with the fact of her suffering along the way, goes on to emphasize her agency both in her escape and in her refusals of Meriaduc's frequent requests for her love (834).

At this juncture in the narrative, the private has become a public prize; Marie reveals the desire for the woman as a competition between men. Guigemar ultimately demonstrates his possession of the lady to Meriaduc when he unties her belt. Marie, however, undercuts even this public witnessing of their mutual love—a traditional narrative avenue for resolving the question of who possesses the woman. Meriaduc refuses not only Guigemar's plea that he return the lady out of kindness, but also his offer to serve as Meriaduc's vassal for two or three years in exchange for her (837–52). Although she loves Guigemar and would clearly choose him (836), her voicelessness combined with his subordinate, feminized position vis-à-vis Meriaduc leave both Guigemar and the lady dispossessed. In making her a territory of dispute, a possession to be defended much like a castle or a holding of land (846–52), Meriaduc initiates a spiral of aggression to which Guigemar, in turn, responds with violence. He renounces his initial covenant with Meriaduc, joining forces with a lord who opposes him and who is delighted to have the additional help in achieving his own ends. In a final, all-consuming irony, because their assault on Meriaduc's castle fails, Guigemar and his new lord resort to besieging the town and starving everyone inside, including, of course, Guigemar's love, whom Meriaduc still has in his possession (853–80).

With this prelude to the lai's "happy" ending, Marie suggests that, in a culture that commodifies women, public conflict inevitably incurs private costs and that personal loss can easily escalate to social disruption and loss. Marie insists that the fiction of discrete, hierarchical boundaries between public and private desire is a kind of facile narcissism with grave human consequences. In a painful reminder of the continued threat of the imbalanced polarization of gender identities, Marie closes her narrative with the unnerving monofocal reassurance that "all [Guigemar's] pain was now at an end" (882). "And the lady's?" we might ask. After all, her quest has only led her to an "other world." We have yet to hear the story of her return.

Lanval: Reenvisioning the Male Gaze

In *Lanval* Marie explores once more the implications of her culture's hierarchical social structure with its polarized gender roles and inherent commodification of women. Here, however, she considers more explicitly the impact of misogyny on men, specifically by reimagining what critics call "the male gaze" through feminine eyes. By exploring the social circumstances that lead the parallel protagonists of this lai to engage in cross-dressing, Marie suggests that the male gaze, with its fictive substitution of public for private desire, can silence not only women but men as well.

Lanval opens with a subtly incongruous portrait of King Arthur, one that Marie uses to depict how the feudal structure of her culture arbitrarily disenfranchises individuals. Arthur, "the brave and the courtly king" (6) of legend, nevertheless is sojourning at Cardoel because the Scots and Picts have invaded his kingdom of Logres and are destroying it. Marie compounds this troubling description of Arthur's passive refusal to defend his kingdom by proceeding with a description of his strangely selective gift-giving at court. Arthur gives generously, she tells us, distributing "wives and lands" (17) to all the counts and barons who serve him. However, he arbitrarily overlooks one of his vassals, quite simply forgets Lanval (13–19). We discover that Lanval is known in the court for his "valor," "generosity," "beauty," and "bravery," but Marie emphasizes that most of the men envy rather than admire these traits in him and can only feign love in their encounters with him (20–26). Excluded by a less than competent king and socially isolated by self-interested peers in a court that cultivates deceptive relationships, Lanval is a man ostracized by his culture. To this public disenfranchisement Marie adds the suggestion of private loss. Although the son of "a king of high degree," Lanval is "far from his heritage" (27–28), "depressed and very worried / . . . a strange man, without friends, / ... very sad in another land" (34–37). Both publicly and privately displaced, Lanval becomes a man without a political or domestic identity.

Marie uses this scenario of the feminized protagonist to entertain the possibility of an inverse quest narrative, one in which the hero does not travel to the "other world"; instead, the other world—where, in a mirror to this one, the feminine is a position of power rather than subservience—comes to his own. In fact, when Lanval one day leaves the city to go for a ride in the country to relieve his sorrow, he pauses next to a river and is approached by two richly dressed girls who seem to come from nowhere and who, in turn, greet him and guide him to their lady (39–76). Celtic literature often uses rivers as symbolic points of transgression or as liminal boundaries between parallel worlds. The regal garments of the serving girls as well as the luxurious ornamentation of their lady's pavilion (80–92) underscore their otherworldly origins.

In an intriguing departure from the rather conventional initial focus on material trappings to indicate this unearthly connection, Marie directs her reader's gaze, as she does Lanval's, to the body of the faery woman, reclining on a beautiful bed within her tent. We have already heard from the serving girls that she is "worthy and wise and beautiful" (72), a threefold description that underscores her ability to combine intellect and appearance. In a strategic move that risks reducing the woman's identity to her body, Marie offers us a detailed topography of what Lanval will see when he enters the tent, though clearly not through the eyes of Lanval himself:

> The girl was inside the tent:
> the lily and the young rose
> when they appear in the summer
> are surpassed by her beauty.
> She lay on a beautiful bed—
> the bedclothes were worth a castle—
> dressed only in her shift.
> Her body was well shaped and elegant;
> for the heat, she had thrown over herself,
> a precious cloak of white ermine,
> covered with purple alexandrine,
> but her whole side was uncovered,
> her face, her neck and her bosom;
> she was whiter than the hawthorn flower.

The knight went forward
and the girl addressed him. (93–108)

Marie's map of the body here differs dramatically from the conventional portraits of idealized feminine beauty that twelfth-century romance narrators create. E. Jane Burns argues that the male authors of these romances "could be said without exaggeration to have suffered from the Pygmalion complex," that their portraits "suggest posed statues rather than living flesh":

> The fetishized bodies of romance heroines are typically frozen in descriptions of isolated body parts, descriptions that most often descend from an initial focus on the woman's hair to a sustained look at the face and its features, passing quickly past the neck and chest to glimpse the hands and hips. Dismembered and objectified by the gaze of the male narrator and/or protagonist whose observation constructs the desired and desireable female, these women's bodies, though they appear in public and are presumed to be clothed, are described nonetheless as if they were naked. The eyes of the beholder seem magically to undress the beautiful anatomy they perceive, or rather imagine. Emphasis falls throughout the standard portrait of medieval beauty on the whiteness of the woman's exposed skin, whether of the face, hands, chest, shoulders, or bosom, and we typically hear of her round, firm—and seemingly bare—breasts. (Burns, 109)

Subverting the *effictio* (head-to-toe catalog of body parts) that Burns describes, Marie's narrator focuses first on the body, then the woman's side, and finally—in a tightly condensed, intentionally abbreviated single line of poetry—on the woman's "face, her neck, her bosom." When she does recall the whiteness of the woman's exposed skin, it is through an analogy to the hawthorn flower, resonant with its dual Celtic-Christic symbolism: otherworldly healing or redemptive suffering.

Virtually free from the fetishizing of the woman's body found in conventional romance depictions, Marie's portrait refuses the sustained and detailed focus on individual body parts. Instead, she describes with nuance what the woman has chosen to wear. In striking contrast to the stasis of the Pygmalion-like portraits of her male contemporaries, Marie creates with this emphasis on self-fashioning-through-clothing the narrative equivalent of motion: a loose shift; a white ermine cloak decorated with purple embroidery that the woman has "thrown over herself."

Finally, in defiance of the Pygmalion fiction of nakedness—what Burns describes as the refusal "to actually expose the woman's nakedness"—Marie shows us the "whole side" of the woman, "uncovered." We see the place where flesh and apparel meet even as Marie refuses to define concretely the boundary between the two. The woman's deshabille, her semi-naked disarray, suggests that she has materially both dressed and undressed herself. With the sinuously erotic vibrancy of her description of this woman from Avalun, Marie works to translate her from object of the male gaze to gazing, self-creating subject.

Just in case Marie's subtle revision of the conventions of fetishizing masculine romance portraits is lost on the audience, or if the woman's powerful, self-fashioning eroticism confuses them, Marie confirms her unorthodox reinvestment of the traditional female "object of desire" with agency by ending the physical description with a focus on the woman's voice: As Lanval approaches, she is the first to speak and the one who directs the conversation that follows (107–33). In a private parallel to Arthur's public gift-giving of wives and lands, the woman grants Lanval "her love and her body" (132). Whereas the transactions Arthur initiates suggest his court's equation of women with property, this woman governs how and under what circumstances she'll exchange herself. She redresses Lanval's economic poverty and the resulting social and personal isolation in Arthur's court by assuring him that he will "never again want anything, / he would receive as he desired; / however generously he might give and spend, / she would provide what he needed" (136–39).

The covenant Marie describes here verbally duplicates the visual promise of Lanval's first sight of the woman. It is a fantasy of achievable desire: one predicated not on Pygmalion-like self-fulfillment but contingent on Lanval's ability to construct his need in terms of what he wants to give others rather than what he hopes to possess (138–39). In this conversation with the woman from Avalun, Lanval chooses to become her vassal (121–30) but is not displaced as he is in the hierarchy of Arthur's court. Although her servant, he nevertheless retains his voice, his autonomy within the relationship in contrast to the objectification he experiences from Arthur and his court. The woman as a source of patronage and revenue does not emasculate but offers the possibility of living within Arthur's court without being defined by its social and moral economics.

The woman's "giving gift" establishes a paradigm of concatenating, reproductive generosity: one that Marie associates with the feminine autonomy that Celtic myth regularly ascribes to the otherworld. The woman gives so that Lanval can give; she, in turn, will give more if Lanval will give more as well. It is possession that requires dispossession. Now Lanval can redefine his position at court through his ability to give rather than receive from others. Equal at last to the material demands of his community, he can restore the public identity he lost when his own material value dropped. The only condition the woman places on her gift to Lanval is secrecy. In a move designed to defend the reciprocity and mutual love of their private covenant from the public manipulation that characterizes Arthur's court, she warns Lanval that he will lose both her love and her giving gift if he makes public their relationship.

Only shortly after Lanval's return to court, the faery woman's attempts to enforce a boundary between private and public worlds prove futile. When Arthur's queen tries to make Lanval her lover, he refuses flatly, excusing himself on the grounds that it would require him to break public faith with his lord. More importantly, he understands that such a move would force him to betray his private covenant with the woman from Avalun: the covenant that, in fact, has allowed him to reconstruct his public identity. The queen, apparently convinced that she could use her position as Lanval's public patron to acquire his private affection (263–64), fumes at his rejection. She sees Lanval's refusal of her love as a comment on her lack of desirability rather than as an indication that his desire is focused elsewhere. Believing her own gender identity called into question, she frames her anger in the form of a reciprocal attack on his:

> In her wrath she insulted him:
> "Lanval," she said, "I am sure
> you don't care for such pleasure;
> people have often told me
> that you have no interest in women.
> You have fine-looking boys
> with whom you enjoy yourself.
> Base coward, lousy cripple,
> my lord made a bad mistake
> when he let you stay with him.
> For all I know, he'll lose God because of it." (276–86)

Marie's use of Old French *talent* for "interest" (280) is significant. Its foremost sense in this context is "desire," but it can also refer to a gold coin or to the skill with which an activity is performed. With her accusation of homosexuality, the queen indicts Lanval's sexual performance, characterizing it as crippling, unnatural in a man. She implies that homosexuality is not merely a private flaw, but that it prevents Lanval from circulating as a commodity in the heterosexual *fin'amor* milieu of Arthur's court. Lanval is a bad investment for her husband, the queen argues, personally, economically, and morally (283–86).

Marie eloquently critiques the rhetoric of the queen's attack, not only characterizing it as misspeaking (Old French "mesparla"; 276), but using a reflexive verb—"s'en curuça" (275)—to emphasize the self-corrosive quality of the queen's narcissistic anger. Lanval reciprocates with his own spiteful declaration that the woman he loves surpasses the queen "in body, face, and beauty, / in breeding and in goodness" (301–302), quickly entering into the queen's attempts to escalate a confrontation about personal desire into a social conflagration. Unwittingly, in publicizing his love's beauty, Lanval makes her an object who must be viewed, a commodity to be exchanged if not literally, then verbally through gossip. He becomes fully implicated in the court's construction of the male gaze, a way of seeing that substitutes public appetite for private desire.

When the queen reports Lanval's remarks about her physical appearance to Arthur, she makes their private spat public by conveniently charging that Lanval asked first for her love. In a move that underscores how fully Arthur's court confuses the private with the public, Arthur swears that he will have Lanval burned or hung (328)—punishments for treason—unless Lanval produces evidence that his love surpasses the queen in beauty. Insisting on his innocence but knowing he will not be able to substantiate it, Lanval agrees to be judged by the court. Most intriguing is the word Marie uses repeatedly for the act of judgment: "esgarder" and its cognates—"to watch," "to gaze," "to see" (380, 388, 477, 577, 583, 611, 629). On Lanval's day of judgment, the court eagerly waits to see if the woman from Avalun will appear. They are more richly rewarded than expected. The woman is preceded by two pairs of serving women so beautiful that the barons and knights who have come to judge Lanval find themselves unable to discern which if any is Lanval's love. Each could satisfy the court's desire for evidence of physical beauty that exceeds the queen's. However, when Marie distinguishes among these women, it is to indicate who is older, wiser, or more courtly (533): a subtle gesture that redirects the gaze of the voyeurs in her literary audience from body to mind.

When Lanval's love eventually makes her public appearance, we see her in a combination of simple linen shift and regal, dark purple cloak that is as complexly revealing and concealing as the array she donned in her earlier private encounter with Lanval (559–62). Marie makes more explicit her earlier revision of the conventional *effictio* portrait, creating here an upward sweep of the gaze from hips to neck to face. Once we pause to examine the woman's face, Marie describes its various components in random order as if to refuse even a simple inversion of the conventional construction of the female body (563–70). Marie rejects the single-minded, fetishizing gaze that the sole appearance of the woman from Avalun might inspire. Instead, the trial scene offers a visual feast that encourages her audience to see women diversely.

The magnificent procession of women with its unembarrassed visual display of physical beauty is certainly proof that Lanval has not misspoken. Yet it is evidence that can be appropriated, commodified if described by the viewing subject alone. With a final narrative stroke, Marie underscores that voice is as significant a criterion for establishing value as material presence. After letting her cloak fall to give her audience a better view of that evidence, the woman from Avalun interrupts the knights' discussion of her beauty to confirm verbally what they have intuited about her relationship with Lanval. She then departs in silence, speaking neither to Lanval nor the members of the court as she rides off. Although the woman has prefaced her arrival with her serving girls' requests that Arthur prepare a place for her to stay, her immediate departure pointedly emphasizes that there really is no place in Arthur's kingdom for a voice like hers. Lanval silently joins her, leaping from the stone usually reserved for heavily armored knights mounting war horses as they depart on their quests and onto the back of the woman's palfrey. If Lanval is ravished, as the Old French "raviz" suggests (644), it is a ravishment that entails none of the violence and territorial aggression associated with rape by men in *Guigemar*. Marie closes the lai with this vivid image of the knight who abandons both the public and private strictures that his culture's construction of male identity requires, reinforcing it with her own powerful authorial claim to silence: "No man heard tell of him again, / and I have no more to tell" (645–46).

Yonec: The Origin Within

In *Yonec* we find Marie narrating a familiar tale about a young woman who is "wise and gracious and very beautiful" (22–23) but trapped in a desperate marriage. Her possessive husband, a rich old man who has sought this union without a thought for her desire but rather to produce an heir (17–20), proves to be inordinately suspicious. He locks her "inside his tower / in a great paved chamber" (27–28), isolating her from his entire household with the exception of his old, widowed sister whom he stations at her door as a guard. The young woman is quite literally immured, and the sorrow of this entombment, with its attendant isolation from human community, gradually leads to her physical and emotional decay (47–50). By beginning the narrative with this description of the woman's living death, Marie points immediately to the radical transgression of physical boundaries that she will explore in the lai: not just wounding, as in *Guigemar*, or imagining the self regendered, as in *Lanval*, but material shape-shifting, both within and between bodies.

To the extent that it explodes virtually all the traditional structural expectations of courtly aventure, *Yonec* is a lai quintessentially about reimagining human experience in order to reconstruct it. In a move that intimately links artistic creation to the process of refashioning identity, Marie describes the inspiration for the woman's aventure as explicitly literary. Despairing because her husband has denied her even the freedom to "go to church / or hear God's service" (75–76), the young woman recalls that she has often heard of aventures "that brought relief to the unhappy," tales of knights and ladies who discover blameless love (91–100). She subsequently prays: "If that might be or ever was, / if that has ever happened to anyone, / God, who has power over everything, / grant me my wish in this" (101–4). In a rich echo of the poetic persona Marie fashions in her prologue, the young woman uses her prayer to align human longing with the powers of memory, literary imagination, and divine creation. She rediscovers in this literary imagining the autonomous self that her husband's jealous enclosure of her nearly annihilates. Marie suggests that it is the lady's gaze that enables Muldumarec, the lover who subsequently flies in through her tower window in hawk form, to morph into human form (113–15). Muldumarec explains his astonishing presence and the healing love he offers the lady as a conjoint effort: the product of their mutual imagining (126–34).

To represent the symbiotic, deeply spiritual quality of their mutual desire, Marie describes the hawk-knight's willingness to take the Eucharist in order to confirm his benevolence to the lady. To avoid discovery when the priest brings the Eucharist, Muldumarec takes on the lady's appearance, not as simulacrum but quite literally transposing his body into hers in a somatic encounter that conceptually reproduces the ecstatic union with Christ described by contemporary female mystics.[29]

Immediately after, Muldumarec and the lady consummate their love. The Eucharist characterizes their procreative union aptly. As a sacramental mystery involving transubstantiation—translation of bread and wine into the body and blood of Christ—it is the ultimate Christian emblem of the flesh made miraculous.

Inevitably the hawk-knight is discovered and impaled on spikes in a trap set by the jealous husband. As Muldumarec prepares to leave so that he can die in his own kingdom, he comforts the lady, tells her she is pregnant, and assures her that the son they have conceived will comfort her and avenge his death once he is gone. The remedy for her future sorrow and suffering is, quite literally, within her: a joint endeavor of his other-worldly inspiration and her own will to author herself. We see immediately the effect of her renewed sense of creative power. When the hawk-knight departs, the lady's deep sorrow moves her to follow him. She miraculously finds the means to escape her imprisoning tower and to initiate her own quest.

Pregnant, dressed in nothing more than her shift, and—as Marie takes care to emphasize—naked beneath this gown (341), the lady leaps from a window more than 20 feet high, survives the fall, and traces the heavy trail of her lover's blood along a road that leads through a dark opening in a hill into the fecund, vernal otherworld of her beloved (337–64). She initiates her aventure in this completely liminal state. Neither dressed nor undressed, with a body quite clearly in its own state of physical transformation, she passes through seemingly impossible material barriers to reach her love before he dies. Most interesting in this description of the lady's journey are the evocative birth-conception metaphors Marie uses: the woman's nakedness, the trail of blood, the journey to light through a dark tunnel. This quest returns the woman to the womb. Her reenwombing allows her to enact inversely the experience she will, upon returning to her own world, deliver to her child. It is a remarkable revitalization of one of the most hackneyed of romance clichés—the quest-as-rebirth—in which Marie emphasizes the inception rather than the conclusion of the journey. Through the feminine topography of this aventure, Marie astutely conceives of the otherworld as a place of origin that is within, not without.

In the final scenes of *Yonec*, Marie reminds us that memory itself is the metaphorical expansion of the womb in which humans come into being. Although the lady would rather die with Muldumarec in his kingdom than suffer her husband's retribution for that love, the hawk-knight insists she return. He gives her two gifts that will protect her and preserve the memory of their love for their son: a ring for the lady to wear that will prevent her husband from remembering her infidelity; a sword for his grown son to use as he sees fit once he has heard the lady's narrative of his father's wrongful death. Both of Muldumarec's gifts emphatically underscore the lady's role as poet-rememberer. They give her the power to reshape the narrative of her personal sorrow.

Marie refuses, however, to romanticize this power of reshaping sorrow. The lady, after telling her grown son the tale of his parents' love and betrayal, faints on the hawk-knight's tomb and dies. She has deferred but finally cannot escape the sorrow of her greatest loss (547–48). Nor can her most intimately authored creation. Moved by the aventure his mother tells—a tale now of his own loss—Yonec decapitates his stepfather with his father's sword. He restores the memory of his parents' union by avenging their sorrow with a painful, violent gesture that signals his own movement between two worlds: indescribable, innocent childhood (Marie describes it in two lines; 457–58) and adulthood, with its complex symbiosis of joy and sorrow.

The legacy of Yonec's parents, inseparably fused in their child, is the legacy of all those who write from the space of the displaced. Womblike, it is a position of expectant, material silence that nevertheless engenders a poesis that values accretion; that revels in the power to double even as it recognizes the potential for creating difference in that doubling. It is the space from which speak, in succession, Guigemar, his lady, Lanval, and his faery, as they voice their experiences of loss and gain, of suffering and fulfillment. And it is, of course, the position from which their creator, Marie de France, herself speaks, even as she remembers the silent sorrows of voices otherwise forgotten.

The Double Intercession: Mary offers her breast, Christ his wounded side to intercede with God for sinful humankind.
Florentine panel painting, ca. 1402.
The Metropolitan Museum of Art, New York, The Cloisters Collection, 1953 (53.37).

CHAPTER 6

Body Broken, Body Whole: Eucharistic Devotion, Fabliaux, and the Feminine Impulse of the Corpus Christi Drama

Corpus Christi: Wholeness or Fragmentation in the Body of Christ?

At the heart of the religious system that shaped Christian Europe during the high and late Middle Ages was the Eucharist. This small, comestible wheat wafer, when consecrated, mysteriously became not Christ's similitude but his "real presence," his body. The ritual sharing of the Eucharistic host among Christians provided an experience of *communitas* grounded in Paul's early equation of the body of Christ with the body of the Church: "For as the body is one, and hath many members, and all the members of the body, whereas they are many, yet are one body, so also is Christ" (1. Cor. 12:12–27). In the Middle Ages, the Eucharist served as the sacramental common ground between individuals with diverse theological, political, economic, and gender perspectives; it offered the hope of binding people together "despite the differences between them in the non-ritual space and time" of daily life.[1] Through the ritual fragmentation and consumption—quite literally the incorporation—of Christ's body, individuals within the Christian community could reassert the unity, the wholeness of the Christian social *corpus* even as they acknowledged the diversity of its members.

In her recent study of Eucharistic theology, Miri Rubin underscores this tension between wholeness and fragmentation. She emphasizes that interpretations of the Eucharist vary considerably according to context; differences in experience, gender, region, age, and occupation all guarantee that its meaning was neither predictable nor univocal (Rubin, 288). Although Eucharistic theology holds up *communitas* as an ideal, Rubin observes that people never experience the ritual "from a unitary position, in a homogeneous way." Their sense of *communitas*, she argues, "is dissolved as soon as the sweat evaporates off the brow of the ritual performer," the priest saying the mass (Rubin, 2).

Corpus Christi, the movable feast introduced during the mid-thirteenth century to celebrate this ritual participation in Christ's body, arrived in England by 1318. Observed yearly at the beginning of summer (between May 21 and June 24), Corpus Christi was celebrated over the next two centuries in a variety of forms: through public sermons; in elaborate processions mounted by Corpus Christi fraternities, local parishes, and civic guilds; and ultimately through cycles of biblical plays that narrated the whole of Christian sacred history. The spectrum of dramatic activity associated with the Feast of Corpus Christi by the end of the late fourteenth century reflects the manifold, often divergent, readings of the Eucharist that had developed. The various dramatic enterprises inspired by Corpus Christi are living events: more heterogeneous, less neatly classifiable than most criticism to date has appreciated (Rubin, 272). In addition to full cycles originating in York, Chester, Wakefield (the Towneley cycle), and Bury St. Edmunds (the probable origin of the N-town cycle), and fragments of cyclical plays from Coventry, Norwich, and Newcastle,[2] Rubin includes dramatic activities as diverse as the tableaux vivants of the Corpus Christi processions mounted by parishes, guilds, or crafts in honor of the feast day as well as the four plays of the Reading Group, the Ipswich Assumption play, and the Croxton Play of the Sacrament (271–87). The celebrations that Corpus Christi kindled varied in content, size, or frequency in response to the differing religious, political, social, and economic dynamics of the towns, villages, cathedrals, fraternities, and guilds that staged them.

The cycle plays, the focus of this chapter, are first mentioned in the records of the city of York in 1376 and subsequently with increasing frequency in the records of various English cities over the next century and a half (Rubin, 213–87). Vast in scope, they dramatize all of salvation history from Creation to Doomsday—including the Creation and Fall, the history of the Jews, the Incarnation, Christ's life, the Crucifixion and Resurrection, and the Last Judgment—often in a single day of performances. They celebrate the Eucharistic paradox of fragmentation as a way to wholeness by staging individual biblical narratives that compose both isolated episodes and a typologically interconnected structure in which Old Testament characters and events foreshadow New Testament episodes. Typology is a paradigm for interpreting the Bible that allows readers to confer meaning retrospectively as well as prospectively, to work toward a definitive understanding of historical or biblical events through the accumulation of multiple interpretations.[3] In the cycle plays, for example, the Old Testament characters yearn for and anticipate relief from the human suffering intrinsic to their post-Edenic existence. The New Testament plays that focus on Christ's life, especially the nativity and crucifixion, stage in turn the fulfillment of the promised redemption from the consequences of sin in a fallen world. As a conceptual framework for the drama, typological staging of scriptural narrative simultaneously invites and defies closure. It is an incorporative system that nevertheless recognizes extensive invention and allows for different understandings of truth.

In their use of typological structure, the Corpus Christi plays imagine human history from the omniscient narrative perspective of God. As V. A. Kolve has argued, the cycles offer in essence "the mimesis of total human time."[4] Yet, although God may see all of human time simultaneously, the authors, players, and audiences for the plays enjoy only a limited form of that kind of divine omniscience. They focus on bits and pieces of human history, understand divine integrity from a variety of perspectives. The dynamic, like the Eucharistic experience, puts the holistic in tension with the fragmented. If the plays argue for logocentric wholeness, they image that wholeness through a host of different configurations of their biblical material.

Women and Typology

Understanding the Corpus Christi cycles in terms of their potential for diversity—especially with respect to the region, social class, and gender of the audiences for whom they were performed—sets the stage for reexploration of gender relationships and the roles women play within the cycle drama as they reflect the paradoxes inherent in Eucharistic theology.[5] Previously, critics have suggested that the typology that underlies characterization and dramatic form in the Corpus Christi cycles limits gender-oriented readings. They argued, somewhat shortsightedly, that the figural structure of the drama necessarily prescribes the roles of female characters, stereotypes them. However, as Theresa Coletti cautions, merely identifying stereotypes "constitutes a feminist approach only in the narrowest sense, for it risks mistaking the perception of a type for an understanding of the dramatic text's representation of gender" ("A Feminist Approach," 79–80). By accepting that these characters conform to scriptural narrative or received moral types and by suggesting that they consequently can do nothing more than perpetuate the stereotypes of medieval antifeminism, we miss an opportunity to understand the relationship between gender and the Eucharistic focus of the cycle plays.

Certainly the biblical narrative as represented by the cycles focuses largely on male characters, casting women in the roles of helpmates and servants, ostensibly at the margins of the action, and seemingly conforming to the Eve-Mary polarities that characterize so much misogynic rhetoric, both medieval and modern. However, because these limits are culturally scripted, the combined product of theological and social influences, they are hardly inert. The cycles function as symbiotic rather than reductive mimetic mirrors, both feeding on and responding to changing cultural anxieties, calling into question the ideological norms of the communities that produced and attended them.

Peter Stallybrass's observations about the nature of ideological boundaries are essential for a reading of the representations of women in the cycle plays. Rather than understanding boundaries as "somehow just there" and transgression of the cultural limits they announce as subversive activity, Stallybrass suggests that we should see boundaries themselves as evidence of earlier changes, as confirmation that an older, once-established division has been trespassed.[6] This is certainly the case with the cycle drama, where the stereotypes used to represent women often call into question their very own parameters. In fact, the plays often overstage their Eve-Mary typologies through comedy, and for precisely this reason should be seen as offering up to scrutiny the Christian *genetrices* of female stereotyping. Noah's wife, for example, for whom Eve is the prototype, is quite clearly a fabliau caricature of the excesses of speech and body assigned to women by patristic commentaries like Saint Jerome's *Against Jovininan*.[7] In the various cycles she repeatedly argues with her husband about entering the ark. She overdresses, consorts with gossips, and drinks too much. Like the parodic, bodily excessive female characters in the fabliaux,[8] Noah's wife is the type done to such an extreme that she calls into question its characteristic features.

Fabliau women inhabit culturally normative positions transgressively. They are wives, mothers, and daughters who insist that their conventional social roles should afford them a degree of subjectivity rather than leave them voiceless within their own society. They derive their powers of speech from the ways in which they commodify their bodies. Of the fabliau-like characters from the cycle dramas, the Virgin Mary and Christ in particular—the archetypal mother and child—use their bodies as points of origin for the power of their speaking voices. The "Joseph's Troubles" plays, for instance, depict Mary as a potential adultress whose physical boundaries are perplexing: at once permeable and impermeable. Participating in an apparent fabliau love-triangle, she conceives Christ while her earthly spouse, Joseph, is away on business, yet manages to convince him of her integrity, both physical and verbal, to her marital vows. Christ in the York *Crucifixion* similarly achieves his transgressive quality through the silent speech of his effeminate and wounded yet redemptive body. He is the inscrutable straight man to crucifiers whose antics resemble a Three Stooges routine. In these plays, Mary and Christ are metamorphic figures not unlike the fabliau women. Their paradoxically shape-shifting bodies—Mary's in her virginal maternity and Christ's in his enfleshed and humanly suffering divinity—manifest what Stallybrass refers to as contingent limits, boundaries whose demarcations are constantly in flux (13–14).

With this idea of contingent limits in mind, Coletti offers a thought-provoking reconception of the function of the Virgin Mary within the cycle plays. The impact of the medieval Marian cult, because of its celebration of Mary's singularity as a woman through her immaculate conception, virgin birth, and perpetual virginity, has most frequently been seen as restricting the conception and status of women ("Purity and Danger," 83). Women are encouraged to model themselves on Mary, but such imitation must fail. At the very least, it is impossible to biologically reproduce her virgin motherhood; her spiritual immaculateness poses an even more daunting goal. In contrast to this focus, Coletti argues that Marian representations "may contest rather than simply reproduce traditional gender roles and meanings" ("Purity and Danger," 66). Misogynic rhetoric can speak against itself, mimetically subvert itself when voiced by female or feminized characters.

Coletti describes an "interplay of difference and likeness" that in the infancy plays of the Corpus Christi cycles results in representations of

Mary that move simultaneously in opposing directions. The roles they invoke for Mary "directly link her to historical women: she bears, cares for, nurses, and protects her child; she marries, has disagreements with her husband, and observes the division of sex roles within the nuclear family unit." But these same representations, Coletti emphasizes, "deploy ideological assumptions about woman's nature and woman's body to emphasize Mary's deviation from those assumptions" ("Purity and Danger," 82–84). She is, after all, a *pregnant virgin* who, according to Church doctrine, was not only herself conceived free from the taint of original sin but remained perpetually virgin after the birth of her son. Representations of Mary's body in these plays refuse the "either/or" logic of dichotomous models, presenting instead a model of the feminine that insists on the "both/and" logic of difference that is characteristic of fabliau.

Coletti grounds her discussion in late medieval understandings of the unstable margins of the female body. Drawing on the theories of Aristotle and Galen, medieval treatises on the humors held that women were excessively moist and cold.[9] The physiological model most prevalent in the high and late Middle Ages suggested that women's several orifices assisted them in purging their bodies of their natural "fumosity."[10] It is a way of constructing the female body that emphasizes its breachable boundaries.[11] Woman's presumed physical susceptibility to illness and external influences almost inevitably was seen as resulting in moral vulnerability as well. Bernard of Clairvaux, for example, understood the human will as Eve, as "woman in collusion with the flesh to eviscerate the soul," Karma Lochrie explains (20). In a description that graphically associates woman's voice with bodily contamination and corruption, he characterizes the will as a scabrous, greasy old woman with infectious breath, who rages and picks at her own ulcers.[12]

We find this larger cultural dis-ease with female fleshly fissures, especially its alignment of voice and reproductive organs in a woman's body, dramatized in the infancy plays of the Corpus Christi cycles.[13] In these plays, Joseph regularly accuses Mary of adultery and cannot initially listen to her pleas of innocence. He finds incredible her vow that her pregnant body is sacrosanct, impermeable in spite of what the visual evidence might suggest. Ultimately, however, he acknowledges her flesh as spiritually regenerative. The infancy plays, then, stage the patristic construction of woman as contaminated both in body and voice only to reject it.

The infancy plays ask us to consider the implications of the boundaries associated with Mary's body, Coletti emphasizes. In doing so, she addresses a substantial gap in criticism of the cycle drama. Most accounts of the Corpus Christi drama suggest that Christ's body is the central, singular focus of these plays. After all, at the center of the Corpus Christi feast—and underlying the cycle plays' uneasy negotiation of divinely impermeable and humanly permeable bodies—is the Eucharist: the sacrificial ritual through which "God and humans could meet and unite, mix and merge ... the disc of baked wheaten dough [which] could embody the saving body of Christ" (Rubin, 1). Like the feast they commemorate, however, these plays dramatize not only the manifest presence of divinity in Christ's body, but they also explore the process through which that divinity is enfleshed in the human matter Mary provides. They stage both the unmaking and the making, the crucifixion and the nativity, of the flesh that is spirit, the female matter that realizes divine logos. Two enfleshed holy bodies, not just Christ's but also Mary's, stand in focal equipoise at the heart of the cycle plays.

Gendering the Drama Feminine: Beguine Origins of the Feast

The cycle drama's double corporeal focus has its origins in the Corpus Christi feast, itself quite literally doubly engendered. Although ultimately supported and ecclesiastically sanctioned by their male counterparts in the Cistercian and Dominican orders, the feast was initially inspired by beguine devotional practice, initiated through the dream vision of one of their most famous saintly women, Juliana of Cornillon (Rubin, 164–69). The beguines, who shared with the male mendicant orders the ideals of poverty, chastity, and religious activity in the world rather than the cloister, make Christ's suffering body their quintessential focus. For these religious lay women, Eucharistic devotion involved an outspokenly erotic exchange with Christ's body. Consuming His body in the Eucharist was a tactile, sensory encounter through which Christ "could be watched, adored, smelt, touched," experienced as "sweet, satisfying, nurturing"; apprehended "not as a judge, or as paternal, majestic or lordly" but as "a man, a husband, a son, resplendent in vulnerable humanity, in the feminine principle" (Rubin, 168).

Juliana's dream vision reverberates with the competing desires for incorporation of and submergence in Christ's body that became the signature qualities of many female mystic experiences.[14] Her Vita's account of her initial dream describes Juliana's vision of a moon appearing in splendor but with a small break in its sphere. In her dream Juliana watches the moon and wonders what its enigmatic break might portend. Twenty years later she dreams once more of the same fragmentary moon, but this time with Christ present to reveal to her "that the missing part of the moon stood for the absence of one feast in the Church, which he would want his faithful to celebrate on earth."[15] It is a dream about the undeniable continuum between fragmentation and wholeness. The missing feast, with its promised completion of the liturgical calendar, registers the very hope for fulfillment that the Church temporal, through its annual, reiterative celebration of individual feasts, both establishes as a focal spiritual desire and acknowledges as materially impossible.[16]

The very feast envisioned as filling the gap, Corpus Christi, celebrates the gaping, feminizing wounds of the crucified, Eucharistic body: flesh fissured to restore the wholeness of the body spiritual. With its analogy between the moon and the Church temporal, this vision genders the Christian social body feminine and asks us to understand the pervious metaphoric flesh of that feminine body as restorative. The gap in the Church's devotional structure that the missing liturgical feast represents suggests that the Church's most vulnerable spaces are also its most redemptive. Juliana's vision, replete with the paradoxes of divinity feminized through its enfleshment, points dramatically to the imagery of contingent limits that inspires the cycle dramas' depiction of both Mary's and Christ's bodies.

Feminine Play, Fabliau Impulse, and Cycle Drama's Devotional Fabric

If beguine devotion, with its emphasis on simultaneous incorporation of and submergence within Christ, provides the feminine matter of the cycles, then fabliau provides the cycle drama with the narrative parameters that encourage the fullest use of Eucharistic theology's startling wholeness-in-fragmentation trope. Fabliau gives the drama its feminine form. It does this by translating the conceptual tension between wholeness and fragmentation into a narrative tension between metaphor and metonymy: respectively the rhetorical figures of "affirmation of resemblance" (narrative as a legible whole) and of "syntagmatic relation" (narrative as the positioning of disparate details).[17]

The cycles' episodic design, which duplicates the Eucharistic tension between wholeness and fragmentation intrinsic to Christ's body, provides a key instance of the fabliau interplay of metaphor and metonymy. Given that a comprehensive representation of salvation history is impossible, selected episodes from the biblical narrative—fragments of scripture, in effect—must necessarily stand for the whole. This metaphoric process is diametrically inverted at the level of individual episodes, however. Here, self-consciousness that the letter of scripture cannot possibly reflect God's unknowable thoughts results in an inquiry into what scripture cannot say. As we will see, the cycle dramatists initiate this inquiry through narrative improvisations that are metonymic in nature: associative and context-specific rather than comprehensive. With their assiduous expansion of apocryphal materials and cultural intertexts, these plays offer a literary mimesis of Christ's Incarnation. They literally flesh out the feminine, voiceless spaces of God's word.[18]

The connection between the English Corpus Christi cycle drama and the French fabliau is one that medieval literary history testifies to.[19] Individual plays from the cycles attest to this influence through similarities in the structure of their narratives. Using the scripture as their form, they dilate—fabliau-style—the biblical history they stage with bits and pieces, fragments from their own contemporary exegetical, cultural, or apocryphal narratives. The Lucifer plays, for instance, draw on patristic compilations of scattered biblical allusions to Satan's fall.[20] Episodes as central as Eve's temptation, Cain's murder of Abel, and the shepherds' visit to Christ at his nativity are fleshed out with references to contemporary manorial conditions and England's hegemonic seigneurial social structure.[21] Christ's Harrowing of Hell builds on details derived from the unauthenticated and uncanonical *Gospel of Nicodemus.*

Noah's wife provides a particularly dramatic example of this narrative strategy. She barely gets a nod in the cataclysmic flood narrative of Genesis 6–9, yet she is a vivid presence in several of the cycles. Her various portraits dramatize a spectrum of stereotypical behaviors familiar from contemporary antimatrimonial literature and fabliaux. *Uxor Noe* repeatedly refuses to enter the ark, arguing and even exchanging blows with Noah in Punch-and-Judy style in the Wakefield play when he refuses to allow her to finish her spinning. In the York cycle, she insists on returning home before the deluge to collect a few personal items, then wants to bring along additional family and friends once she returns to the ark. In the Chester play, she procrastinates by drinking with her gossiping friends before boarding. Mrs. Noah's excesses dilate the narrative by exaggerating contemporary misogynic commonplaces about "wyked wyves."

In fact, like the fabliaux, these dramas regularly make woman's body or the feminized male bodily sites of inquiry and dramatic fiction making. In the N-town *Birth of Christ*, for instance, Mary's perpetual virginity is questioned by the apocryphal midwife, Salome, who helps deliver Christ. She attempts to guarantee, through a gynecological exam unscripted in scripture, the miracle of a hymen that remains impermeable postpartum (a doctrinal claim for Mary that, similarly, has no scriptural ground). The elaborate tortures featured in the scourging, buffeting, and crucifixion plays of all four major cycles offer the audience members a kind of tactile voyeurism that not only graphically delineates the breached boundaries of Christ's flesh but implicates those who gaze on that flesh as contributing agents of his anguish. In fact, this kind of extrabiblical speculation frequently reveals an affective curiosity about the relative permeability of the human body's fleshly margins, the synergy between rupture and redemption.

If the Corpus Christi feast celebrates the experience of community that results from the sharing of Christ's body, then the drama, fabliau-like, repeatedly explores the impulses of fragmentation that underlie such a desire for mythic homogeneity. The individual cycle plays understand scripture as gaping, wounded, and explore these gaps not to fill them univocally but to consider a variety of narrative possibilities. The diverse presentations of shared biblical episodes among the cycles stand as vivid testimony to this. The comedy of the York *Crucifixion* contrasts strikingly with the decorous lamentation of the analogous play from the N-town cycle. Some authors even explore this kind of plurality within a single cycle. The Wakefield Master, for example, wrote two Shepherds' plays, apparently staged in alternate years, with each play clearly referring to local figures as well as to characters within the alternate play. This intertextual economy celebrates the circulation of tales in much the same fashion as the fabliaux, where body parts lost in one narrative almost magically reappear in another.[22]

Even as the plays saturate the gaps of scripture at the level of narrative structure, similarly at the semiotic level they resolve those spaces through resonant rhymes, puns, and extensive verbal doublings that, as in fabliau, simultaneously undercut and multiply meaning. The pairings in the York register of the professions of individual guilds and the plays they present offer splendid instances of the playful, parodic relationships between players and plays that animate these cycles. Just a few examples suffice. The Plasterers play *The Creation*; the Shipwrights, *The Building of the Ark*; the Fishers and Mariners, *The Flood*. The Tilethatchers use their performance of *The Nativity* with its shabby, leaky Bethlehem stable to plug their roof-mending skills. The Bakers play *The Last Supper*. On a darker note, the Butchers are responsible for *The Death of Christ*; the Pinners, makers of pegs and nails that join wood, play *The Crucifixion* discussed below.

These connections are not simply, as some critics have suggested, a quaint attempt by the various guild players to "find themselves" in their material—some odd stab at medieval method acting—but a genuine understanding of the semiotic extension of the biblical word to their own lives. If Christ is the word made flesh, then these cycles, which dramatize the historical buildup to and denouement from that climactic moment, mirror the process of enfleshing the consonances and contradictions inherent in God's word as it applies to their daily, lived experience. They celebrate the "feminine principle" of social interactions inherent in the medieval community's focus on Eucharistic theology.

Uncovering God's Feminine Body: The Stooges Crucify Christ

The passion sequences from the cycle dramas, as Kolve first emphasized, consistently make Christ into a game figure who is both victim and object of his torturers' desire (175–205). The York *Crucifixion of Christ*,[23] with its brassy, bungling crucifiers and their irreverent, comic dismemberment of Christ's body, stands out among these for its sustained development of a comic narrative. Christ's visibly bursting sinews and painfully silent, feminized body functions like the dismembered bodies of the fabliaux.[24] The play suggests that cycle dramas can share with fabliaux even their darkest humor. Although the York *Crucifixion* hardly seems to fit the Eucharistic devotional model for the cycle drama grounded in Juliana of Cornillon's vision, in fact, Christ's body in this play provides the perfect fictive ground for the convergence of female mystic and fabliau discourses. The fabliau impulse endows Christ's body with the Eucharist's morphic, feminine quality and gives Juliana's mysticism a comic bite. The play's scandalous laughter translates the corruption that misogynic rhetoric assigns to the female or feminized body into a position of power.

To begin deciphering the York play's shocking correlation of crucifixion and comedy, we should turn to its closest fabliau analog: "The Crucified Priest," a tale of a crucified, castrated priest-lover's hasty escape and unintended theft of a cross.[25] In this tale, a sculptor suspects that his wife is having an affair with a local priest. To catch the illicit lovers together, he tells his wife that he is going to town to sell one of his statues, but he bides his time on the road to town until he is certain he will catch the lovers together. Indeed, after his departure, the wife invites her lover over, only to be interrupted by the unexpected return of her husband. She urges her illicit priest-lover to disrobe and hide amongst the statues in her husband's workshop. In order to disguise himself better, the priest climbs onto one of the unfinished crucifixes, in effect substituting himself for the absent image of Christ.

The husband astutely discerns from the priest's absence in his wife's bedroom that he has probably hidden himself among the sculptures. He then sharpens a knife, goes to his workshop, locates the crucifix appropriated by the priest, and informs his wife that he has made this particular image badly and will quickly "amend it," with the implication that he will improve on it by adding to it. The husband amends the image, of course, by cutting off the priest's penis and testicles. When the wounded priest runs out of the studio with the cross still on his shoulders, the husband cries out to those outside his home to stop the thief who is stealing one of his statues. The priest is captured, and the husband collects a 15-pound fine from him in compensation for the stolen goods. The tale concludes with a firm moral: Priests who love women will end up like "this priest, Constans, / who left his hanging there" (99–100).

The tale's opening description emphasizes the sculptor's craftsmanship with a razor-sharp pun that anticipates the climax of the narrative. He is "a prudent craftsman, good in his affairs / Who knew well how to make images / And to sculpt crucifixes carefully [bien entaillier crucefis]" (3–5). I am thinking specifically of the double sense of Old French "entaillier": "to chisel" or "to sculpt" as well as "to trim, cut, prune." The creative act is simultaneously an act of desecration. To take the pun one step further, the additional sense of "entaillier" as "to place oneself in the midst of" implicitly sets up an analogy between this sculptor/creator and his divine counterpart who fashions his son's crucifixion as a way to mediate between sinners and Himself. The "franc mestre" of "The Crucified Priest" enacts a parodic crucifixion in which the priest plays a guilty and very male Christ who literally ends up paying for his sins twice: initially through the castration of his genitalia and ultimately to the tune of 15 pounds.

As parodic Christ-type, the priest is a dismembered shape-shifter who plays a sequence of roles throughout the narrative, each simultaneously displacing and including the former: priest, priest-lover, priest-lover-parodic Christ. Even as the list of metaphoric personae expands, he is literally metonymically reduced, ultimately defined by the absence of penis and testicles. Like many of the cycle drama episodes, this comic tale works not only "to subvert the social, but to reinforce it as well." The implicit tongue-in-cheek moral, what Bloch calls "the socially recuperative thrust of the [fabliau] joke," is that dismemberment really is also amendment (*Scandal*, 120).

This notion of comedy as that which, through metonymic displacement, simultaneously subverts and reinforces the social is the fabliau influence most central to the York *Crucifixion*. Through similar images of crucifixion and dismemberment, the play draws on the comic double weave—the recuperative subversion—specific to fabliaux. Like "The Crucified Priest," the York *Crucifixion* considers the kinds of authorial power the soldier-crafters of the crucifixion can exercise over their "creation," Christ. Yet if "The Crucified Priest" locates its humor in masculine agency, the authorship of the male artisan within the poem (specifically, the sculptor's ability to rewrite the conclusion to the subversive love narrative that his wife and the priest author), then the York *Crucifixion*, in contrast, derives its humor from focusing on the ultimate authorial/creative power of the shape-shifting, fissured body at the heart of the narrative: the feminine flesh that the crucified Christ has taken on.

The barest plot outlines of Christ's crucifixion are familiar, no doubt. Let me describe in further detail the comic activity that surrounds the literal process in the York play of attaching Christ's body to the cross. The guild dramatizing the crucifixion is of course the Pinners guild, a group of carpenter-craftsmen whose success is invested in the seamless joining of wood. With a kind of brilliant perversity, the opening dialogue of the play depicts the soldiers who crucify Christ as artisans proud of their "werke" or craft, the crucifixion itself as the product of creative virtuosos in wood. They caution each other to work with utmost care, demonstrate genuine pride at acquiring and arranging the crucifixion implements with efficiency (25–48). Ultimately, they will measure the quality of their work by their success at flaying Christ's body.

Their craftsmanlike pride, however, quickly devolves into a display of their ineptitude—a slapstick routine in which one excruciating mistake after the next simultaneously amplifies the audience's laughter and Christ's pain. The humor is both agonizingly funny and nauseating, the product of a horrific accretion of handyman's glitches that tear Christ's body apart. As the soldiers stretch Christ's limbs to the boreholes they have drilled, they find it difficult to nail the first hand to the cross and search for a nail big enough to go all the way through the sinews. They subsequently realize as they reach for the other hand that they have mismeasured the width between boreholes by over a foot. Their solution is simply to stretch the body until its "sinous go asoundre" (132). They groan about the difficulty of stretching the body; whine about the weight of the cross as they try to set it upright; worry about future back problems; argue with each other about whether the distribution of weight is equal as they lift the cross. They fail at this and drop the cross to the ground as the audience watches Christ's not-so-firmly attached body sway against the momentum of its own flesh. These loud-mouthed soldier-craftsmen comically transfer Christ's visible, silent suffering to themselves as they work.

When they lift the cross a second time, they drop it again, this time into the mortise in order to avoid further injury to their backs, then argue about who made the mortise too wide, so wide that the cross sways back and forth in its base as does the fragmented body hanging on it. These "pinner-soldiers" even misplace the hammers they need to wedge the cross in place (239–40). Their mordant routine is an anticipatory improvisation on Christ's final words at the play's end—"Forgiffis thes men that dois me pine. / What they wirke wotte they noght [Forgive these men who inflict pain on me. / What they work, they know not]" (260–62)—the equivalent of the gospel's "Father, forgive them, for they know not what they do" (Luke 23:34). The process objectifies the experience of pain through metonymic reduction of the suffering whole of Christ's body to its constituent parts. The dramatist renders the biblical Latin's "faciunt" with "wirke," not "do," to underscore the crucifiers' hapless artisanship. Christ may play the straight man to their antics, but his final words—a pun that in its semiotic slippage doubles the craftiness associated with woman's tongue[26]—leaves him the last laugh.

Both "The Crucified Priest" and the York *Crucifixion* share a focus on dismembered bodies and an interest in using metonymic displacement as a ground for dark comedy. However, the cycle play ultimately can invert the "creator-created" nexus it appropriates from the French fabliaux because of the unusual dual status accorded Christ's feminine flesh. Christ's body is what the fabliaux refer to as "desnaturer" or denatured: a mutilated version of its natural form that can metamorphose into something more than a suffering corporeal presence. Here fabliau and female mystic discourses converge. Christ's fissured flesh duplicates the site of disruption from which women devotional writers author their visions (Lochrie, 6).

The most prevalent physiological models in the Middle Ages, the Galenic and Aristotelian, explain female anatomy as a specular but denatured version of male anatomy. If the male body is defined in terms of its corporeal integrity, the female body is seen as composed of pervious flesh unable to render adequately the components of male anatomy without distorting their limits.[27] The semiotic extension of this concern that the female body corrupts the male form finds its clearest expression in the "woman as riot" topos popular in much medieval literature (Bloch, *Medieval Misogyny*, 17–22). The riotous woman is one whose speech is abundant, uncontrollable, illogical, indecipherable, deceptive, or enigmatic. Her discourse in its exuberance is as semiotically overdetermined as her body in its viscosity, its fluidity.

This misogynic connection between fissured body and enigmatic speech serves as the conceptual substratum for the narrative reversal of the York *Crucifixion*: the startling shift from comic to tragic mode in the final moments of the play. In "The Crucified Priest," the garrulous, love-talking priest's ultimate silence is a guilty voicelessness that results from his emasculation. The York *Crucifixion* inverts this speech-silence dynamic. Christ is silent for most of the play, but it is not the stalwart, manful virtue held as an ideal in monastic spiritual communities (Newman, 24). His body speaks somatically, instead, through the kind of graphic suffering that plays a central role in the female mystic's experience.

When Christ finally uses his voice, it is to make a cosmic joke that underscores the literal ineptitude of his torturers. He emphasizes his physical suffering through an extrabiblical addition to scripture's rendering of Christ's dying words: "Forgiffis thes men *that dois me pine* / What they wirke wotte they noght" [my emphasis]. Christ's final words in the play mark his voice as woman's. His connotative doubling of "wirke" as both "inflict" and "create" collapses the semiotic boundary between desecration and creation. With this verbal slippage, he draws attention to the material incongruities of divinity enfleshed: He is both objectified, suffering body and omniscient, omnipotent creator. With his doubling of "wirke," Christ explodes the crucifiers' deceptive use of "wirke" and its cognates throughout the play to identify their various torturous activities singularly as craftsmanship. Like the feminine shape-shifting of the fabliau trickster and like the somatic speaking of the female mystic, Christ's combination of physical suffering and linguistic play gives him a body and a voice impossible to invest "with univocal interpretation" (Bloch, *Scandal*, 67–68).

To alleviate their guilt, the torturers exploit their culture's misogynic link between the physical fissures of the female body and its verbal excesses. In their need to find a semiotic justification for their feminizing torture of Christ's body, the soldier-crucifiers capitalize on the bizarre fabliau logic of making the victim's crime fit the punishment, rather than the punishment fit the crime. In fact, Christ's crucifiers ultimately accuse him of speaking like a woman. They begin by comparing his words to the jangling of jays and the prating of magpies (265–66): familiar aviary analogues from medieval bestiaries for women who are both verbally and sexually excessive. They indict him specifically for his false "sawes" or soothsaying (274), accuse him of producing "gaudis" and "bourde[s]" (125, 149, 200; tricks and jests), and try to contain him by insisting that he is powerless "for all the kautelles that he couthe kaste" (278; tricks, devise). Their agreement that they should leave the dying Christ to "hinge here stille, / And make mowes [grimaces] on the moon" (285–86) parodically resonates with the description of Juliana's originary vision for the Corpus Christi feast: the fragmented moon to be completed only by a celebration of Christ's body enfleshed in female matter. Through the linguistic economy of their accusations, the York dramatist subtly threads together characterizations of the voice of the fabliau poet-trickster, misogynic portraits of female voice, and the female devotional substrata of the feast that the plays celebrate.

In this play, Christ is for his crucifiers worthy of their torture because he is a deceptive, sorcererlike worker of miracles who might take advantage of them: in short, a match for the most anxiety provoking, stereotypical qualities assigned to women by antifeminist rhetoric. For the audience, however, he is the wry but merciful equivocal trickster that even fabliau aligns with divinity doubled through its human enfleshment: the "bon doublere" or "good doubler" as Christ is called in the fabliau "Brunain, the Priest's Cow,"[28] who Mary-like "feeds and bleeds," nourishing sinners by lactating his redemptive blood into the Eucharistic cup.[29] His fissured flesh is like woman's in that its vulnerability not only provides "the gap through which the self fell from God and from itself" but the means through which it may yet return. If the fragmented female body is a site of "perversion," it also offers, as Bernard of Clairvaux argues following Augustine, the possibility of redemption (Lochrie, 20–22). The semiotic extension of this body—Christ's punning, "female" request that God consecrate the desecrating work of his torturers—uncovers the combined disruptive and recuperative powers of the feminine voice in these plays.

Recovering the Redemptive Female Voice:
The Wakefield *Salutation of Elizabeth*

In the York *Crucifixion*, Christ as word-made-flesh reauthors God's Word in a way that demonstrates its intrinsic feminine plasticity and suggests, fabliau-like, the contingency of all language, even God's, when given feminine voice. The crucifixion certainly offers the hope of redemption; however, its graphic staging of the evisceration of Christ's body presents the audience with the tragicomic paradox of social wholeness achieved through fragmentation. Mary's visibly pregnant body in the nativity plays similarly acknowledges a breaching of boundaries. Yet it also insists on the self-containing unity of that breach. Mary is, after all, absolutely inviolable according to doctrine: immaculately conceived as well as perpetually virgin before, during, and after her conception and birth of Christ. But in carrying a child she clearly demonstrates the elastic, movable boundaries of her female body.

For medieval culture, Mary's virgin body serves as the emblem of immaculateness. The cycle drama, however, circumvents the obsession with her hermetically sealed womb familiar from patristic exegesis on female chastity (Lochrie, 24–25). It does so by entertaining a bivalent view of Mary's body: from without and from within. The nativity plays focus equally on questions surrounding the access to and the contents of Mary's womb. Her body can, on the one hand, register cultural dis-ease about the female body's lack of fixed boundaries as Coletti demonstrates in her readings of the "Joseph's Troubles" plays. However, it also stands as analog for the social body's capacity for recuperative, Eucharistic difference: for separate entities—here child *in utero* and nourishing mother—sharing the same sustaining flesh. Bynum reminds us that it is this physiological role of the mother, "whose uterine lining provides the stuff of the foetus (according to medieval medical theory) and whose blood becomes breast milk" that underlies the sense of at least one female mystic that "Christ is mother more than father when it is a matter of talking of the Incarnation."[30]

The Wakefield *Salutation of Elizabeth* celebrates this link between flesh, woman, and God's body; then takes it one step further, not simply underscoring Christ's humanity but celebrating Mary's material embodiment of the Holy Spirit. In complementary opposition to the disordered, fragmented community that the profaned, crucified body of Christ represents,[31] the material elasticity of Mary's pregnant body in this play becomes emblematic of the sacralized symbiosis of the social body. The flux of her womb is not a function of the divinity who fathers this child; rather it is the characteristic she shares most vitally with other female bodies less miraculously inseminated: a point of material identification with other women. The *Salutation* dramatizes a conversation between two visibly pregnant women who compare their bodies as a way of discussing the health of the social body they participate in.

In his brief introduction to the Wakefield *Salutation*, David Bevington suggests that the play "serves chiefly as a vehicle for the 'Hail Mary' and *Magnificat*"(368). He astutely observes that extrascriptural additions to the text aim at "personalizing the situation, rendering it comfortably familiar to medieval audiences," and describes the conversation between Mary and Elizabeth as "innocent family gossip about absent loved ones." However, his characterization of these additions as "inconsequential" is somewhat startling. Certainly the *Magnificat* is the focal point of the narrative, appearing as it does at the center of this brief whisper of a play. Yet of the 90 lines that make up the *Salutation*, more than two-thirds are dedicated to what Bevington characterizes as "innocent" and "inconsequential." As with representations of women in other cycle plays, it is crucial here to discern the interplay between the center and the margins of dramatic activity since this graphically doubles as a paradigm for the historical displacement of women in late-fourteenth- and early-fifteenth-century England.

Although the *Magnificat* at the heart of the *Salutation* (49–78) renders Luke 1:39–56 verse by verse, the Wakefield Master complicates this fairly straightforward duplication of scriptural structure with a striking shift in its verbal matrix. The Wakefield Master's dramatized version of the opening of the biblical *Magnificat* reads almost like a stanza from a love lyric:

> My saull lufys my Lord abuf,
> And my gost gladys with luf
> In God, that is my hele.
> For he has bene sene agane
> The buxumnes of his bane,
> And kept me madyn lele. (49–54)

In place of the biblical emphasis on Mary's rejoicing spirit, the dramatic Mary's praise of God resonates with the erotic language of beguine mysticism's "mystique courtoise," which subtly synthesizes eros and agape (Newman, 139–40). Her "buxumnes" (53) evokes the fruitful bridal self who is both carnal and spiritual partner to the divine Beloved and points to the play's pervasive doubling of the enfleshed and the incorporeal. Following this pattern, the dramatist reshapes scripture's characterization of God as "saviour" through Mary's description of Him as "my hele": a word that refers both to physical health and spiritual salvation. This fabliau-like semiotic play on the double sense of "hele" is a dynamic that is dramatically reproduced by the spontaneous *in utero* leap through which the prophet John "makys joy" in recognition of the unborn Christ. John's adult role of proclaiming Christ as messiah, literally enwombed, suggests the very material connection between the promise of salvation that the biblical Salutation celebrates and the intimate talk of health and family that Mary and Elizabeth share in the Wakefield *Salutation*.

The emphasis on "hele" in the drama establishes the theme that the frame discourse—Mary and Elizabeth's remarkably consequential gossip about family health—richly tropes. Their exchanges emphasize in domestic terms the salvific devotional continuum between the different genders and generations that compose the diverse social body that is audience for the play. The first 30 lines of the *Salutation* focus on Mary's and Elizabeth's mutual inquiries into the well-being of their respective families. Mary first asks about Elizabeth's health (7), then congratulates her that she "with child in elde gang" (11). Elizabeth, who calls Mary "doghter" (8) and "dere kins-woman" (15), wants to know how Mary's mother and father are faring. Through Elizabeth's explicit characterization of Mary's mother, Anna, as her niece (23), the dramatist subtly reminds the audience that the participants in this exchange span three generations. And, not coincidentally, he describes the connections matrilineally. This detail, derived from patristic tradition, suggests how fully the cycle dramas can transform "masculine" text through its "feminine" spaces. We discover that the kinship between Christ and his prophet John—and, presumably, between Christ and all those human "cousins" who in future generations will testify, prophetlike, to Christ as messiah—has its origins in the wombs of these mothers.

In its closing passages, however, and with characteristic lyrical intensity, the Wakefield *Salutation* urges its audience to understand the enfleshing capacity of Mary's womb not merely as point of origin for Christ but as commensurate with His Eucharistic power. In a final negotiation of scriptural form and boundary-breaching dramatic play, the *Salutation* focuses on Mary's departure, as described in Luke 1:56, but actually concludes with Elizabeth's apocryphal farewell not texted in scripture:

> *Mary:* Elezabeth, min[e] awnt dere,
> My lefe I take at you here,
> For I dwell now full lang.
> *Elezabeth:* Will thou now go, Godys fere?
> Com kis me, doghter, with good chere,
> Or thou hens gang.
> Farewell now, thou frely foode!
> I pray the[e] be of comforth goode,
> For thou art full of grace.
> Grete well all oure kin of bloode.
> That Lord, that the[e] with grace infude,
> He save all in this place. (79–90)

Structurally these final two stanzas follow the stichomythic pattern of exchanges and trinitarian groupings of lines—evident in the six-line, interlocking *aabccb* rhyme scheme—that the dramatist uses throughout the play. The stichomythia works to suggest that Mary's and Elizabeth's experiences mirror each other. The trinitarian groupings, subtle throughout, take on a new resonance here, however. Elizabeth addresses Mary first as God's "fere" (82), a word whose homophones and connotations vibrate with physical and spiritual doublings. Mary is, at the simplest level, both physically and spiritually "fair." More complexly she is his enfleshing and spiritual "companion": mother and lover of God as her lyrical *Magnificat* richly suggests.

This second doubling prepares us for Elizabeth's pun at line 85, a playful suggestion that Mary, as "frely foode," is coequal with the Eucharist her enfleshment of the divine makes possible. Of course "frely foode" can mean "noble person" or "noble companion" as most glosses of this line suggest, but it has carnal valences as well. Mary's pregnant body, "with grace infude" [infused with grace] (89), provides the "foode" that makes Christ's body Eucharistic food. The overtones of an "alternative trinity" tradition here, with its substitution of Mary for the Holy Spirit, are inescapable. The Eucharistic resonances of her maternal role as food for Christ bring to mind sapiential Mariology's iconographic tradition of the "Double Intercession" in which both Mary and Christ appear as joint intercessors for the Christian community, with Mary offering up her lactating breast as Christ offers his wounded side.[32]

If the cycle plays are about the Christian social body, then they are most richly about the movable female boundaries of that body. They offer a symbiotic, double experience of the body that is distinctly feminine: Christ's open wounds paired with Mary's incorporating breaches. The silent, exhausted, broken body of Christ—what Peter Travis calls the *sermo humilis* of the York *Crucifixion* (33)—finds a recuperative voice in the Wakefield *Salutation*. Mary's conversation with Elizabeth, with its emphasis on the joyous, bulging bounds of Mary's womb, reverberates with the complex reality that the unified community imagined as the outcome of Eucharistic devotion is constituted of divergent, self-articulating members.

The Bodleian Library, Oxford. MS Douce 195, folio 152v.

By permission of The British Library, London. MS Harley 4431, detail of fol. 290r.

In the *Roman de la Rose*, Jean de Meun describes Venus, a figure of lust, breaking through the defenses of a castle representing the female body (ll. 21251 ff). Replying to Jean, Christine de Pizan erects a new female defense in her *Book of the City of Women*.

CHAPTER 7

The Female Speaker in Dream Vision: The Problem of (Women's) Language

In the English Corpus Christi plays discussed in the previous chapter, the way in which a character speaks, as well as his or her biology, determines gender identity. Mary and Elizabeth speak women's language, and so does the Christ of the York passion play. His verbal responses to the executioner's tortures make Him—for them—woman. Equating women and language is a frequent feature not just of Eucharistic drama but medieval literature generally. As we saw in chapter 1, medieval verbal theory imagined that language, like the womb, lends material form to a spiritual essence—words spoken or written clothe an idea with sounds or letters just as the body clothes the soul. Hence different uses of female sexuality can represent different uses of language: Mary's giving birth to the transcendent Word may stand for language's capacity to connect humans to the realm of ideas, whereas Eve's seducing Adam to eat the forbidden fruit may symbolize language's habit of straying from the truth.

Medieval texts often use a woman's sexuality as a self-conscious metaphor for authors' preoccupation with whether their own words are true. The question of textual truth is displaced to the problem of women's sexual fidelity. This displacement is especially the case in dream vision. In this genre a narrator, usually male, dreams that an allegorical female figure engages him in philosophical discourse. Normally the two discuss the questions (1) which is more real, ideas or matter? and (2) how does language represent reality? Quite often, in addition, they touch on women's moral nature. In dream vision, then, women are both topics to be debated and skilled debaters who outwit inferior male opponents.

What a female debater tells us about her creator's views on women, however, is a complex question, and depends on the philosophical assumptions of the poem in which she appears. If a text locates reality in the Platonic ideal or if it believes that language transparently conveys ideas, its female debater tends not to reflect well on actual women. As the symbol of a pure idea, she may be a virtuous foil for human women who occupy the vicious material world, her truthful language a contrast to their lying tongues. The majority of dream visions I survey fit this mold; to generalize an observation that Toril Moi makes about Andreas Capellanus, each of these authors "conveniently represses the fact that he has unmasked a problem of general linguistic and epistemological importance (how can language convey truth?) and blames it all on the deviousness of women."[1] Boethius in his *Consolation of Philosophy*, as we will see, blames the problems of language on the allegorical Muses and Fortune. Alan of Lille's *Plaint of Nature* sees an allegorical Venus as the source of linguistic and sexual deviance. Both Andreas in *De Amore* and Jean de Meun in the *Roman de la Rose* put women at fault; yet Jean exceeds Andreas in his vilification of the feminine by placing the allegorical heroines of his precursors—the Ladies Reason and Nature—among the guilty party.

But not all dream visions blame women for problems of language or see them as inherently false. If a text distances itself from Platonism and instead imagines that the spiritual and physical worlds mutually inform each other, its female speaker may be an ideal that human women can reach, her speech a model for them to emulate. Christine de Pizan in her *Book of the City of Ladies* brands the philosophical underpinnings of the dream vision tradition as inherently antifeminist, and pagan to boot. She composes in response a vision with a Christian theory of language and offers herself and her patron, Saint Christine, as model speakers for her female readers.

The source of most dream vision conventions, including its female pedagogue and concern with questions of reality and language, is Boethius's *Consolation of Philosophy* (524)—next to the Bible, the most influential text of the Middle Ages.[2] The *Consolation* opens with Boethius, once a high-ranking Roman official, wrongly imprisoned for treachery to the state. Boethius presents himself as the anguished victim of false accusations: "Perjury and deceit are ... covered by the color of lies."[3] A majestic woman, Lady Philosophy, appears and tells the prisoner that he is not suffering because he is imprisoned but because he, like his accusers, has a mistaken notion of truth. He will continue to suffer as long as he remains like those who "fix their attention on their own feelings rather than on the true nature of things" in the ideal realm (Bk. 4, Pr. 4; p. 87).

Philosophy, furthermore, blames Boethius's false perspective on his frequenting of wanton women. First, he was taken in by the "deceitful antics" of his "mistress" Fortune (Bk. 2, Pr. 1; p. 22), who with her ever turning wheel personifies the world's arbitrary award of favor or scorn; Boethius erred in assuming that such a mistress could ever be true.[4] Second, even in prison Boethius dallies with "wounded muses," "whores from the theatre," who represent the elegiac poetry with which he has lamented his imprisonment; these poems can only cement his concentration on his sufferings, not assist him in escaping them. For the muses' sexuality is "sterile" (Bk. 1, Pr. 1; pp. 3–4), unproductive of truth.

Banishing the muses, Lady Philosophy teaches Boethius how to speak truth by the example of her own speeches: "I shall use the sweet persuasion of rhetoric," she says, "if it does not contradict the truths of philosophy" (Bk. 2, Pr. 1; p. 21). In the course of the *Consolation*, Philosophy's speeches grow longer and longer as they instruct Boethius about such heady topics as the nature of good and evil and the relationship between providence and free will. The work ceases to be a dialogue as Philosophy's becomes the dominant and then the only voice.

But although Boethius stops speaking as a character, he continues to speak as an author, through the mask of Lady Philosophy. For she emerges as not an independent figure but an aspect of Boethius, that part of the mind that deals with abstract concepts; as she tells Boethius, she must take her rightful place in his mind (Bk. 1, Pr. 5; p. 16). *Philosophia* is pictured as feminine because of the gender of her Latin name, and Boethius is generally careful to keep her in womanly character—she is said to cure Boethius, a task consistent with medieval women's role as healers, and is maternal in her solicitude for him. But Philosophy—although she could at times offer a model for medieval women who claimed the rights of study and composition[5]—is simply a feminine persona of her male creator. Boethius is his own guide, and the reader's. The truth Philosophy claims for her speeches is really the claim Boethius makes for his book.

Boethius's imitators in the dream vision tradition tend like him to use allegorical goddesses as figures for their own best selves, yet some go beyond him by defining truth as an idea apprehended only by male minds. Alan of Lille's *Plaint of Nature* (ca. 1165), for one, creates an imaginary world that contains no female humans, only feminine ideas. The *Plaint* is significant in allegorical tradition for featuring as its presiding goddess Nature, who represents the material world.[6] Like Philosophy, Nature's purpose is to expose sexual sin as an aspect of bad language. Men, she complains, disdain her by practicing homosexuality and bad Latin grammar—with both vices humanity "introduc[es] barbarisms in its arrangement of genders."[7] Such perversity, Nature continues, results partly from wrongful interpretation: Mankind has taken literally Greco-Roman myths, like that of Jupiter and Ganymede, that seem to advocate homosexuality, instead of treating them allegorically. Using a common metaphor, she teaches that a reader should look for deeper significance within these stories, "so that when the outer shell of falsehood has been discarded the reader finds the sweeter kernel of truth hidden within" (140).

Nature, of course, speaks for Alan, who through her teaches that his book, like mythology, is to be read allegorically. *The Plaint of Nature* is a difficult poem, and, aside from condemning unnatural vice and bad poetry, modern commentators disagree about what its message is.[8] Yet whatever the moral, it is aimed at a purely male audience. Alan's opening declares that the root problem of unnatural vice is the emasculation of men by Venus, who represents the power of generation; she was good before Adam's fall but afterward degenerated to lust: "Venus now changes 'he's' into 'she's' and with her witchcraft unmans man" (67). To communicate his moral vision of a world where men are men, Alan invents a fantastic realm peopled with both female and male allegories: Nature, her daughter Truth, and Venus; Nature's husband Genius, Cupid, and Hymen, the god of marriage. But although Alan's imagined world contains both sexes, his real world does not. In the *Plaint*, women function only as symbols for either male virtue or vice—and predominantly the latter, since a man's fallen state is figured as a transformation into a "she."

Viewing men as real but women as symbols, as Alan does, is commonplace in the Middle Ages. Texts often urged male readers to abandon human women and sublimate their desires with figures like Ecclesia, Athena, or Philosophy.[9] Such an appeal would have seemed unremarkable to the readers of works like the *Consolation of Philosophy* and *The*

Plaint of Nature; since these were Latin texts, they would be read by male clerics, who as at least nominal candidates for ordination should remain celibate. The university-trained clergy, however, if unaware of any ethical problem in reducing women to allegories, were concerned with the logical problem that feminine personifications presented: How could allegorical women be good if real women, as antifeminist tradition held, were so bad? The potential contradictions of using women to represent philosophical ideas, the divide separating human from allegorical women, is taken up in Andreas Capellanus's *De Amore* and Jean de Meun's section of the *Roman de la Rose*. Andreas's work (ca. 1170) is not a vision, but, like dream texts, uses women as a locus for discussing how language communicates truth. It at once announces its self-conscious concern with words—Andreas, purporting to advise his young friend Walter on how to win love, notes that the best course is "fluency of speech": "For an elaborate line of talk on the part of the lover usually sets love's arrows a-flying."[10] Andreas adds that he will illustrate this idea "as briefly as I can"—a claim certainly tongue in cheek, for Andreas's "brief" illustration, a series of dialogues between men who woo and women who reject, occupies the great bulk of the work—105 of 185 pages in Parry's translation.

The men in the dialogues attempt to cajole, flatter, threaten, or fool the women—that is, use every verbal trick in the book—into having sex with them. The women deflect the men's assaults principally by denigrating male verbal skill: The potential lovers, the women charge, speak empty words (51), obviously contradict themselves (66), use obscure allegorical narratives (73), interpret too literally (130), and generally lie (passim). One woman sums up the action of the dialogues when she says, "Although some men ... utter foolish, almost crazy, remarks," "clever women are in the habit of turning away fools and unwise men in contempt" (60).

The women of the dialogues are indeed "clever women" who discuss the nature of truth and its relationship to language as if they were Lady Philosophy or Nature. The positive image of women as profound interpreters and teachers, however, is overturned as soon as Andreas finishes his exemplary dialogues and turns to other topics. Bits and pieces of misogyny pepper Book II (see 143, 146, 150), but these passages simply presage a swelling up of virulent misogyny in Book III of *De Amore*. There Andreas urges Walter never to practice love—primarily because of the vicious character of women, about which Andreas goes on for 10 pages (200–10): Women are greedy, irrational, deceptive, garrulous, lustful, and "prone to every sort of evil" (208).

The antifeminist ending of *De Amore* obviously conflicts with the respect accorded eloquent women at its beginning. Andreas is quite aware of the contradictory nature of the two parts of his text and explains it away by stating that the two halves of his text operate on different philosophical planes: The first part gives "the theory of the subject," whereas the second part offers practical advice (187, 211). I would reword this division to concentrate on Andreas's treatment of women, to say that part one of *De Amore* offers a portrait of women who, in spite of their resemblance to courtly ladies, are theoretical, that is, allegorical women; they represent the ideal of truthful discourse and teach it to the reader, just as Boethius's or Alan's ladies do. The second half of the book, in contrast, presents real women as if they were all Boethius's poetical whores and offers the same practical advice as Philosophy had: Avoid them. By making the discrepancy between "good" theoretical women and "bad" real women so stark, Andreas exaggerates how literary tradition had illogically used feminine allegories to castigate feminine vice: It is as if dream visions like Alan's had taken the idea of "woman" and divided it in two, using one part to laud philosophical ideals and the other to denigrate evil, and sometimes women as well.

This division of the feminine is emblematized by Andreas at the end of his final dialogue, where a lover and a lady debate whether one should love the upper part of a woman—which has "attributes peculiar to the nature of man"—or the lower parts—which "are in no wise differentiated from brute beasts" (136). The question is ridiculous, as Andreas means it to be. No one can love only the top or bottom of a woman. But the writers of dream vision have chosen to love half of a lady, loving only the ideal feminine while denigrating the carnal. Andreas further underscores allegory's routine division of allegorical from biological gender with his last words, when he vests Walter in the moral attributes of feminine allegories: He advises Walter to marry Christ the Bridegroom in the persona of a Wise Virgin (211–12; cf. Matt. 25:1–13). Walter paradoxically is to avoid women by becoming one himself.

Jean de Meun's portion of the *Roman de la Rose* replicates *De Amore*'s techniques for emblematizing dream vision's distinction between allegorical and biological gender and goes considerably beyond them. The *Roman*, one of the most influential works of the Middle Ages,[11] was begun about 1230 by Guillaume de Lorris, who composed a little over four thousand lines describing how his dream self—called the Lover—wanders into a garden where he falls in love with a Rose. The Lover's attempts to win his beloved are abetted or repulsed by personifications of the psychic, biological, or social forces motivating him and the Rose. Guillaume died before finishing the poem, leaving the Lover frustrated of his goal, but it was completed about 1280 by Jean de Meun. Jean concludes the Lover's search with scabrously hilarious metaphors: The Lover, garbed as a pilgrim, consummates his desire by penetrating a secret shrine where he scatters seed on the rosebud, then cuts the rose. This narrative and sexual climax is, however, anticlimactic, coming at the tail of the cacophonous discourses that compose most of Jean's continuation. For Jean does not so much conclude Guillaume's poem as inflate it. Bringing the number of lines to nearly 22,000, he takes the figures inhabiting Guillaume's garden, adds others, and has them address the Lover in gargantuan speeches. These ostensibly concern how he should or should not pursue the Rose but veer off into a miscellany of questions concerning philosophy, love, sex, religion, science, and—of course—interpretation.

Jean's section of the poem quotes swathes of text from *The Consolation of Philosophy*, *The Plaint of Nature*, and *De Amore*, and Jean is just as self-conscious about the truth value of language as his predecessors are, if more lighthearted in his claims for truth in his words. Like authors of earlier texts, Jean describes his protagonist's visit by a divine personification—Lady Reason—who teaches him to read allegorically. In the course of advising the Lover to abandon the madness of desire, Reason tells the story of "Saturn, whose testicles Jupiter, his hard and bitter son, cut off."[12] She explains that the Lover should interpret this myth allegorically in order to learn the "truth hidden within," "the secrets of philosophy" (136).

Although Reason does not say what truths Saturn's testicles hold, she is dead serious that a spiritual idea will be conveyed via such an unlikely image. The tenor and vehicle here are divorced from each other, absurdly if not shockingly so—but that is precisely Jean's point. As David Hult argues, the real secret revealed here is that Reason's theory of language—the same theory animating most dream vision—sees no inherent connection between word and object, representation and meaning. Reason confesses that she names things "at my pleasure," arbitrarily—she could just as well have named testicles "relics" and relics "testicles" (135). The image of Saturn's castration, Hult continues, brilliantly emblematizes the nature of Reason's theory of reading: The rupture between objects and their names, between myth and allegorical meaning, is as great as that between Saturn and his testicles.[13] Like Andreas, then, Jean implies that an allegorical hermeneutic cuts off words from their meanings in the material world; and like Andreas he uses a dissected body—although a male one—to represent that cut.

Jean does subject women to rude treatment in his further investigations of language; the female figure who comes under attack is Reason herself, who falls victim to the Lover's verbal theory, which differs significantly from her own. When Reason has finished telling the Lover about Saturn's testicles, he answers that he will waste no time on her poetic fables, for he wants to think only of the Rose (136–37). He twice reproves Reason for her speech: She was wrong to mention the word testicles, a word "shameless and excessive" (115). "I do not consider you courteous," he tells her, "when just now you named the testicles to me; they are not well thought of in the mouth of a courteous girl" (133). As Hult again points out, the Lover's peculiarly ambiguous choice of words, like Lady Reason's discourse, draws attention to how words represent things: The Lover means to say that the word "testicles" doesn't belong in Reason's mouth, but the plural pronoun "they" can refer grammatically only to testicles themselves—which the Lover, through his agreement problems, has put in an inappropriate place (Hult 116).

The Lover, unlike Reason, is not explicit about what linguistic theory he holds to, but certainly his hermeneutic opposes Reason's: Where she reads allegorically (the word "testicles" points to philosophical truth), he reads literally ("testicles" means testicles); where she views words as disjoined from things, he sees words and things so intertwined that they are indistinguishable ("testicles" are testicles). The Lover, in short, is about as literal and carnal as a reader can be.[14] For him, words refer to material things, especially the body, especially those members that seem to embody carnality.

The Lover's carnality renders him unable to recognize Reason as a personification of his own reason or of rational judgment in the abstract. Faced with a female allegory, he treats her as a flesh-and-blood woman, and he treats women as he does the Rose, simply as an orifice for his penetration. The Lover's stuffing "testicles" in Reason's mouth doesn't differ much from his assault on the Rose. Indeed, both the Lover and Jean de Meun treat feminine allegories as if they were Boethius's Muses or Alan's Venus, ascribing to them the carnal significance that human women carried in medieval thought. Jean's version of Nature, for example, because of her verbosity includes herself when she states that "Women have too many devious and malicious ways in their hearts" (317, 301). And she is not the only character to offer up misogynist cant. A Jealous Husband concludes that "All women are whores" (317). The Lover's Friend pretends to defend women but reports that he has never found a good one (177), and his speech cites antifeminist authorities (169). Genius lists the usual catalogue of women's vices—fickleness, greed, lying, and garrulousness (276–81). And every kind of female vice is incarnated in the Old Woman, the Rose's disreputable duenna, who declares that "all men betray and deceive women.... Therefore we should deceive them in return" (269).

Obviously Jean de Meun's portion of the *Roman de la Rose* is replete with misogyny. But is Jean himself a misogynist? His readers have argued the question since at least 1400, when the participants in the *Querelle de la Rose* began to debate the literary and moral value of the *Roman*. Jean's defenders have always argued that he did not concur with his women-hating characters but used their speeches to address philosophical ideas. Jean, they say, wants us to read the poem allegorically, as Reason directs, so that we may apprehend those pure concepts. One of the participants in the *Querelle*, for example, calls Jean "excellent philosopher" and accuses his critics of not being "capable of understanding so high a conception or of attaining to its mystery."[15]

As my analysis of Reason's dialogue with the Lover implies, I agree with Jean's defenders that his primary interest in the *Roman* is philosophical, self-consciously linguistic. But I do not agree that this absolves him of misogyny. Even if an author does not agree with the antifeminist sentiments he voices, his expression of them may and does lead to social misogyny, with women suffering the consequences. This argument was advanced against the *Roman de la Rose* by Christine de Pizan (1365–1430), the most vocal of the participants in the *Querelle*. In one of the documents of the *Querelle*, she tells of a jealous husband who took the *Roman*'s depiction of women as gospel truth. As he read the antifeminist passages aloud, he would kick and beat his wife (136). Ideas have political consequences, Christine argues, and cannot be excused simply because they are ideas.

Christine de Pizan was France's first professional female writer, turning to the pen to support her three children, mother, and other dependents after her husband's death left her a young widow. Christine is unusual among medieval female authors—she was not a nun or otherwise attached to a religious community; she was married and a mother; she was prolific, composing 10 works in poetry and 11 in prose; and she was famous and successful.[16] As a writer she was familiar with misogyny as a literary tradition, and as a woman she knew it as a real-life phenomenon. For Christine, as her vignette of the readerly jealous husband shows, life and art were inseparable.

Recognizing the intertwined nature of literary and social misogyny, she combated both. Christine's fullest response to misogyny is her masterwork, *The Book of the City of Ladies* (1405). Christine tells us that she wrote *The City of Ladies* to provide women with a defense against misogynist attacks—hence the title of the work, referring to an allegorical fortress that Christine "builds" as a refuge for women.[17] Christine constructs the city by telling stories drawn from mythology and from classical, medieval, and biblical history about women whose lives belie antifeminist stereotypes—wise women demonstrate that not all women are irrational, chaste women show that not all women are driven by lust, and so on. Although the narrative contents of *The City*, as explicit responses to misogynist claims, deserve considerable attention, what is most intriguing about the book is its form. *The City of Ladies* is a dream vision that reinvents the conventions of the genre even while invoking them. By remodeling the machinery of the dream vision, Christine is able to call into question the philosophical underpinnings of that machinery, and thus to question not just misogyny but the larger epistemological and hermeneutic foundations on which it rests. These she replaces with strategies of knowing and reading that she finds more conducive to her pro-woman enterprise.[18]

Christine attacks the philosophical foundation of misogyny by making *The City of Ladies* an imitation of *The Consolation of Philosophy*, yet an imitation that questions the sort of consolation philosophy affords women. *The City* opens with a distraught Christine consoled by not one but three goddesses, Jean de Meun's Lady Reason and the Ladies Rectitude and Justice. Like Boethius, Christine laments that she has been imprisoned—not in jail but within a female body (5). But when Reason diagnoses Christine's illness, its cause is the opposite of Boethius's. Whereas the Roman writer suffered because he had forgotten philosophy, Christine suffers because she knows it far too well. Christine feels contempt for "myself and the entire feminine sex" (5) because she believes the misogynist harangues of "all philosophers and poets and . . . all the orators" (4). Christine names Aristotle, whose biological theories argued for the inferiority of women's bodies, and she implies the culpability, too, of Plato, whose followers assumed the inferiority of female minds.

Just as Christine's disease is the obverse of Boethius's, so too is the cure for it. Lady Philosophy told Boethius to contemplate ideal truth. But

Reason tells Christine that if she wishes to know the truth, she must forget philosophy, which is not gospel truth but only opinion. As Christine puts it in the *Querelle*, "human understanding cannot attain to a perfect knowledge of absolute truth ... so men draw conclusions from opinions rather than from certain knowledge" (*Querelle*, 116). *The City* shows up philosophers' statements as only opinions because "these same philosophers contradict and criticize one another." Faced with contradictory philosophical authorities, Christine must reject them and look for truth elsewhere—in her own experience, for "it is evident and proven by experience" that philosophers are wrong about women (7).

Christine's skepticism about knowing absolute truth is crucial to her feminist project, for Platonic epistemology enabled one strain of medieval misogyny. Plato held that true reality lay not in objects but in the single, unchanging idea of the object—there are not multiple women, only the idea of Woman in which all women partake. Grounding themselves in this epistemology, misogynists claimed that if you knew one woman, you knew them all—and alleged some nefarious stereotype to be true of the whole sex. In attacking the misogyny voiced in the philosophical dream vision, Christine points out that she does not oppose valid criticism of particular women for particular vices, but only totalizing statements about them. Jean de Meun angered her when he defamed "without exception an entire sex" (*Querelle*, 56). Her experience taught that she and other women were not wicked; thus, as Reason says in *The City*, "attacking all feminine conduct is contrary to the truth" (17).

When Christine adopts an empirical epistemology that discovers truth in the material realm, she adopts with it a compatible theory of signification. Allegory entirely suits dream vision's Platonic epistemology because it sees truth as an idea hidden inside words and images, both material objects to be thrown away; as we saw, Lady Nature taught Alan's dreamer to discard "the outer shell of falsehood." Because exterior images are false, they have, as Jean de Meun's castration image wittily depicted, no intrinsic relation to the truth they convey but can be cut loose. But Christine rejects the notion that a sign has no connection to its signified. Rather, she adopts a Christian hermeneutic that asserts that words and images are not arbitrary signs but have a material relationship with what they signify. As Augustine explained, just as Christ, while still remaining the Word, became flesh, our ideas, even while remaining ideas, become words.[19] Christian signs are part of what they represent, the medium is part of the message—the Eucharistic bread does not just signify the body of Christ but *is* that body. This Christian hermeneutic particularly suits Christine's feminist revision of dream vision; since a sign has a material relation to what it represents, a feminine idea like reason can be expressed only by a biological female—like Christine herself. The real goddess of *The City*, then, is not the abstract Reason, but the flesh and blood Christine who incarnates her.

Christine most vividly represents her use of a Christian hermeneutic in the scene where Reason, Rectitude, and Justice first appear, recalling the biblical moment when the Word became flesh, Gabriel's visit to Mary. The female trio, a remodeling of the Trinity, delivers an annunciation to Christine imagined as type of the Virgin: As Mary in illustrations of the Annunciation, Christine sits reading in a chair when the Ladies approach her with Gabriel's words, "Do not be afraid." There is even a hint that Christine conceived *The City of Ladies* as Mary conceived Jesus, for when the Ladies appeared, "I suddenly saw a ray of light fall on my lap," as golden rays convey the Word to Mary's womb (6).[20]

The City's annunciation scene, like the gospel's, imagines language as a place where all of human experience comes together: the mind and body, God and humanity, idea and word. Christine regularly attributes this sort of completeness to women. She says they are inclined to "integrity" (31), and her overall figure of the city of ladies is strongly suggestive of physical wholeness, for this impregnable fortress is her transformation of the castle, representing the female body, that the Lover and his armies breach in the *Roman de la Rose* (*Roman*, 340). Christine's insistence that women naturally possess moral and physical integrity is a significant part of her response to counter misogynist philosophies, for it directly responds to Aristotle. This thinker claimed that women's inferiority to men was obvious in their smaller and weaker, hence "deformed," bodies; the Greek physician Galen (131–201) added that a woman's lack of a penis marked her as "mutilated."[21] Christine reviews pagan theories of generation in *The City* (22–23), and Reason refutes them by telling the Genesis 2 story of creation, which she interprets—not without precedent—as teaching that feminine and masculine bodies, both created directly by God, are equally good, as are the souls inside them: God formed Eve out of Adam's side so that she would "stand by his side as his companion," not lie at his feet like a slave (23).[22] As regularly in *The City of Ladies*, Christine rejects what she sees as pagan antifeminist lies for Christian pro-woman truth.

Reason's, however, is not Christine's full reply to Aristotelian-derived theories of women as defective men. Elsewhere in *The City* Christine turns the tables on misogynists to argue that they, not women, are deformed. Reason, to Christine's question about the causes of misogyny, replies that sometimes impotence makes men woman-haters; frustrated by their inability to fulfill their desires, they blame the objects of their lust. These misogynists' physical deformities render them less than men. They "are moved by the defect of their own bodies," "have impotent and deformed limbs" (19). Ovid, whom Christine blames for beginning the misogynist tradition in his *Art of Love* and *The Remedy for Love*, was "castrated and disfigured" (21).

Christine's reference to Ovid's castration recalls the importance Jean de Meun placed in Saturn's castration in the *Roman de la Rose*. That castration is alluded to yet again in *The City of Ladies*, in the story of Saint Christine. This saint is Christine's special patron, and this life represents her own, for it tells the story of a woman who speaks despite male attempts to silence her.[23] Christine's opponents had attempted to unvoice her in the *Querelle* of the *Rose* with the usual misogynist arguments, impugning her as emotional and irrational by nature (61, 93); one had, echoing Jean de Meun's language, compared her to a whore (183).

Christine compares herself, however, to a saint. Saint Christine is a typical early virgin-martyr, tortured by pagans for her refusal to worship idols. Saint Christine's passion, however, takes an atypical form: Because she keeps calling out the name of Jesus, the executioners cut out her tongue, not once but twice. Still, the saint is able to pray "even better and more clearly than before" (239). It is not far-fetched that Christine's story of her patron's severed tongue imitates and answers Jean's castration scene—particularly when we note that the idol Saint Christine is ordered to worship is Jupiter, the perpetrator of the crime against Saturn (235, 237). The documents of the *Querelle* record Christine's repulsion at Reason's talk of Saturn's castration, how inappropriate she found the language there (117–18). That scene ended with the Lover's verbal thrusting of testicles into Reason's mouth. Christine wittily transforms severed testicles into severed tongue and has her saint speak in spite of the incision—a declaration that she, the saint's namesake—and Christ's—will not be silenced by illegitimate male authority. Clearly the saint's speech is a miracle, but the author's speech and her book, too, possess divine authority. "God ... has truly placed language in women's mouths," Reason tells Christine in yet another troping of Jean's testicles (30). Christine thus invests her book with the highest authority. It speaks not for philosophy, nature, or reason, but for God.

Althogh his lyfe qweynte be · the resemblaunce
Of hym hath in me so fressh lyflynesse
That to putte other men in remembraunce
Of his psone · I haue heere the liknesse
Do make to this ende in sothefastnesse
That they that haue of hym lost thought and mynde
By this peynture · may ageyn hym fynde

The ymages that in the chirches ben
Maken folk thynke on god and on his seyntes
Whan they the ymages · beholden and seen
Where as vnsight of hem causeth restreyntes
Of thoghtes goode · whan a thyng depeynt is
Or entailed · if men take of it heede
Thoght of the liknesse · it wole in hem breede

Yit som holden oppynyon and sey
That none ymages sholde y maked be
They erren foule · and goon out of the wey
Of trouthe · han they skant sensibilitee
Passe ouer now · that blessed trinite
Vpon my maisters soule mercy haue
ffor hym lady eke · thy mercy I craue

Moore other thyng wolde I fayne speke and touche
Heere in this booke · but such is my dulnesse
ffor that al voide · and empty is my pouche
That al my lust is qweynt with heuynesse
An heuy spirite · comaundeth stilnesse
And haue I spoke of pees · I shal be stille
God sende vs pees · yf it be his wille

Portrait of Chaucer, literally breaking the boundaries of his text. Hoccleve, *The Regement of Princes*. By permission of The British Library, London. MS Royal 17 D VI, fol. 93v.

CHAPTER 8

Chaucer, Rape, and the Poetic Powers of Ventriloquism

As we saw in the previous chapter, Christine de Pizan insists in the *Querelle de la Rose* that individual women belie the stereotypes that misogyny assigns wholesale to their gender. Her focus on the possibility of reimagining gender identity is one that also runs throughout the work of one of her most famous English literary contemporaries, Geoffrey Chaucer. Like many medieval poets who write dream visions, Chaucer often uses female sexual fidelity self-consciously as a metaphor for his own preoccupation with poetry's efficacy as a vehicle for textual truth.[1] He is fascinated with the concept of the female body as allegorical terrain that, when mapped by the male poet, will answer his questions about how fully reality can be represented through language. Chaucer, however, is also clearly aware that the portrait of woman that emerges from the dream vision's central gender fiction—the polarization of matter and spirit—is inherently invasive and divisive. At best, the dream vision female pedagogue can appear in her own body but only if she speaks with a voice not her own: that of "male" reason. At worst, the deceptive quality of language is underscored through the misogynic association of linguistic ambiguity (fictional narratives as lying words) with her "intrinsic" carnality. It is a portrait of woman that disjoins mind/voice and body. In its mind-body split, it mimics conceptually the literal dynamics of the nonconsensual sexual assault of rape: a radical attempt to divest body of voice.

In his own poetry Chaucer repeatedly acknowledges his discomfort with this strategy by using narratives that hinge on rape to rework the metaphoric equation of deceptive language with female infidelity. He explores the powers of ventriloquism to work through the implications of rape's silencings. In "Adam Scriveyn" he employs the concept of rape to explore what happens in a metaphorically gendered textual exchange between author and scribe, whose wranglings compromise integrity of voice in the feminine text. *The Legend of Philomela* reveals both the suffering and power that obtain when that suppressed voice is no longer simply feminine, but viscerally female. When Chaucer tropes rape in *The Wife of Bath's Tale*, he uncovers the all-too-familiar double-talk of his culture's rape law and the uneasy choice it offers between private revenge without social redress and public satisfaction at the expense of individual protection.

Defending Dido or Aeneas?

Over the past two decades, many new critical focuses have emerged for Chaucerians. The function of gender in Chaucer's poetry is proving one of the most exciting and most vexed topics of inquiry. Gender studies provide us with a polychromatic spectrum of theoretical contexts: history, cultural anthropology, religion, psychoanalysis, and sexuality, to name a few. It is a rich array of critical figurations for assessing how Chaucer structures both female and male subjectivity, how he creates versions of the self as well as how he constructs his own identity.[2] Indeed, given Chaucer's dual interest in the advantages and consequences of the gender-play produced by his androcentric culture, it is hardly possible to read fifteenth-century Scottish Chaucerian Gavin Douglas's assessment that his poetic "mastir," "venerabill Chauser," was "evir (God wait) al womanis frend [always, God knows, all woman's friend]"[3] with the literal-mindedness of early Chaucer scholars who understood Douglas's allusion as testimony to Chaucer's sympathy for historical women. A single phrase—"al womanis frend"—complicates both syntax and diction here, making us wonder about the nature of the relationship Douglas imagines between Chaucer and women: Was he "the friend of all women"; "always a friend of women"; what kind of "friend" was he? For gender-conscious readers from the late twentieth century, Douglas's claim is fundamentally ambiguous.

Reading Douglas's comment in its literary context gives us an even more specific sense of its attendant ironies. Douglas makes the remark in the Prologue to Book I of the *Eneados,* his Scottish verse translation of Virgil's *Aeneid,* in which he considers the authenticity of various translation strategies while describing and justifying his own methodology for readers. In this prologue, he compares his own work as translator with that of his most immediate literary mentor, Chaucer. He chides "venerabill Chauser" for having "gretly ... offendit" Virgil, their mutual poetic patriarch, with his version of Virgil's narrative of Aeneas's and Dido's love in the *Legend of Good Women* (II:25). Tongue in cheek, Douglas singles out Chaucer's admonishment of Aeneas for abandoning Dido as a mistranslation that can be excused perhaps because of his empathy for women. He sees it, nevertheless, as an attack not only on Virgil but also on the poetic forefather of English romance, Aeneas.

> But sikkerly of resson me behufis
> Excuss Chauser fra all maner repruffis
> In lovyng of thir ladeis lylly quhite
> He set on Virgill and Eneas this wyte
> For he was evir (God wait) all womanis frend. (II:445–49)

Douglas backhandedly acknowledges his immediate literary progenitor while subtly asserting the greater legitimacy of his own status and that of his Scottish literary peers as inheritors of the classical poetic tradition through which Britain had, for the previous three centuries, claimed itself rightful heir to Troy's legacy, the Roman Empire.[4]

Douglas's accusation testifies, on the one hand, to Chaucer's pervasive association of his own problems establishing "auctoritee" with the alleged excesses of woman's voice (too much speaking as well as too little).[5] Yet Douglas's tribute is at best subversive, a masculinist poetic gesture. He implies that Chaucer's poetic activity of mistranslating Virgil is as riotous a site for language as the female body, traditionally the site of linguistic chaos for the Middle Ages,[6] and attempts to neutralize Chaucer's paternal powers of influence by aligning him affectively with women, by making him an ally of Dido rather than of Aeneas. Douglas identifies Chaucer fully with the feminine, unmans him in order to underwrite his own literary fame as well as his country's historical-mythic status.[7] Interestingly, the strategy is one that Gayle Margherita associates with one of Chaucer's own narrators, the seemingly naive voyeur-reader of *Troilus and Criseyde*.[8] The irony, I am suggesting, is that although twentieth-century readers may characterize Chaucer's narrating persona as masculinist, one of his near contemporaries assigns him to the poetic purgatory of the effeminate. Whereas late-twentieth-century readers may find Chaucer's empathy for women limited by his gender, a near literary peer finds it too far-reaching.

In fact, the poetic personality doubled through identification with both genders is one Chaucer plays with throughout his poetry. Almost invariably, the subjectivity of his female characters can never be understood in isolation from men. Their identities are shaped—and often distorted—by their interactions with male characters. Writing within a culture in which the male-female gender hierarchy systematically denies women the "capacity to judge and act on the basis of a fully developed moral consciousness,"[9] Chaucer nevertheless creates a series of intelligent, witty, disturbing female characters whose capacity for autonomous thinking disrupts, even redirects, masculine narrative patterns. The Wife of Bath, May, Griselda, and Criseyde are all products of a poet keenly aware of the fiction his society perpetuates about the object status of women: that they inhabit only the space of the privatized when, in actuality, they are exchanged as public commodities as well.[10]

Chaucer writes with considerable irony of his patriarchally structured culture's habit of setting up a dual-use value for women: desiring their worth as objects of public exchange to secure political domains or to ensure dynasty, while relegating them to the space of private possessions, where they are at the disposal of individual male fantasy. The lie here, that woman is alternately public object or private possession as convenience dictates, is grounded in medieval misogynic rhetoric's central dichotomy: that Woman is either virgin or whore, Mary or Eve. It is a bipolar cultural fiction that masks the confluence of these extremes in the concept of Woman-as-excess: either quintessentially inviolable (too good, like the Virgin Mary) or inherently flawed (too bad, like Eve).[11]

As Derek Pearsall suggests, Chaucer is troubled not only "by the inhuman stupidity" of the denial of women's rational and moral equality with their male counterparts but also "by the consequences to men if the rights of women as individuals are allowed" (Pearsall, 138). If Chaucer is "al womanis frend," it is not without a certain degree of self-interest. Nowhere is this more uncomfortably apparent for readers of Chaucer than in recent discussions of the implications of what Carolyn Dinshaw has described as "the one biographical fact everyone remembers about

Chaucer ... that in 1380 Cecilia Chaumpaigne apparently threatened to accuse him of raping her" (*CSP*, 10).

Chaucer, Fourteenth-Century Rape Law, and the Rape Accusation Release

On May 4, 1380, Cecily Chaumpaigne brought a deed to the Chancery of Richard II that released the poet Geoffrey Chaucer from "all manner of actions such as they relate to my rape or any other thing or cause."[12] Witnessed three days earlier on May 1, 1380, by several prominent members of the court of Richard II,[13] the deed was then enrolled on the close rolls: that is, "recopied by a clerk," as Christopher Cannon explains, "on the back of those sheets of parchment used to record the 'closed' or sealed letters sent by the king" (74). Although the original deed was presumably written, certainly signed and sealed on May 1, 1380, it "passed for good into Chaucer's possession, and then, ultimately, into oblivion" (Cannon, 90). Until Cannon's recent discovery, the only record we actually had regarding Chaucer's rape of Cecily Chaumpaigne—the one discovered by F. J. Furnivall in 1873[14]—was that provided by the release recopied onto the membranes of the close rolls on May 4, 1380.

Scholarship related to this release has focused almost exclusively on the meaning of "*de raptu meo*"—the phrase at the center of the document that raises, Cannon observes, "the troubling possibility that Chaucer was a rapist" (75). Although the Latin *raptus* can be translated both as abduction (which may or may not involve sexual violence) and as rape (nonconsensual forced coitus), scholars who examined the document during the first half of this century found the fourteenth-century use of the term too ambiguous to discern what Chaucer had actually been accused of. Most recently, however, Cannon has examined the release in its original context—that of the language and practice of English law—and argues compellingly that the term in this instance almost certainly means rape. He demonstrates that the use of the noun *raptus* in the Chaumpaigne release in isolation from some form of the verb pairing of *rapere et abducere* (to ravish and to abduct) decisively tells us that Chaumpaigne was releasing Chaucer from an accusation of rape as sexual assault and not ravishment or abduction.

Even if rape is established decisively as the accusation from which Chaucer was released, the document still raises as many questions as it answers. Chaucer's most recent biographers, Donald Howard and Derek Pearsall, consider a range of possibilities: that the accusation was entirely a case of falsified charges (i.e., that no crime was committed); that the accusation of rape was trumped up as leverage to force a compensatory settlement for some other crime; that the charge was a legitimate one that Chaumpaigne settled out of court to secure some kind of financial compensation for a crime that English law could not recognize.[15] Evidence for the first two of these three possibilities is less than compelling. Howard, however, offers a disturbing if unverifiable suggestion for why Chaumpaigne might drop charges of rape in favor of an out-of-court settlement: that she was pregnant.

Howard explains that "by a maxim of medieval law it was believed that a woman could not conceive if she had not consented" (320) to sexual relations. The maxim derives from the Galenic physiological model popular in medieval medical treatises on the body's humors. Galen's account emphasizes that heat is of critical importance to sexual excitement and conception, and that women who conceived did so only by achieving orgasm. As Elizabeth Robertson observes, this view "could lead to disastrous consequences in rape cases, since the rape victim who conceived was deemed to have given the consent necessary to achieve conception."[16] If Chaumpaigne discovered that she was pregnant after accusing Chaucer of rape, her accusation would not have held up in court. Both Pearsall and Howard mention that Chaucer acknowledged an apparently out-of-wedlock child, "little Lewis," who was 10 years old in 1391, when Chaucer dedicated his *Treatise on the Astrolabe* to him. Pearsall describes the suggestion as conjecture and characterizes the evidence for it as "merely circumstantial" (138). Howard explains that "if the rape or seduction had occurred not long before the release was signed on May 1, nine months would just barely have gone into 1381" (320). The ambiguities these biographers underscore suggest that we can do no more than speculate about whether Chaucer committed the rape Chaumpaigne names in her release.

It would obviously be absurd to characterize the rape accusation as the most important influence on Chaucer's writing. His poetry mirrors too richly his culture's diverse literary, theological, political, and social influences—both English and continental—to be treated so reductively. However, the significance of the rape accusation for representations of women in his poetry is, I would argue, of singular importance. We do not need a precise biographical record establishing Chaucer's guilt or innocence of the crime to find intriguing the marked increase in narratives of rape in his poetry after 1380 until his death in 1400.

A few examples from poems in which rape figures as a central motif suffice to suggest the pervasiveness of the imagery in Chaucer's later work. In *Troilus and Criseyde* (1382–1386), Chaucer interweaves epic, mythic, and courtly narratives of rape in a way that quite pointedly draws attention to the continuum between private and public commodification of women. He connects the epic and lyric levels of the narrative through a deft portrait of the continuum between rape and courtly love. Rape is the specific narrative focus in the tales of Lucrece and Philomela in *The Legend of Good Women* (1386–87); abandonment, betrayal by false male lovers, and suicide figures throughout. Chaucer also peppers *The Canterbury Tales* (1388–1400) with narratives in which rape or abduction, although less focal, play a part. In *The Wife of Bath's Tale*, as we will see, he substitutes rape for murder as the crime its protagonist-knight is found guilty of and must atone for. In *The Franklin's Tale*, he narrates the story of the courtly heroine Dorigen, who finds herself compelled by both her husband, the knight Arveragus, and her would-be lover, the squire Aurelius, to pay off a wager she made with Aurelius by having sex with him. Chaucer confirms his suggestion in *The Merchant's Tale* that May's marriage to the much older January, although socially and legally sanctioned, has the qualities of rape by invoking the mythic tapestry of Pluto and Proserpina for its conclusion. Custance, the heroine of *The Man of Law's Tale* and clearly an emblem of the fluid exchange of women between men, is subjected to repeated attempted rapes.

Nor do we need a transcription of Chaucer's contributions as a member of a commission investigating a similar case seven years after the Chaumpaigne release to acknowledge the importance of Chaucer's participation in *raptus* proceedings from both the perspective of the accused and the investigator.[17] I am not recommending a biographical approach that might document images of rape as literary mirrors of Chaucer's "personal experience" of rape. (We can't know what that experience might have been at a remove of 600 years any better than we could at a remove of 60 minutes.) I am suggesting, however, that we explore how his familiarity with the legal rhetoric surrounding rape in late-fourteenth-century England might have translated into his literary representations of the difficulties women meet in establishing autonomy in a culture that recognizes male subjectivity foremost.

Most scholars responding directly to the Chaumpaigne release have focused their energies on determining the nature of her accusation or the degree of Chaucer's guilt or innocence. Few have actually noticed the frequency with which Chaucer subsequently makes narratives of rape the context for his poetic discussions of women's voices. In fact, critical consideration of Chaucer's literary uses of rape is a fairly recent phenomenon.[18] Cannon's evidence, however, for the fluctuation of the term *raptus* and the resulting confusion of the implications of the terms *rape* and *abduction* in legal documents during the thirteenth and fourteenth centuries opens up a splendid new critical space for this kind of inquiry. His discovery of an additional memorandum related to the Chaumpaigne release—one that suggests that Chaucer was himself interested in the self-fashioning power latent in the semiotic continuum between rape and abduction—allows us to see how intimate the relation between rape as a narrative trope and poetic ventriloquism is in Chaucer's poetry.

Cannon emphasizes that instances in which a *raptus* accusation can, without question, be equated with rape (as opposed to abduction) are in the minority. In fact, rape and abduction were often tried using the same procedures and were frequently linguistically conflated as a result (79–84). Cannon's newly discovered record of the Chaumpaigne release tellingly illustrates the influence of the linguistic gray area between rape (a felony) and abduction (a trespass) in English medieval law. In a memorandum dated May 7, 1380, and recorded in the *coram rege* rolls (a form of the original release recopied for the more frequently consulted rolls of the Court of the King's Bench), the most striking phrase from the less frequently consulted close rolls release—"*de raptu meo*"—has been eliminated. In its place, the memorandum releases Chaucer from "all manner of actions both concerning felonies, trespasses, accounts, debts, and any other actions whatsoever."[19] Cannon entertains the possibility that Chaucer himself sought the revision: a revision that suggests that the noun *raptus* was so bold that three days after the close rolls release, "whether by coercion, persuasion, or some more complicated manipulation in the court of the king, this strong word—this mention of rape—had to be quietly, but emphatically, retracted" (94).

Regardless of whether Chaucer literally authored the substitution, he seems (unlike twentieth-century critics obsessed with differentiating between abduction and rape) to have been aware of and to have availed himself of the complexities, both legal and semiotic, of the continuum between these two terms. Although himself clearly charged with rape, Chaucer or someone acting in his interest takes advantage of the prevailing legal conflation of the terms *rape* and *abduction* in order to revoice, ventriloquistlike, the original close rolls release. If the close rolls release constitutes a more "private" record of the rape accusation, the substitution of the more general term *felony* for *rape* in the more frequently consulted *coram rege* rolls memorandum suggests a dramatic refashioning of Chaucer's public persona[20]—a fictive renarration of the self as innocent, at least of the implications of rape.

It is a legal narrative that doubles that of the initial accusation release and that allows Chaucer to inhabit both the role of masculine agent of the crime and femininized victim of the accusation. This double legal persona, as we will see later, is one Chaucer translates into his poetry in myriad forms: to consider the possibilities of rape as a metaphor for poetic ventriloquism ("Adam Scriveyn"); to explore the manifestations of voice beyond literal speech through a kind of reverse ventriloquism in which women, as disenfranchised speakers within his culture, present their experience (*The Legend of Philomela* from *The Legend of Good Women*); and to experiment with constructing not only a voice for the accused but a voice for the victim as well (*The Wife of Bath's Tale*).

"Adam Scriveyn": Troping Rape to Construct the Doubly Gendered Self

One of the clearest instances of overlap between the confusing legal language concerning rape and Chaucer's poetic troping of rape occurs in the single-stanza lyric, "Adam Scriveyn"[21]:

> Adam scriveyn, if ever it thee bifalle
> Boece or Troylus for to wryten newe,
> Under thy long lokkes thou most have the scalle,
> But after my makyng thow wryte more trewe;
> So ofte adaye I mot thy werke renewe,
> It to correcte and eke to rubbe and scrape,
> And al is thorough thy negligence and rape. (AS, 1–7)

Some literary historians have tried to identify the "real" Adam, the reckless fourteenth-century scribe Chaucer chides. The biographical impulse to do so is certainly understandable given the evidence for scribal intervention in manuscripts of *Troilus and Criseyde*, one of the two poems Chaucer's narrator here explicitly accuses his scribe of corrupting.[22] However, the highly self-conscious literary quality of this poem is evident as well from the "book curse" form it takes.

Popular throughout the Middle Ages, book curses were often appended to manuscripts by authors and scribes to discourage not only the literal theft of a manuscript but its textual, and consequent conceptual, corruption as well.[23] In fact, miscopying is both literally and metaphorically an assault on the flesh of the textual body, and Chaucer's curse gruesomely reflects this continuum between physical and mental activity. He wishes a parasitic infection, "the scalle," on Adam unless the scribe begins to copy more accurately, even designating a location for the disease to strike: "under thy long lokkes." The homophonic pun on "scalle" and "scolle" (Middle English for *skull*)[24] suggests the retributive equation of punishment with crime that is characteristic of such curses: a parasitic skin plague is doubly appropriate since both the scribe's activity of copying texts and his inability to reproduce them whole are parasitic. The flaking skin that Chaucer wishes on his scribe also provides a physically graphic double for what Chaucer has to do to amend the mistakes the scribe introduces when he miscopies Chaucer's texts: "rubbe and scrape" the vellum, flake off its flesh, and then smooth its surface again. Chaucer can then inscribe the corrected version on the clean subdural layer underneath.

Particularly striking in this context is Chaucer's characterization of Adam's activities in the final line of the poem as "negligence and rape." *Rape* is univocally glossed by Chaucer editors, Dinshaw observes, as *haste*. Too much speed in copying results in careless transcription ("haste makes waste"). But clearly the mind-body continuum that Chaucer's curse underscores invites readers to explore the implications of the word's sexual denotations as well. Dinshaw suggests that, given the culpability implied by the Chaumpaigne accusation, it is ironic "that Chaucer should position himself in 'Adam Scriveyn' as raped, not as rapist" (*CSP*, 10). In view of the implications of the recently discovered *coram rege* memorandum, however, it seems hardly surprising. In fact, the verbal redressing of *rape* with the more ambiguous term *felony* in this memorandum, because it functions as an act of fictive renarration, involves an eerily similar double figuration of the self. Clearly in "Adam Scriveyn" rape affords an opportunity for a revenge narrative that silences the female voice of accusation.

In creating his narrative persona here as profaned "auctour," it is not that Chaucer imagines himself as inhabiting only the position of victim. He implicates himself in the sins of his scribe as well. Certainly his scriveyn, Adam, violates Chaucer's poetry in terms of both its physical appearance and its meaning; however, Chaucer characterizes his own reparative efforts in language that is at least as materially invasive: He has to "rubbe and scrape" and ultimately reinscribe the text in the vellum. The act of renewal is itself an assault. In fact, Chaucer's reversal of the pedestrian process for correcting a text—first "scraping off the old ink and then rubbing the surface smooth again"[25]—achieves the end rhyme between "scrape" and "rape" that both visually and aurally affiliates poetic making, scribal transmission, and rape, and thus subtly encourages the reader to draw analogies between Chaucer's scribe's activities and his own. The difference, of course, is that Adam's "rape" of the text is destructive and perhaps deliberate; by using the word *negligence*, Chaucer mercifully allows for a kind of obtuseness or oversight—rather than malicious destruction—and mirrors the contemporary practice of prosecuting some rapes as abduction. Chaucer's, on the other hand, is intentional but restorative. Each is simultaneously guilty and innocent. Whether as scribal defamation or as authorial amendment, the literary troping of rape here is as conflictive and apparently as malleable as the fourteenth-century legal language surrounding *raptus*.

If Chaucer positions himself as a victim of rape in this poem, it is as a secondary victim: His "woman-text" has been both raped and abducted, in effect revoiced, by his resonantly named scribe. Chaucer suggests that by distorting the poetic narrative (his poetic "Word," so to speak), his scribe Adam falls, like first Adam in Genesis, into postlapsarian language's displacements of meaning.[26] Chaucer works to restore that voice's prelapsarian integrity. Their vying for possession of the poem's "body" by extension amounts to a dispute over who finally authorizes the text's voice and how: whether the text will remain (Mary-like) the consummate masculine fantasy of integrity or find its value (Eve-like) disfigured, prostituted, and transformed through exchange.

Chaucer constructs his narrator-author as doubly gendered: as inhabiting not only the space of feminine victim but also of masculine procreator, contending with his scribe for possession of the female text's body and voice. He suggests that this kind of possession may itself manifest as redemptive or violent, depending on whether author and scribe construct the voice of the female text as Mary or as Eve. Chaucer's ventriloquism in "Adam Scriveyn" allows him to multiply his fictive personae. However, his use of rape here as a literary trope for masculine textual exchange encourages poetic self-multiplying with a price that Chaucer explores fully only in later works: that of feminine silence.

Philomela's Tongueless Speech

In the *Legend of Good Women* (c. 1386–87), Chaucer considers whether that feminine silence can be made to speak. Certainly it is inviting to read the *Legend of Good Women* as the embodiment of female voicelessness, "as a series of negatives, absences, or denials" (Delaney, *NT*, 59). In this collection of nine tales, Chaucer presents us with a gallery of portraits of good women whose physical descriptions he never includes and whose goodness is controversial at best.[27] He draws his heroines from classical mythology, giving us an essentially saintless hagiography in which the female protagonists, all martyrs for love, testify to woman's truth with their mutilated or dead bodies. Even the framing voice for these tales fits this pattern of lack, for all are told by a male narrator who has been accused in the prologue to the *Legend of Good Women* of lacking empathy for and therefore misrepresenting women; a narrator who, as Carolyn Dinshaw has observed, regularly softens or elides the violence, recrimination, and revenge of his primary Ovidian source for these legends, the *Metamorphoses* (*CSP*, 75).

The naive, impotent, or inadequate narrator is so familiar in Chaucer that it becomes a type within his poems. We find Chaucer exploring it in works written both before and after the *Legend*: works as varied as *The Book of the Duchess*, *The House of Fame*, *The Parliament of Fowls*, *Troilus and Criseyde*, and *The Canterbury Tales*. Chaucer uses his various narrators' silences—whether explicit and self-conscious suppressions of information or inadvertent narrative bunglings—to draw attention to what is not said. It is a kind of voiceless yet audience-interactive strategy that allows Chaucer to speak to his readers while challenging them to read autonomously. In the *Legend of Good Women*, for instance, Chaucer's narrator repeatedly and explicitly identifies his key sources, even suggesting we consult on our own the "auctour" from whom he borrows most directly: "But who wol al this letter have in mynde, / Rede Ovyde, and in hym he shal it fynde" (*LGW*, 1366–67). The narrator's recommendation may be a defensive ploy intended to ensure his own authority and to disinterest his audience in narrative gaps. Or perhaps it is a subtle directive to explore the possible ironies of his voice. In either case, it announces the intertextuality of his *Legend* and marks its narrative silences as spaces in which readers may find his female characters' voices competing with what he renders in the letter of the text. Some critics see these silences as part of a strategy of suppression, a fragmenting of the textual body that discards compromising parts and retains only those that mute women's voices. *The Legend of Philomela* provides an example of omissions so disturbing—textual cuttings (so to speak) of its Ovidian source that are so dramatic—that critics have argued they actually mimic the rape and severing of the tongue of the *Legend's* heroine. I would like, however, to argue for the power of these silent places in the text: a power that provides spaces for female voices.

In this narrative Chaucer follows Ovid fairly closely until the end of the tale. For the most part, he narrates faithfully the broader details of Tereus's inauspicious marriage to Procne and her subsequent desire, after five years of married life in Thrace, that her sister Philomela visit her. He describes Tereus's journey to Greece to ask Pandion, the father of Philomela and Procne, to allow him to return to Thrace with Philomela. And Chaucer details, although not as graphically as Ovid, the story of Tereus's lust for Procne's younger sister:[28] the resulting rape, mutilation, and imprisonment of Philomela; his lie to Procne that Philomela is dead; the tapestry that tongueless Philomela weaves to reveal to her sister the circumstances of her rape and imprisonment; and finally Procne's search and discovery of Philomela.

What Chaucer omits most strikingly, however, is Procne's and Philomela's concluding revenge: their murder of Procne's son, Itys, and their decision to serve his boiled, roasted flesh to his father, Tereus. It is an enormous narrative gap, one that baldly shifts the focus at tale's end from a crime that transgresses all social and familial human bounds (not simply familial murder, but maternal infanticide as a revenge for incestuous rape, resulting not merely in cannibalism, but in a father's consumption of his firstborn son and heir) to one that in Chaucer's time was clearly culturally less anomalous: rape. But to what ends? Dinshaw argues compellingly that Chaucer's elision of the infanticide-cannibalism lessens "the violent rupture of death, the sudden shock of metamorphosis … as Philomela and Procne are simply left sobbing in each other's arms" (*CSP*, 75). She suggests that the revised conclusion falls into a larger narrative pattern of the *Legend of Good Women*: one in which its heroines are stripped of strong action, of their self-defining or self-signifying potential. Perhaps. But it also shifts the narrative emphasis from *the* archetypally heinous female crime to the most pervasive cultural form of male violence against women.

Rape, as Chaucer clearly knew from his familiarity with fourteenth-century legal practice, was a crime often redressed through judicial rhetoric that no longer acknowledged the specific, individual violence done to victims; a crime that could, in fact, even be elided from legal record if the accused had the proper connections. Both practices involve a cultural silencing of the female victim that Chaucer responds to in *The Legend of Philomela*. In shifting the focus of this tale, he refuses to highlight, as Ovid does, the anomalous, monstrous "female" behavior. He omits the actual revenge not to silence Philomela or Procne but to underscore emphatically the emotional wake that such a violent experience leaves. Chaucer cannot justify the revenge, but he can paint the sorrow and anger behind the promise of retribution.

The final embrace between the sisters need not be read as an episode of passive, pathetic mutual collapse. Procne's response upon seeing Philomela's tapestry depiction of her rape makes clear that her sister's missing tongue does not lead simply to silence. Procne's initial deathlike hush upon reading the tapestry is actually bivalent—silence born not only of "sorwe" but "ek for rage" (2374)—and shortly explodes into "the wo, the compleynt, and the mone" (2379) of inchoate mourning for the living. It is a poignant instance of the reverse ventriloquism that metamorphosis of silence involves. Whereas the ventriloquist speaks through a lifelike but silent dummy, here, in contrast, one human's voicelessness metamorphoses into another's speech.

With this context in mind, minor omissions that Chaucer makes in his version of the Philomela legend take on, in retrospect, a much fuller resonance. They prepare us to recoil at the especially invasive, familial betrayal this rape involves and to see Tereus's irrational behavior as part of the social fabric's weave. Chaucer omits any mention of the birth of Procne's and Tereus's son, Itys, thereby circumventing the inauspicious portents that Ovid assigns to it. He diverts attention from the culminating cannibalism of Ovid's narrative, emphasizing instead the marriage celebration as ill omened and illuminated solely by the Furies' "mortal brond" (2252): a union silently fated for disaster from its inception. And although Chaucer remains silent about the obsessive, lustfully voyeuristic fascination that Tereus displays while watching Pandion's fatherly affection for Philomela in Ovid (*Metamorphoses*, 147), he does so to underscore the double horror of an incestuous brother-sister rape through Philomela's own vocal admonishment of her rapist: "Where is my sister, brother Tereus?" (2315). He translates Philomela's explicit threat to make the story of her rape public knowledge among Tereus's people (a threat that, in Ovid, inspires Tereus's rage and makes Philomela perversely at fault for his dismemberment of her tongue) into a paranoic and morally empty suspicion on Tereus's part that she will shame him publicly: "and yit this false thef / Hath don this lady yit a more myschef, / For fere lest she shulde his shame crye / And don hym openly a vilenye, / And with his swerd hire tonge of kerveth he" (2330–34). The change in narrative does not empty Philomela's speech of substance; rather it points the finger at Tereus and makes audible his unspoken fear of female voice as public contagion.

Tereus's misogynic construction of female voice as contagion is, ultimately, ironic and self-reflexive given Chaucer's opening characterization of the infectious quality of Tereus's lust. He describes Tereus's rapist's desires as diseaselike and explains that they are so potent that even their narration "enfecteth hym that wol beholde / The storye of Tereus, of which I tolde" (2242–43). It is a haunting feature of Chaucer's vivid portrait of Tereus. In the final lines of the tale, he traces the consequences for women of the spread of this disease among men:

> Ye may be war of men, if that yow liste.
> For al be it that he wol nat for shame
> Don as Tereus, to lese his name,
> Ne serve yow as a morderour or a knave,
> Ful lytel while shal ye trewe hym have—
> That wol I seyn, al were he now my brother—
> But it so be that he may have noon other. (2387–93)

This infection of desire might strike as close to home as one's brother, the narrator cautions unnervingly. And although it does not make all men "serve" women as Tereus "served" Philomela (2384)—as rapists or murderers or knaves—it certainly calls their ability to remain "trewe" into question. By evoking this continuum, Chaucer suggests unblinkingly that rape in his culture is not the anomalous, episodic stuff of myth and legend, but an especially violent, frequently repeated example of the pervasive power of men over women.[29]

In this closing passage, Chaucer sets up a remarkable analogy between the male agency of the rape he narrates and his own authorial decision to cut the text off short. But whereas Tereus cuts out Philomela's tongue to foreshorten her ability to tell the tale of her rape, Chaucer foreshortens his narrative, eclipses Ovid's concluding description of maternally procured father-son cannibalism, in order to allow the rape narrative to speak for itself. His reiteration of "served/serve" twice within 10 lines works as a pointed pun that reminds readers of the unnarrated scene of Philomela and Procne's revenge in which they literally serve Itys on a platter to his rapist-father. Although the literal announcement

of Philomela's victimization is pregnant with the eclipsed Ovidian conclusion, in fact it underscores that it is Tereus's silencing of her voice
rather than the clearly horrific and anomalous cannibalism, that we
should attend to. For Chaucer, men serve women vilely, not women
men. The force of the unnarrated crime is lent the one told. The poet's
power to create speaking silences works to avenge the cultural silencing
of women's voices.

The tapestry Philomela weaves for Procne offers us a powerful
reminder that some forms of silence can be as potent as—and can even
substitute for—the discursive powers of pen and voice. A comparison of
Chaucer's fashioning of this part of the myth with two essential sources
underscores this point. In Ovid, Philomela weaves her tale in a fashion
that suggests its pictorial rather than narrative force: "Cunningly she set
up her threads on a barbarian loom, and wove a scarlet design on a white
ground, which pictured the wrong she had suffered" (*Metamorphoses*,
150). In a well-known medieval analogue, Chrétien de Troye's "Lai of
Philomela" incorporated into the *Ovide Moralisé*, she is granted the powers of a consummate artist; not only skilled weaver, she "knew the *auc-
tores* and grammar / And could write and compose verses" (Delaney, *NT*,
218). In Ovid, Philomela's creativity is exclusively female. In Chrétien,
her power to write is carefully delineated through context. She writes out
of the same tradition of learning as her male contemporaries: from a
knowledge of the *auctours* and of grammar. Chrétien praises her because
not only can she weave like a woman, but she can write like a man.
Although neither description is explicitly misogynic, both versions of
Philomela participate in a more conventional, essentialized portrait of
the female artist.

Chaucer's portrait provides a striking contrast:

> This woful lady lerned had in youthe
> So that she werken and enbroude couthe,
> And weven in hire stol the radevore
> As it of wemen hath be woned yore ...
> She coude eek rede and wel ynow endyte,
> But with a penne coude she nat wryte.
> But letters can she weve to and fro,
> So that, by that the yer was al ago,
> She hadde ywoven in a stamyn large
> How she was brought from Athens in a barge,
> And in a cave how that she was brought;
> And al the thyng that Tereus hath wrought,

> She waf it wel, and wrote the storye above,
> How that she was served for hire systers love. (2350–65)

He depicts Philomela's creative activity as a combination of the conventional association of women's voice with weaving and the powers of the male imagination grounded in writing (Delaney, *NT*, 218). Philomela can work, embroider, and weave as women of yore; she can also read and "endyte" or compose poetry. And although she cannot write with a pen, she can weave the letters that narrate the images she presents. Her inability to use a pen is a "lack" with spectacular results: a manifestly intertextual narrative that juxtaposes the vivid visual tapestry representation of the rape with the woven letters of "the storye above." By presenting the narrative of her rape in two media, it transforms the text into a doubly voiced, living body less susceptible to the violations of scribal corruption, of textual rape, than the flesh of the manuscript that Chaucer confronts in "Adam Scriveyn."

As Lisa Kiser has observed, Philomela "enacts the role of the giver of forms," the Christian God whom Chaucer invokes at the outset of the *Legend of Philomela*.[30] Chaucer uses this invocation—"*Deus dator formarum* [God is giver of forms]"—uniquely within the *Legend of Good Women* as "a prayer to a deity recognizably Platonic and Christian in its eternity and creativity" (Delaney, *NT*, 213). In the image of God the creator, Philomela uses her artistry to make letters into forms and informs them with the body of her visual art. Her silent artistry mimics more closely than poetic practice the prelapsarian wholeness that the narrator of "Adam Scriveyn" desires: one in which words are not as susceptible to the ravages of their readers.

Philomela can, of course, finally only shadow rather than achieve the inviolability of God's language. Nevertheless, she at least avenges the manifest evil that, the narrator pointedly emphasizes, God "suffer[eth]" (2228–37; either "endures" or "allows") in his creation: Tereus. Although the tapestry's message—"that [Philomela] was *served* for hire systers love" (2365; my emphasis)—makes clear that both Philomela and Procne are victims, it also contains the imaginative seed for their revenge. Though tongueless, Philomela replaces Tereus's fictional account of her death (an account that eerily parallels Chaucer's fictive revision of Cecily Chaumpaigne's rape accusation) with the vivid narrative of her loss and survival. Although Philomela's and Procne's final embrace tells the tale of their mutual suffering, it also confirms Philomela's endurance and, ultimately, silently promises that retribution will be served.

155

The Wife of Bath and her Tale:
Redressing the Accusation of Rape

Chaucer's portrait of the Wife of Bath is arguably his most brilliant and most complicated act of gender ventriloquism. More than any other female literary character, the Wife is seen as verisimilar and identified with historically real persons, from Christine de Pizan to Simone de Beauvoir. As Elaine Hansen observes, early feminist critics see her as a "plausible foil to the idealized views of femininity found in prescriptive texts of the period; possibly even 'a truly practicing feminist'; and indubitably a survivor and spokeswoman."[31] Hansen reconsiders the shared optimism of these readings from a considerably darker perspective, emphasizing the powerlessness, self-destructiveness, and silencing that belie her apparent rhetorical power and underscore the fiction of her verisimilitude.

At issue in the debate between optimistic and dark views of the Wife is how successful a ventriloquist she is. Does the misogynic rhetoric she brings into play when paraphrasing the authors she has heard during her fifth husband Jankyn's recitations from his book of "wikked wyves" (666–95) multiply or limit the power of her voice, give her autonomy or typecast her? When she paraphrases Jerome's synopsis (in his treatise *Against Jovinian*) of Theophrastus's descriptions (in his *Golden Book of Marriage*) of lustful wives obsessed with clothes, jewelry, and wandering around after dark (224–450), is she playfully aligning the material excess that misogynic literature attributes to women with the verbal excesses and incestuous ventriloquism evident in its own authorial borrowings? When she characterizes her attitudes toward marriage and sexuality in terms that echo the patristic antifeminist hermeneutics of Jerome's exegesis on Paul's First Letter to the Corinthians (1–23), is she a brilliant mimic of patriarchal discourse, enacting the more vicious stereotypes of woman not to subvert but to reform that discourse (Dinshaw, *CSP*, 114–20)? Does the Wife recite the maxims of misogyny to make transparent their absurdity; does she, in the Irigarayan sense, rehearse the discourse with a difference? Is she finally trapped by the rhetoric, both consciously and unconsciously endorsing these antifeminist stereotypes? Is she thus able to speak for herself "only in terms provided by the dominant language and mythology of [her] culture" and finally paid for her "deceits" by the beating Jankyn gives her after she tears three pages from his book (Hansen, 32)? Is the Wife, in her sexual poetics, redemptive flesh like Mary or a mutilated, carnal Eve?[32]

Although a direct source is not known for *The Wife of Bath's Tale*,[33] fourteenth-century audiences would have been familiar with other versions of Chaucer's narrative of a knight, accused of a crime, who exchanges a promise of marriage for advice from an old hag and who is then rewarded for his atonement for that crime by her transformation into a young, radiant beauty. The central narrative question of the knight's quest—"what do women desire most?"—is one found in several analogues from the late fourteenth and early fifteenth centuries. Chaucer makes two essential changes in his presentation of this popular tale. Almost too obvious to mention and discussed at length by recent critics is his choice of a woman's voice to narrate the tale. In addition, Chaucer alone among his contemporaries identifies the crime that the knight must atone for as rape.

John Gower, Chaucer's contemporary at court, tells a version in the *Confessio Amantis* (narrated by the male allegorical figure Genius) in which the knight-protagonist, Florent, must go on a similar quest but to atone for his accidental murder of another knight.[34] In the anonymous *Wedding of Sir Gawain and Dame Ragnell*, the crime with which King Arthur, the narrative's knight-protagonist, is charged amounts to real estate fraud; he gives to his loyal knight, Gawain, lands that are not his to give.[35] In these tales, the atonement is related to the crime in more metaphorical, ungendered ways (usually as a punishment for excessive willfullness). Chaucer, in contrast, uses the narrative of rape to make visceral his culture's ambivalence about female "sovereignitee" and to explore the implications of giving women voice.

Chaucer's changes juxtapose rape and ventriloquism as in "Adam Scriveyn" but activate an aspect of the continuum between the two that is more familiar from *The Legend of Philomela*. Rather than characterizing the production of his art as the exchange of a voiceless female text between male author and male scribe, here Chaucer creates a woman-narrator angered by the compromises her culture's mandate of female silence requires. She tells a tale of rape doubly redressed: rape that can be atoned for only indirectly, by abandoning the desire for private retribution in lieu of the public compensation promised by abduction proceedings.

In *The Wife of Bath's Tale*, Chaucer reinstates what is silenced in the narrative refashioning of the *coram rege* memorandum of the rape accusation release: the mention of rape. However, he does so with a twist. He simultaneously draws attention to the historical-mythic pervasiveness of rape while comically implicating his own culture in the sanctioned voyeurism and dispossession of women characteristic of romance. Following the conventions of romance, Chaucer sets the tale in "th'olde dayes of the Kyng Arthoure" (858). He juxtaposes the mythic feminine world of a "land fulfild of fayerye" in which "the elf-queene, with hir joly compaignye, / Daunced ful ofte in many a grene mede" (859–61) with his contemporary England, a place where "lymytours and othere hooly freres" circulate throughout the land "as thikke as motes in the sonne-beem" (866–71). These holy men bless everything in sight with a pious indiscriminacy that sets us up brilliantly for the ambiguity of the alleged contrast Chaucer draws between these "hooly freres" and the "fayeryes" they replace. "Wommen may go saufly up and doun," his Wife slyly reports; "in every bussh or under every tree / Ther is noon other incubus but he, / And he wol doon hem but dishonour" (878–81). In fourteenth-century England, Chaucer suggests tongue in cheek, women can move safely; the raping male incubi of fairy days have been replaced by friars. It is a loaded comment given his description (in the *General Prologue* to *The Canterbury Tales*) of the "wantowne … merye" Friar who, Chaucer implies, uses his religious purview to identify desirable sexual partners and then arranges suitable marriages for those who find themselves pregnant (208–14).

In fact, the opening passage of the Wife's tale is threaded with allusions to two of the culture's master narratives of extramarital conception: that of Arthur and that of Christ. Although the offspring in each case sanctions the union and makes it retrospectively redemptive, in both narratives the most problematic aspect of the sexual relations described is the woman's consent. The legendary first ruler of a unified Britain is conceived as a child of rape. Utherpendragon, who fathers Arthur, takes on the shape of his ravaged battlefield opponent, Gorlois, Duke of Cornwall, with the aid of Merlin's magic in order to seduce the Duke's wife, Ygerna. And although Utherpendragon and Ygerna ultimately "live together as equals, united by their great love for each other" after Gorlois's death, the story of King Arthur's conception is, after all, a supplantation narrative.[36] Chaucer follows this very clear example of a violation of consent with an allusion to the Blessed Virgin's conception of Christ. Medieval exegetes and popular Marian lyrics regularly explain the miracle of her virgin conception by comparing it to the penetration of a ray of sunlight through glass. Here Chaucer's description of the friars as specks that thickly populate an analogous sunbeam of God's "blessynge" (869) reminds us of the culture's evident need for reassurance that the union between God and Mary, although required by God, was one that involved her consent as well: that Christ was not a child of rape.

By framing his subsequent narration of the knight's rape of a woman with allusions to these two culturally redemptive supplantation narratives, Chaucer creates a poetic context that shifts concern from individual culpability to public restitution. It is a movement that mirrors and exposes the fiction making intrinsic to the legal discourse surrounding rape and abduction during his time.[37] Joseph Hornsby suggests that Chaucer probably did not consider rape and abduction as different crimes.[38] As I will argue below, however, the evidence from *The Wife of Bath's Tale* recommends otherwise. Chaucer's troping of rape in this tale suggests that he is aware not only of the different implications of each crime but also of the ways in which contemporary legal discourse cloaked these differences in order to prosecute rape as an offense against property, not person.

Christopher Cannon describes in detail the different uses of rape law—both to manipulate or avoid marriage strictures and to prosecute rape—and the resulting blurred lines between forced coitus and abduction. In theory, abduction was primarily a crime of monetary gain for which the abducted victim's family usually sought monetary compensation from the accused for goods carried off along with their offspring. Rape, in contrast, was a crime of sexual violence for which an individual victim usually sought punishment of the accused. The hybrid language of court records in the late fourteenth century, however, suggests that rape victims who wanted only monetary compensation and not personal retribution could prosecute for abduction instead. Abduction, in turn, could "easily shade over into something that is hardly to be distinguished from sexual assault," Cannon observes (88). Although women in some instances could apparently derail unwanted marriages or leave their husbands by allowing abduction, Cannon emphasizes that the benefits of such control "were offset by the collapse of their legal recourse for sexual violence."[39]

Certainly Chaucer understands rape as a crime that reduces a woman to the status of object by divesting her body of her voice and, consequently, of her person. His punning rhyme of "heed" and "maidenhed" in his initial description of the knight's rape—"maugree hir heed, / By verray force, he rafte hire maidenhed" (887–88)—clearly identifies the knight's obliviousness to the need for the woman's consent as a dual violation of her voice and her body. However, Chaucer follows through with a tale that circumvents the retributive justice theoretically available to rape victims who want to appeal the crime directly with a sentence of death for the rapist. Instead he explores the pattern of fictive displacement of women's voices in a legal discourse that shaded the distinction between rape and abduction.[40]

Chaucer begins the tale, tellingly, with the silence of the victim herself. Even though he frames the knight's quest as a challenge to discover "what thyng is it that wommen moost desiren" (905), he pointedly elides this particular "mayde['s]" desire: We never hear her voice and she disappears physically from the narrative after the initial accusation. Her theoretical legal power to seek punishment for the crime is instead transferred to the court's community of women, "the queene and other ladyes mo" (894), who plead with King Arthur not to punish the knight with the death sentence. They desire compensation rather than retributive justice and stipulate that the knight go on a quest to discover what women desire most in exchange for release from the death sentence. This is a transfer that, by making atonement an alternative to the exacting punishment of Arthur's death sentence, mirrors subtly the possibility of prosecuting a particular rape with the forms commonly used to prosecute abductions.

Theoretically, at least, the compensation desired is reimagined from the perspective of the women. Chaucer transforms the conventional monetary reimbursement associated with abduction proceedings—with its implicit equation of violated victim with "the value and quantity of goods carried off" (Cannon, 82)—into an experiential remittance in which the knight, while journeying across the land, asks a spectrum of women what they most desire. The knight pays for his failure to hear one woman's voice by listening to many. Ultimately, however, the tale's emphasis on compensation rather than retribution reproduces the central fiction of rape law in late-fourteenth-century England: Although prosecution for abduction in place of rape could be manipulated to allow women greater choice in whom they married, it did so at the price of their control over their bodies since it precluded legal recourse for sexual violence (Cannon, 81). Rape victims in medieval England were treated, in effect, "as no more than damaged goods" (Hornsby, 120).

In fact, the satisfaction demanded by the women is mercifully negotiable, and the knight takes full advantage of it. He does not need to identify a single, univocally true response to the question "what do women desire most" in order to guarantee his life; he need name just one, his female adjudicators inform him, which is "suffisant in this mateere" (909–10) and which reflects some kind of redemptive learning. The women's assessment of the response the knight provides when he returns to the court for the conclusion of his trial underscores Chaucer's subtle emphasis on corporate satisfaction at the expense of individual voice: "In al the court ne was ther wyf, ne mayde, / Ne wydwe that contraried that he sayde, / But seyden he was worthy han his lyf" (1043–45). No one proclaims or even expects the truth-value of his words; they simply agree that his response makes him worthy of life rather than of death. It is a decision that, although it endorses the value of communal forgiveness, does not afford retribution to the "mayde," the original victim of the crime.

Indeed, in a sly inversion of the dispossession of the rape victim's voice, Chaucer makes the ownership of these "wise words" unclear. In contrast with the tale's analogues, we never actually hear the counsel of the hag because she whispers her advice to the knight: "tho rowned she a pistel in his ere" (1021). When the knight answers before the court that "Wommen desiren to have sovereynetee / As wel over hir housbond as hir love" (1038–39), we are presumably hearing *his* understanding of the hag's words rather than her words themselves. But even that understanding is ambiguous and contains the shadow of her voice: Do women want "sovereynetee" over both husbands and lovers (what the knight fears), or do they want "sovereynetee" over their husbands as well as their own say in love (what the hag desires)? It is, of course, impossible to establish whether the knight, by reconfiguring the hag's words, has substituted his voice for hers, or whether the hag is "speaking through the knight" as a ventriloquist might speak through her dummy.

Chaucer negotiates the gap in perspective between rapist and victim with parallel narratives of male and female fantasies: respectively of clemency and of reform. In doing so, however, he foregrounds, even identifies as focal the male protagonist's individual desire and admits, finally, that in Arthur's court the cost of implementing female influence is the displacement of individual suffering of the raped maiden through communal voice. The knight's posttrial negotiations with the hag contrast with the request of the women at court for clement compensation and spiritual redress. His marriage to the hag, suggestive of the traditional settlement for a charge of rape through consensual marriage between the rapist and his victim,[41] is a verbal bond that the knight acknowledges, yet he tries to escape the physical consequences of his covenant with her.

Having succeeded in defending himself at the trial largely because the hag invests his voice with the appropriate words, the knight attempts to repay this final debt—the loan of her voice—by substituting the kind of material satisfaction afforded by abduction proceedings rather than rape prosecution in the fourteenth century. When the hag confronts him with his contractual obligation to marry her as reciprocal tender for the lifesaving words she provided, the knight pleads with her, "Allas and wey-lawey! / I woot right wel that swich was my biheste. / For Goddes love, as ches a newe requeste! / Taak al my good and lat my body go" (1058–61). His readiness to substitute property for body in order to prevent his verbal bond (his "biheste") from being turned against him suggests foremost that the knight has failed to learn from the clemency offered him by the women's court. It also recalls the initial rape (with the rapist this time the victim, if only metaphorically) and functions as a pointed reminder of the too easy substitution of financial redress for personal grievance when rape is prosecuted as abduction. In his presumption that body and voice are somehow separable, discrete, disconnectable, he recreates the "logic" of his initial crime.

The uncomfortable implications of the knight's persistence in severing body and voice serve as the inspiration for the choice the hag offers him on their wedding night. After the hag makes one final attempt to reeducate the knight with a short sermonlike discourse endorsing "gentilesse" (nobility achieved through worthy action rather than through birth, class, or rank), she tests the knight once more to see if he has at last absorbed the lessons of his quest. The choice she presents him with is a standard ingredient of these "loathly lady" narratives, but Chaucer deftly reshapes it not to polarize body and voice but to emphasize their intrinsic connectedness.

Chaucer does this by changing not only the narrative timing but also the nature of the choice. In both Gower's *Tale of Florent* and the anonymous *Wedding of Sir Gawain and Dame Ragnell*, the repulsive old hag has already transformed into a young, beautiful woman when she offers the protagonist the choice of having her privately beautiful at night (read "in bed") and publicly ugly during the day (read "in full view of the court"), or the reverse. In each of these narratives her beauty is bait for the knight, and the nature of his pride is tested. The condition of the woman's body, the choice implies, will necessarily reflect on its possessor. He may opt for private or public satisfaction, pleasure in bed or the admiration of his courtly peers. Which is more vulnerable, these narratives ask: his private or his public ego?

In contrast, Chaucer's hag presents her knight with the alternatives while still a hag. There is no tantalizing incarnate promise of physical satisfaction here. Chaucer even implies that the knight's appreciation of her ultimate transformation, which offers a combination of moral quality and physical youthfulness, is contingent on his ability to see truly: "And whan the knyght *saugh verraily* al this, / That she so *fair* was, and so *yong* therto, / For joye he hente hire in his armes two" (my emphasis; 1250–52). Although in the analogues either choice guarantees physical beauty for at least half of a twenty-four-hour day, the choice Chaucer's hag presents is a deliberately specious "either-or" contract, seemingly between youth and age, between beauty and ugliness, each with its attendant rewards and consequences. The dichotomies she baits him with are the false oppositions with which misogynic rhetoric constructs women.

> "Chese now," quod she, "oon of thise thynges tweye:
> To han me foul and old til that I deye,
> And be to yow a trewe, humble wyf,
> And nevere yow displese in al my lyf,
> Or elles ye wol han me yong and fair,
> And take youre aventure of the repair
> That shal be to youre hous by cause of me,
> Or in som oother place, may wel be
> Now chese yourselven, wheither that yow liketh." (1219–27)

Age assures the pleasure of fidelity but through a "foul" body; youth brings with it a "fair" body but opens the possibility of infidelity. The price of a reliable voice, then, is a bad body; the price of a fair body is a potentially false voice. From the knight's perspective, the choice is an irreconcilable double bind: possession without desire or desire without satisfactory possession.

The dichotomies presented here offer, at first glance, the familiar misogynic dynamics of insatiable desire at play in *fin'amor* love lyrics. Chaucer, however, qualifies them subtly and complicates them semiotically in order to allow us to align our voyeuristic gazes with the hag's vision as well as the knight's. The hag couches her old self's fidelity in terms that could be understood to include both physical and emotional pleasure, since her promise to the knight "nevere yow to displese" reverberates with the erotic pleasure that romance associates with its courtly love talk. And she gives a decidedly feminine twist to the threat of female infidelity posed by her younger self by characterizing it as the knight's "aventure," the noun used to describe quests in romance. The hag even transforms the presumption of female infidelity into the male game of sexual possession—cuckoldry—by suggesting that the youthful, fair woman's faithfulness will depend on the quality of visitors ("the repair") her knight-husband allows to frequent his household. A reading of the choice grounded in the knight's point of view will reproduce the ethos of possession that divests the female body of voice—an ethos shared, not surprisingly, by fourteenth-century English rape law. On the other hand, one that takes into account the intricacies of the hag's verbal play suggests that the woman's body ultimately should be more her own possession than her husband's.

In the analogues to Chaucer's tale, the choice actually involves making a decision about distributing the body's fragmented manifestations: The protagonist must assign both the body's ugly and beautiful incarnations to different temporal spaces. Chaucer, on the other hand, reminds us through the ironic ambiguities of the hag's wording of "the choice" that the female body is invested with a will, a mind, and a voice of its own, even as he suggests through his focused portrait of the knight how potentially alarming that may be to men who desire women. Chaucer draws on this narrative tension for the suggestive ambivalence of the hag's closing reconciliation with the knight:

> "Kys me," quod she, "we be no lenger wrothe,
> For, by my trouthe, I wol be to yow bothe—
> This is to seyn, ye, bothe fair and good.
> I prey to God that I moote sterven wood,
> But I to yow be also good and trewe
> As evere was wyf, syn that the world was newe." (1239–44)

On the one hand, the adjectives she uses to describe her promised behavior—"fair," "good," and "trewe"—suggest an idyllic union of physical and metaphysical qualities. However, she qualifies the promise by framing it with the master narrative of "innocence compromised" from Genesis where "the world was newe." Inherent in this prelapsarian, Edenic promise are its postlapsarian consequences of fall and subsequent redemption. What kind of "wyf" will the hag prove to be: one like Eve or one like Mary?

If we work back through the various layers of ventriloquism Chaucer uses to frame the tale, we discover once more the poet's intricate troping of rape. The Wife, who is the most immediate ventriloquist for the hag, structurally anticipates the hag's concluding remarks in her narration of her troubled relationship with her fifth husband, the cleric Jankin: "God helpe me so, I was to hym as kynde / As any wyf from Denmark unto Ynde, / And also trewe, and so was he to me" (823–25). The verbal echoes between these passages ("also trewe," "good and trewe," "as any wyf," "as evere was wyf") confirm any suspicions we might have about the extent of the hag's irony. Through the key East-West trade connection that the Wife names—"from Denmark unto Ynde"—Chaucer introduces a further analogy between the fall from Eden and the commodification of women as goods to be possessed or exchanged.

Most suggestive, perhaps, are the analogies to be drawn with the ultimate ventriloquist's voice. The final promise of the hag at the end of Chaucer's Wife's tale—to be "as evere was wyf, syn that the world was newe"—echoes the legal language of the *coram rege* memorandum that assures Geoffrey Chaucer of his release from

> all manner of actions both concerning felonies, trespasses,
> accounts, debts and any other actions whatsoever that I ever have
> had, do have, or shall have been able to have against the said Geof-
> frey *from the beginning of the world until the day of the making of
> presents* [my emphasis].[42]

At just the point where this document elides the close rolls' mention of "rape" and substitutes "felonies," we hear what in theory should be Cecily Chaumpaigne's voice but is more likely Chaucer's: a bond that releases Chaucer "syn that the world was newe" from a partially silenced series of grievances.

The absence of the charge of *raptus* certainly gives the memorandum document a different look from that of the close rolls. Chaucer discovers that rape can be fictively redressed as felony. In fact, fourteenth-century rape law itself is full of vagaries and strange silencings that condone the rapist's behavior as much as redress the victim's grievances. The tale resonates with this desire divided between empathy for the victim's silent suffering and clement hope for a rapist's reform. A feat of double ventriloquism that leaves readers at the close of the narrative facing a fairy-tale ending bitterly compromised by the Wife's final curse, it vibrates with the nervy irresolution of the hag's final invitation to the knight to "cast up the curtyn, looke how that it is" (1249).

CHAPTER 9

Revaluing the Female Body, Reconceiving Motherhood: Mysticism and the Maternal in Julian of Norwich and Margery Kempe

Writing the Body

Although western Christianity's mystical continuum reaches back to the earliest centuries of its first millenium,[1] its most richly creative period is that of the high and late Middle Ages (c. 1100–1450), a time not only marked by magnificent music and art but characterized by great social change and crisis as well. During this period, traditional social boundaries collapsed as the feudal system gave way to capitalism and cities burgeoned with the development of a new middle class. New constructs of individualism emerged in devotional circles, among them increasing opposition to the institutional structures of monasticism and a heightened emphasis on devotion to Christ's humanity. This new conception of the divine, sometimes referred to as affective piety, allowed for a more material identification with God in his most vulnerable, fleshly form.[2] Elizabeth Petroff describes mystics as the teachers of this age, "the inspired leaders who synthesized Christian tradition and proposed new models for the Christian community."[3] In particular, they emphasized devotional practices that addressed quite explicitly the needs of female religious exploring their spirituality both inside and outside the protective environment of the cloister.

Mystical experience typically includes a call to a higher life marked by successive insights and revelations about the nature of the divine. These ecstatic experiences transform the mystic and direct him or her along a lifelong spiritual journey that aims ultimately at complete, self-effacing union with God. Religious within this tradition write not only to witness their own experiences of God but also to share knowledge, instruct, guide, and offer direction. Mysticism can take myriad forms; however, it is inherently difficult to define given that its most essential ingredient—the unmediated, spontaneous experience of God—is intensely personal and can vary greatly from individual to individual. As Petroff emphasizes, the sheer diversity of social origins among those we count as mystics makes clear that there is "no identifiable mystical type" (*Body*, 5).

Medieval mystics could be male or female with varying levels of education; they came from diverse social strata and professions, and hailed from Eastern Europe, the Mediterranean, Scandinavia, England, and every country in between. The diversity is especially characteristic of female religious in the late Middle Ages who, whether noblewomen, bourgeoises, or peasants, could be virgins, mothers, wives, or fugitive widows. They were affiliated with the Church in a variety of ways: as anchoresses, recluses, beguines, and nuns from a variety of orders.[4] Their mystical experiences took similarly diverse forms. Although sometimes "so abstract as to elude any verbal formulation" (Petroff, *Body*, 5), they were more often concretely auditory, visual, or otherwise sensory, especially the experiences of later female mystics, both continental and English.

Julian of Norwich, for instance, England's most famous anchoress, describes her mystical visions as "bodily sights" not only because they focus on the physical, visible manifestations of Christ's suffering (his face alternately suffused with blood or desiccated beyond recognition) but also because her visions literally emanate from her body, from the physical suffering she experiences during an illness she requests from God that brings her to the threshold of death. Margery Kempe, Julian's slightly younger, more secular contemporary, manifests her ecstatic experiences of Christ in a similarly visceral fashion. Through her effusive devotional tears and irrepressible holy laughter, she challenges her culture's dissociation of flesh and spirit. As we saw in chapter 8, Geoffrey Chaucer, their most famous literary contemporary, similarly unveils this polarization of female voice and flesh through his poetic troping of rape. Yet he finally cannot escape the uncomfortable position of ventriloquist writing woman from the voyeur's perspective—outside rather than within her body. Julian and Margery reclaim the perspective from within that eludes Chaucer; they ground their mystical writings in their experiences of the female body.

Because mystics attempt to articulate real and direct encounters with the divine that often are beyond words, their mystical narratives are what Petroff calls an "oxymoronic proposition" (*Body*, 5). To communicate their experiences of God as directly as possible, later mystics, both male and female, use language rich in symbolism of the body and its functions. The images of the body predominant in monastic bridal mysticism—a celebration of virginity and especially virgin motherhood—are handled very differently in the thirteenth century by women who aspire to the religious life but find existing monastic structures unable to accommodate their increasing numbers and, as a result, develop less cloistered forms of the religious life.[5] In particular, a group of female religious known as the beguines imagine a more materially erotic courtly mysticism. They offer in their writings perspectives on the body that are distinctively female (Newman, 137–81) and that allow both contemporary and subsequent generations of female mystics to rework monasticism's allegorization of motherhood in more material terms. From the thirteenth century on, female religious increasingly use metaphors grounded in physiological processes. Their images of a more material maternity, in particular, enable them to describe their devotion as an experience generated from within the body.

Medieval culture delimits the value of the female body in ways that make it virtually impossible for flesh-and-blood women to combine motherhood and sainthood. As a result, in the spiritual narratives of female religious we find with alarming frequency portraits of maternal martyrdom that emphasize a "tragically alienated experience of motherhood" (Newman, 247). These depictions are characterized by pressure for women to abandon, even sacrifice, their children in order to participate fully in the religious paths they chose. Responding to this more pessimistic manifestation of the material maternal, Julian of Norwich and Margery Kempe, fourteenth-century England's two most famous female mystics, resist their culture's assumption that motherhood and religious devotion are incongruous. Both create mystical narratives that find positive valences in motherhood but that draw on the maternal for very different purposes and to very different ends.

Julian grounds her discussion of Christ-as-mother in the physiology of maternity; she reshapes and deepens this trope, initially favored by twelfth-century monastics, through the more somatic perspectives offered by thirteenth-century feminine spirituality. Margery, building on her very real experiences of motherhood, reimagines the model of maternal martyrdom popular during the later Middle Ages as a means for fictive self-generation. Whereas Julian tropes conception as the quintessence of the doubling of self through which ecstatic union with God can most intimately, most privately, be achieved, Margery—the mother of 14 children—transforms her literal reproductive expertise into a paradigm for engendering a spectrum of biblical personae to reveal a multivalent, very public spiritual self.

Male and Female Mysticism: The Body's Different Voices

Both male and female mystics understand the physical world as an integral starting point for the *via mystica*; both are concerned with how perception in the material world shapes mystical vision. Richard of Saint Victor, for instance, imagined four gradations of vision—two physical and two spiritual—that establish a continuum between material and spiritual realms.[6] Female mystics are similarly interested in the experiential quality of vision but reveal through their writings a demonstrably more somatic kind of mysticism: one that understands the body "not so much as hindrance to the soul's ascent as the opportunity for it."[7]

Although Francis of Assisi may have been the first on record to experience the stigmata (and even this is uncertain, Caroline Bynum tells us), the most bizarre bodily occurrences—stigmata like Francis's, incorruptibility of the cadaver in death, mystical lactations and pregnancies, miraculous anorexia, eating or drinking of pus, and visions of bleeding Eucharistic hosts—are associated with women and appear with increasing frequency in their writings from the late twelfth century on (Bynum, *FR*, 186–94). The *vitae* of thirteenth- and fourteenth-century women report "trances, levitations, catatonic seizures or other forms of bodily rigidity, miraculous elongation or enlargement of parts of the body, swellings of sweet mucus in the throat ... and ecstatic nosebleeds," all phenomena seldom reported of male saints (Bynum, *FR*, 186). As Bynum observes, although male writers "use extremely physical and physiological language to speak of encounter with God," they do not make their own bodies the site of their mystical experiences as female mystics do. The male voice, she argues, is more impersonal, often lacking in the immediacy found in women's spiritual narratives. "However fulsome or startling their imagery," Bynum emphasizes, "men write of '*the* mystical experience,' giving a general description that may be used as a theory or yardstick, whereas women write of '*my* mystical experience,' speaking directly of something that may have occurred to them alone" (*FR*, 190), often describing it in terms of their most visceral bodily experiences.

For male mystics writing in the tradition of "Brautmystik," or bridal mysticism, the ascent to God requires a transcendence of the flesh often represented metaphorically. Bonaventure, following the Franciscan model of literal and spiritual itinerancy, describes a journey into the mind of God;[8] the Cistercian neoplatonist William of Saint Thierry, a ladder of ascent to heaven (Szarmach, 6). Male mystics imagine themselves putting off a body that, because of its quintessentially female carnality, is an obstacle to the soul's ascent. William even describes the ascent in explicitly gendered terms as a process of spiritual growth in which *anima*, the feminine soul, is transformed into *animus*, the masculine mind or spirit. In a letter to the Carthusian monks of Mont-Dieu he explains, " 'When [the soul] begins to be not only capable but also in possession of perfect reason, it immediately renounces the feminine gender ... For as long as it is *anima* it is quick to slip effeminately into the carnal; but the *animus* or spirit thinks only on what is virile and spiritual.' "[9] His designation of the female as carnal and the male as spiritual polarizes the flesh and spirit, makes the body the soul's prison, and genders the union with God as exclusively masculine.

In representing their mystical experiences, female religious found themselves contending with the dualism inherent in Christian culture's essentialist views of femininity. As Elizabeth Robertson explains, "the Middle Ages inherited two opposing views of a woman's spiritual nature, the Platonic notion of the soul's gender neutrality, and the Aristotelian view of the soul as differentiated by gender."[10] Although these two views vied with each other during the high and late Middle Ages, theological commentary on women is pervasively Aristotelian and results in a view of woman as inferior both in body and in soul. Men were seen as only spiritually implicated in the carnality of their bodies. Their souls, although threatened by appetitive desires, were understood to be separate from the body. Women, on the other hand, were thoroughly and quite literally identified with the carnal; both in life and after death, they were perceived as unable to transcend the flesh. Robertson suggests that "women were viewed—and perhaps indeed viewed themselves—as trapped inescapably in a body designated and disparaged as female" (149). It is, then, hardly surprising that sexuality and notions of the female body become central concerns for women pursuing the *via mystica*. Both male and female religious seem to have accepted as a given that women could not simply put off their bodies in their pursuit of the *via mystica*. However, they diverge markedly in their assessment of the spiritual value of the female body as somatic voice. As Barbara Newman demonstrates in her comparison of early bridal and later courtly mysticism, the function of the body in female religious experience could be constructed in dramatically different ways, depending on the gender of the one imagining that experience.

Defining the Female Body's Limits: Virginity in Monastic "Brautmystik"

The allegorized eroticism of bridal mysticism devised by the predominantly male authors of twelfth-century monastic "literature of formation"[11] provided a spiritual paradigm that assigned positive value to the female body only in its most physically static state: virginity. Monasticism addresses the female body's inescapable carnality by recommending in its formation texts that women prevent their biological essence from interfering with their devotional practice by preserving the body in its purest form. These works in praise of virginity, addressed to both men and women and used interchangeably by religious of both sexes, underscore the monastic ideal, grounded in the Pauline principle of "Oneness in Christ," that both female and male religious transcend gender.[12] However, as Newman cautions, formation literature was largely written by male authors who, although "voicing their views of a life they regarded in principle as gender-free," do not divest themselves "of androcentric perceptions and stereotypes" (22).

Newman aptly describes the dissimilar value placed on male and female virginity by these writers. Virginity was seen not simply as an equivalent ideal for both sexes, but as the "great equalizer" that enabled a woman to aspire to the spiritual in spite of her sex. For male religious, lost chastity—even lost virginity—was not an irreparable impediment to "present grace and future glory." Consecrated women, on the other hand, were deemed sacrosanct: "recruited as virgins, defined as virgins, guarded as virgins, and ideally canonized as virgins" (Newman, 31–32). Their virginity was understood not as an achievement, but as a part of their essence to be preserved: a condition of being as opposed to doing.

As a result, the portrait of the religious woman offered by patristic authors is incongruous at best: Even as they characterize her virginity as an attribute of her body, passively achieved by virtue of being female, they hold that the female virgin, because a member of "the weaker sex," has more to overcome in her pursuit of the divine, and can aspire, as a result, to greater holiness. Augustine suggests that Felicity and Perpetua, two of early Christianity's most famous female martyrs, at their deaths endured not so much the fear of dying but the sorrow of leaving behind their infant children. Their martyrdom, he continues, is all the more glorious, their souls "assuredly more virile," because they chose martyrdom in spite of their motherhood (Bloch, *Medieval Misogyny*, 67). Paradoxically, woman's body—both in its capacity for virginity and maternity—proves simultaneously a greater obstacle to and surer guarantor of grace than man's: Its constitutive virginity makes the body simultaneously more vulnerable to and potentially freer from the threat of its carnality; the literal and emotional weight of the offspring it might bear is a more daunting hurdle to transcend.

This incongruity extends in more practical terms to the metaphors used to describe the roles of cloistered religious women. Unlike their male contemporaries who are never, as Newman shrewdly observes, allegorically described as husbands, nuns were encouraged to imagine themselves as inhabiting those gender-specific roles based on the secular sexuality they were renouncing, as well as the social world they were leaving behind (31). As the female protagonists of the narratives of bridal mysticism, they play not only the role of desirable virgin bride to Christ but also obedient wife and fruitful spiritual mother of virtues. Tellingly, the only role not available to them in this paradigm (given the eternal nature of Christ as divine spouse) is the one that afforded secular medieval women the greatest degree of private and public autonomy—that of prosperous, self-subsistent widow. In fact, those women who took advantage of their widowhood, leaving their children in order to serve God more single-mindedly, found themselves encouraged to think of their new religious life as an opportunity to escape the distractions and demands of earthly family in order to display a "truer" maternal compassion for the infant Christ (Newman, 93).

As virgin bride of Christ, the female protagonist in the narratives of bridal mysticism could occupy a range of allegorical personae, but each required some kind of displacement of earthly emotion, whether erotic longing or maternal desire. It is, however, in the role of double for the Virgin Mary that we can identify the source of discontent among female religious with bridal mysticism's emphasis on metaphoric feminine rather than embodied female spirituality. The Virgin Mary—anomalous in her ready consent to divine supplantation, her perpetual virginity, and her painless maternity—provides bridal mysticism with a body that, although it confounds the threat of physiological pollution assigned to woman's body in misogynic exegesis, elides as well both the violence of rape and the physical experience of childbirth encountered by flesh-and-blood women.

Bridal mysticism's stringent endorsement of virginity as the defining characteristic of female religious veils a gender double standard about the threat of sexual transgression. As twelfth-century theologian Idung of Prüfening makes clear, male religious were assumed by nature to be immune to loss of virginity by violence (Newman, 28). Women, on the other hand, not only were vulnerable to loss of virginity through violence but also were blamed for instigating instances of sexual intercourse regardless of whether they were victims of rape or consenting parties (Newman, 23–28 and 61–63). *Raptus*, or ravishment, one of the words used both in bridal and beguine mysticism to describe ecstatic encounters with God, offers a fine example of this double standard. It is a term as complex in its devotional contexts as in its legal usage during the high and late Middle Ages. Kathryn Gravdal observes that in devotional literature from as early as the end of the twelfth century, "ravishing" could refer not only to rape but also to spiritual exaltation and sexual pleasure.[13] Gravdal characterizes the obvious "slippage or *glissement* from violent abduction to sexual pleasure" as one that announces the desire of the rapist rather than demonstrates empathy for the victim of the rape, and that assumes "that whatever is attractive begs to be ravished: carried off, seized, or raped" (5). It is a connotative transformation that dramatically revises "rape," sanitizes its inherent violence so thoroughly that Gérard of Liège, in praising God in his *Quinque incitamenta amoris*, "actually trie[s] to imagine God as the best rapist."[14]

In fact, the Virgin Mary as model for spiritual *imitatio* in bridal mysticism is so thoroughly asexual—eroticized, but only allegorically—that cloistered males in the twelfth century cross-sexually identify with her not only in envisioning themselves as virgin brides of Christ, willingly awaiting divine rapture (Newman, 31), but also by idealizing and ultimately appropriating her mothering role. Cistercian abbots, in some cases with the specific duty of overseeing novices in the monastery, used maternal imagery to counterbalance their identities as "authority figures qua rulers or fathers," relying on the feminine to imbue their composite portraits with "nurturing, affectivity, and accessibility" (Bynum, *JM*, 154–56). These male authors construct their feminine selves through pervasive use of breast and nurturing metaphors. However, in their appropriation of the maternal, they avoid the kinds of images biologically specific to women: womb images marked by radical physical pain, especially those of conceiving and giving birth (*JM*, 150). In bridal mysticism, the key marker of the Virgin Mary's experience—the concept of pleasurable *raptus* with its elision of the violence of rape and the construction of painless birth—both displaces the biologically female and also intellectualizes and sanitizes the physical and emotional experiences of women.

Resisting the Body's Bounds:
Abjection in "Mystique Courtoise"

The monastic model, although apt as a *feminine* spirituality that cloistered religious of both genders might entertain, could not address the more diverse needs of the expanding population of *female* religious in the thirteenth century who increasingly remained in the world, either as tertiaries affiliated with mendicant orders, as beguines, or as "irregulars." Usually taking a vow of celibacy, they were women hungry for an organized religious life but unable to leave the secular world because of family obligations. Many became social reformers who focused on practical works of mercy, caring for the poor, the ill, the despairing; tending to the bodily and spiritual needs of children, pregnant women, the sick and aging. Petroff emphasizes that female mystics worked as "active agents in the transformation of their society" (*MWVL*, 21). She describes Bridget of Sweden's and Catherine of Siena's roles in returning the papacy to Rome as an example of influence that led to ecclesiastical reform. However, female mystics gained their reputations as social reformers most profoundly not through their impact on their society's powerful ruling structures but by caring for its outcasts, its marginal figures.

From the thirteenth century on, the ministerings of various kinds of female religious reveal increasingly their graphic identification with the sufferings of the poor and the sick. Bynum describes how these women came to express their identification with Christ's suffering by feeding and caring for the bodies of the sick as if they were Christ's own: "Like Catherine of Siena, who drank pus, and Catherine of Genoa, who ate lice, Angela of Foligno drank water that came from washing the sores of lepers. One of the scabs stuck in her throat, she said, and tasted 'as sweet as communion'" (*HF,* 144–45). Beguine mysticism in particular responded to monasticism's negative stereotypes of the female body with a genuinely new, female devotion: one that embraced the body in both its delight and pain and that valued the body bivalently as torment and as beloved companion that would rise at the end of time. As Christina Mirabilis promised, the body, "purified of all corruptibility ... [would be] joined in eternal happiness with the soul [it] had as companion in present sadness" (*FR,* 236–37).

Rather than celebrating the pseudomasculinity that bridal mysticism's ideal of virginity offers, or embracing exclusively its allegorical eroticism, the beguines inspire a wave of female religious in the thirteenth century to reengage the flesh in their mysticism, to restore the power of the visceral to spirituality. Newman describes courtly mysticism as "a hybrid of court and cloister": a blending of the spiritual exaltation of bridal mysticism with its joyous confidence in an ultimate, transcendent union with God, and the melancholic turbulence of erotic experience characteristic of the courtly self who plays out the cyclical pattern of desire and fulfillment with a more pronounced emotional range, alternating "moments of adoration and abject submission" with "moods of rebellion and rage." (143).

Whereas the bridal mystic achieves union with God by putting off the body, the courtly mystic understands that union as a fusion of mystic lover and Beloved that requires her "to negate not so much the body as the separate, individual ego" (Newman, 159). Through courtly mysticism, the beguines redefine union with God as involving not transcendence of the self but self-effacement—self-annihilation that allows for immersion in the Godhead. They imagine the ecstatic union with Christ as one achieved through a meditation on his glorified human nature, a meditation that yokes together violent physical forces and the charged eroticism of courtly love. At the core of their mysticism is a kind of self-determining sexuality through which martyrdom can be pursued; a self-directed abjection, "a kind of death wish, a desire for 'unbecoming' that will dissolve the mundane self, its world, and its limits."[15] As the graphic examples of somatic piety mentioned at the beginning of this chapter make clear, beguine mysticism's material spirituality, simply stated, means accepting the body so completely that its significance as a marker of difference from spirituality ceases to exist. The beguines and the female religious they influenced from the thirteenth century on regularly insist that the reviled body, situated by virginity literature in bipolar opposition to the spirit, is itself the ground for the enterprises of the spirit.

Abjection and the Maternal

With its emphasis on erotic union and a more enfleshed spirituality, beguine mysticism introduces among female mystics the possibility of seeing motherhood, too, in more fleshly ways. Celebration of carnal motherhood responds at several levels to "Brautmystik's" allegorical portrait of the virgin as "mother of virtues." Monastics, of course, underscore the importance they assign to Mary's intact virginity and motivate virgin nuns to preserve their most precious spiritual commodity by describing pregnant women in grotesque physical detail. Osbert of Clare concentrates in his portrait of earthly pregnancy on what he describes as the sallow, hollow face of the expectant mother; he then foregrounds the woman's swollen, distended belly with a description of its "vitals torn apart within by the burden of pregnancy." Peter of Blois emphasizes his disgust with what he imagines as the emotional disarray and moral turpitude of the pregnant body by admonishing that "daughters of this world ... conceive in sin, bear in sorrow, suckle in fear; they are constantly anxious about the living and inconsolably grieved for the dying." He states baldly the spiritual consequences for physical procreation: "If you wish to bear, you wish to perish" (quoted in Newman, 32).

Thirteenth-century female mystics draw on precisely these features of physical, emotional, and moral disorder to describe the spiritual power of the maternal: a power not unlike erotic abjection in its ability to "dissolve the mundane self, its world, and its limits." Because female mystics acknowledge rather than suppress the spiritual potential of the physical and emotional pains of maternity, they reconceive the maternal through a whole new range of metaphors that allows them to explore the reciprocity between mother and son. What becomes important for female mystics in their assessment of Mary is not her inviolability, but rather the flesh she gives to Christ and the kinds of emotional bonds that flesh carries with it.

From the thirteenth century on, female devotional narratives focus increasingly on the mother-child dynamics intrinsic to Christ's myriad personae: as sacrificial child, as suckling infant, as birthing mother (Bynum, *JM*, 151–52). In their most alienating form, narratives from this period hold up for *imitatio* Mary's acquiescence to the sacrifice of her son. In imitation of God's mother, women with domestic ties who aspire to be among the female religious and follow this conceptual vein construct themselves as unnatural mothers, as maternal martyrs who abandon—sometimes even come perilously close to literally sacrificing—their own children so that they can pursue a religious vocation (Newman, 76–107, passim). These maternal martyrs prepare to approach the Godhead, lose themselves to God spiritually, by literally losing the living flesh that was at one time part of them.

In the writings of Julian of Norwich and Margery Kempe, however, we find the inverse of this dynamic explored: not separation but the reciprocal desire between mother and child characteristic of primary narcissism. Mutually absorbed in each other's joys as well as in each other's sorrows, mother and child evoke in their relationship the charged reciprocity between mystic lover and Divine Beloved characteristic of courtly mysticism. It is a paradigm that celebrates the cocreative forces of Mary and Christ. By understanding Christ not only as Beloved (the specular, mirroring relationship modeled on *fin'amor*), but interchangeably as beloved child and loving mother, Julian and Margery can describe their mystical encounters with God as infinitely self-generating. They attempt the female mystic's central goal—the dissolution of the self, its world, its limits—not through abject "unbecoming" but through infinite self-engendering.

Private and Public Bodies:
Julian of Norwich and Margery Kempe

In terms of religious vocation and style of devotion, Julian of Norwich (1343–1413) and Margery Kempe (1373–1439) are as different as imaginable: one living in devout isolation, the other fully engaged with the social world; one versed in the classic texts of the Church's contemplative tradition, the other in texts of popular devotion. Their mystical narratives reflect these differences as well. Julian's is a private puzzling out of her uncanny visions of Christ; an intimate dialogue with the enfleshed Divine in whom, ultimately, she finds her physical and spiritual double. Margery's narrative, a spiritual autobiography, focuses on the ecclesiastical disapproval and communal slander she suffers when she reveals her mystical experiences; by design she makes public her personal relationship with Christ. Yet both, finally, draw on their experiences of the female body, especially the maternal body, to construct their different experiences of God.

Although Julian and Margery are both familiar with a spectrum of contemporary mystics, Julian clearly has had the more traditional education and pursues the path of devotion more conventional for women. In Showings,[16] she reveals a profound knowledge of the Latin Vulgate text of the Bible and is also thoroughly familiar with the spiritual writings that form the backbone of the monastic contemplative tradition.[17] Her position within the religious establishment is similarly more orthodox than Margery's. The form of religious devotion Julian chooses is one condoned by prevailing ecclesiastic institutions; shortly after her first vision in 1373, she enters into the solitary life of an anchoress, a female recluse, enclosed within an anchorhold. Although Sarah Beckwith has characterized life in the medieval anchorhold as a form of devotion symbolic of burial, of death to the outside world,[18] Julian challenges its restrictive limits in both her literal and metaphorical uses of its space. Even while living in her anchoritic cell, Julian remained in contact with society beyond its walls through visits with those who sought her out as a spiritual teacher and counselor as Margery Kempe herself did during an extended visit sometime before the summer of 1413.[19]

During this visit, Julian corroborates, even sanctions, Margery's effusive weeping, one of her most material and essentially female manifestations of devotion.[20] As we will see, both the sensual quality of the imagery and the structural dynamism evident in Julian's double narrative of her Showings underscore that she understands her enclosure within the anchorhold not as suffocating entombment but as regenerative enwombment; as a place from which to endorse a distinctively female spirituality. As Robertson has suggested, Julian, although hardly a revolutionary, is a "subtle strategist" who in spite of the circumscribed devotional life of the anchoress seeks to undo her culture's assumption that women, understood to be essentially carnal, are spiritually inferior. She provides, "in an

Irigarayan sense, a new celebration of femininity through contemplation of Christ's 'feminine' attributes."[21]

Indeed, Julian's visions in the *Showings* reveal the unusually visceral quality of her spiritual imagination. They reflect her sense of the mystical journey as rooted in a body distinctively female. Julian's revelations spring directly from her desire for a "bodily sight" in which she can literally suffer with Christ. She tells us that her graphic initial vision of the crucified Christ—"the red blood trickling down from under the crown, all hot, flowing freely and copiously, a living stream" (*ST*, 3, 129)—is born out of her own "bodily sickness," her near-death experience at the age of 30. And she describes an actual physiological ebb and flow between Christ's suffering body and her own: a symbiotic exchange of pain and joy that becomes paradigmatic for subsequent visions (*ST*, 2–3, 128–29).

Julian's *Showings* form an intrinsically processual rather than static narrative. Soon after her initial vision, she writes her Short Text, with its detailed and sensually vivid descriptions of that first vision and 15 ensuing revelations. Twenty years later, in 1393, Julian revises this narrative in her Long Text, including subsequent visions as well as revised explications of revelations that she only gradually came to understand in full. As Nancy Coiner has suggested, the dialectical relationship between Short and Long Texts mimics the growth and development of pregnancy. Interjections varying in length from the frequent brief addition of a new phrase to the extended interpretive digression of the 20-chapter parable of the Lord and the Servant give us "the sense that something new is growing inside the initial text: the Short Text is torn apart as if in labor."[22] Coiner observes that Julian's text moves from a striking opening "concern with death and pain to a concern for transformation, rebirth, renewed life—from images of the Passion to images of the maternal body" (323). The maternal body, in fact, provides the perfect metaphor for the synchronous pain and joy that characterizes Julian's mystical experience of the Divine.

Hints at the maternal and its related physiological conditions suffuse Julian's opening vision of bodily pain. Robertson emphasizes Julian's "extraordinary and idiosyncratically female uses of blood imagery." She argues that the expanded description of Christ's crucifixion in the Long Text—with its more graphic characterization of the drops of blood that issue from under Christ's crown of thorns as "brownish red ... very thick ... [which] as they spread, turn bright red" (*LT*, 7, 187)—is "even more evocative of menstrual blood" than the Short Text's depiction of the scene (154–55). Citing a description found in a fifteenth-century English gynecological handbook (Sloane MS. 2463) of the menstrual process as bleeding that purges, cleanses, and restores health, Robertson suggests that Julian sees Christ's sustained bleeding as "matching her own natural purgation of excess."[23]

The physiological analogies Robertson sees, I would add, extend to the symptoms with which Julian characterizes her near-fatal illness at the outset of the text. In particular, Julian's descriptions in both the Short and Long Texts of a loss of sensation in the lower half of her body—the feeling that her body "was dead from the middle downwards" (ST, 2, 128; LT, 3, 179)—echo those used in the Sloane gynecological handbook to describe women afflicted with interrupted menstrual cycles.[24] The anonymous author of this handbook characterizes the resulting retention of blood as the result of a fault in the "mother" [M.E. moder], the contemporary medical term for the uterine "skin in which the child is enclosed in his mother's womb" (Rowland, 61). The remedies that the treatise describes all aim at repairing the faulty "mother" by restoring the natural flow of blood so that the woman's uterus will be ready again for a healthy conception.

Intriguing in this context is Julian's emphasis on conception rather than birth in the maternal images that form the focus of her discussion of the "spiritual sight" of Christ's "familiar love" that accompanies her initial "bodily sight" of Christ's Passion (ST, 4, 130). Coiner draws attention to Julian's unusual depiction of Mary "at the time of the Annunciation" to explain Julian's description of Christ's "'homely' love" as an infant's enfolding or swaddling cloth (316). It is this vision of Mary at the moment of her conception of Christ rather than at the culmination of her pregnancy that characterizes the uncanny doubleness of the Divine for Julian. He is not only the divine love that promises to enfold maternally, but also, by taking fleshly shape in the Virgin's womb, the child that will be enfolded in human love (ST, 4;131). In Christ's dual role as mother and child, the boundaries between divinity and humanity collapse.

In her mystical union with Christ, Julian in effect reproduces this double self. Whereas monastic contemplative tradition, as we have seen, encourages putting off the female carnal, for Julian the female body is the ground for a more profound spirituality. By imagining Christ in roles that articulate or interact with the female body, she can fashion herself in the course of her narrative in His image and likeness without denying her female self: first as mother, then as child. Julian's evocative opening portrait of her conception of Christ vibrates with a succession of harmonic doubles: the fruit of receiving Christ not merely as beloved but as beloved child. She is a receptive womb quickened twofold: both *by* and *with* her vision of him. The vision inaugurates for Julian a reverse chronology through which she can turn death away not by engaging it as Christ does but by returning to the womb. In a striking inversion of her relation to Christ, even as he proceeds from the womb of her imagination, fully enfleshed as a "bodily sight," Julian finds herself resorbed into his body. As Coiner points out, the halfway point of Julian's revelations is marked by the resurrected Christ's smiling invitation to Julian to enter into the wound in his side. The Short Text in which Christ gazes "very merrily and gladly" into his side makes plain that joy is commensurate with the place of the wound.[25] This stepping into Christ's side provides Julian with an understanding of plenitude from within.

With this shift in perspective, Julian alerts her reader to her most expansive elaboration of the Short Text, a discussion of Christ's motherhood that culminates in her comparison of Christ's Passion to the travail of a mother's labor, his Eucharistic nurturing to "the suck of ... milk" a mother provides her child (*LT*, 60, 298). It is a spiritual paradigm deeply rooted in the physiology of conception. At the most fundamental level, Julian evokes her culture's Galenic understanding of blood and milk as homologous: specifically, the process of dealbation in which menstrual blood is transformed into milk during pregnancy so that a mother may eventually nurse her newborn.[26] As the Sloane treatise explains, women during pregnancy "do not have this [menstrual] purgation, because the child in the womb is nourished with the blood instead" (Rowland, 59–61). With this reminder that the enwombed child feeds on Christ's blood both before and after birth, Julian playfully offers the possibility of understanding Christ not only conventionally as nursing mother but more atypically as pregnant mother, nurturing the human soul in all the "sensuality" that he derives from Mary.

For Julian, Christ is "our Mother of mercy in taking our sensuality" (*LT*, 28, 294). As Robertson observes, "the feminized body of Christ, rather than leading the contemplative to a transcendence of the sensual, redeems the sensual by uniting the contemplative's 'substance' with Christ" (156). Christ recovers human loss, provides the bond between humanity and divinity through the very carnality with which, ironically, patristic tradition denigrated women. Julian's suggestive portrait of a pregnant Christ is the ultimate in female enclosure and intimacy. It effaces all boundaries of identity by making possible the joyful immersion of the self within the

Divine: first enwombed and nurtured by Christ as the child within; then experiencing the intimate reciprocity of Christ as nursing mother.

In dramatic contrast with Julian's role as reclusive, ecclesiastically sanctioned spiritual teacher, Margery Kempe makes clear the commercial quality of her spiritual self-production. In her autobiography, Margery emphasizes her investment in the role of public apostle through her many descriptions of public encounters with audiences, lay and religious, both combative and sympathetic. It is often through these encounters that she satisfies or displays her voracious appetite for scripture and contemporary mystical texts.[27] In fact, Margery self-consciously structures her spiritual narrative episodically around conversations: between herself and Christ (and his immediate family), her husband, her neighbors, local merchants, both local and prominent ecclesiastics, and fellow pilgrims. Whereas dialogue for Julian involves an intimate, both ruminative and visceral devotional exchange between herself and Christ, for Margery it is a marketable commodity to be passed between conversants and valued as it is multiplied. She understands her verbal exchanges as assets through which she can develop her spiritual identity and circulate her own devotional experiences.

Margery is clearly acquainted with the power and wealth that her society associates with the process of self-production. Daughter of John Brunham, five-time mayor of the prosperous medieval port of Lynn and a powerful burgess with considerable social responsibility, when Margery leaves her father's household to marry John Kempe in 1393, she joins a family that, although not as prominent as the Brunham family, nevertheless appears in the Lynn records as well (Windeatt, 10). She describes herself as a woman who, before "enter[ing] the way of everlasting life," vied with her neighbors for prestige "out of pure covetousness, and in order to maintain her pride" (I:2; 44–45). Prolific although discontent as a mother (married at the age of 20, she had 14 children within the next 20 years through a series of difficult pregnancies and births), she turns her energies from the domestic to the public marketplace, developing her skills first as a brewer, then as a miller so that she can pursue "the desire for economic success and security, for political power and social recognition" characteristic of Lynn's elite.[28] Even as it pervades her social environment, this "cash nexus" pervades Margery's consciousness.[29] After both businesses fail, she begins to reconceive her maternal role in economic terms as capital that she can invest in developing her spiritual identity.

If Julian is interested in how physiological images of the maternal can evoke the private spiritual self's distinctively female qualities, Margery is quite publicly engaged with reconstituting her literal experience of motherhood to adapt the life of religious devotion to the circumstances of her material world. Although Julian opens her *Showings* with a description of Christ's Passion that aligns literal conception with mystical conception of the divine, Margery begins the narrative of her spiritual journey with a description of her own difficult first pregnancy: how, "despair[ing] of her life" because of the "labour-pains she had in childbirth and the sickness that had gone before," she sends for her confessor to relate the details of her spiritual struggles (I:1, 41–43). Her postpartum depression gives rise to an opportunity for spiritual self-narration.

This episode inaugurates a narrative replete with analogous instances of self-disclosure or revelation that Margery intimately connects with her experiences of the maternal. Newman describes Margery's two most explicit mentions of her 14 children as markers of her spiritual progress, but she suggests that Margery otherwise represses the presence of her children, who serve as "the all too obvious reminders of her lost maidenhood" (91). To the contrary, I would argue that Margery quite deliberately and frequently threads her narrative with subtle although specific allusions to her pregnancies. In addition to these, she includes more general descriptions of both her personal and her public encounters with the maternal. Margery uses such episodes to structure her spiritual self-narration as a series of confrontations between carnal and spiritual motherhood.

Among the episodes of the maternal that Margery includes, her encounter with Julian looms large. Margery pointedly tells us that she undertakes the trip to Norwich because Christ has urged her to "bear no more children, and therefore commanded her to go." She agrees, even though she is just "newly delivered of a child ... [and] feeling faint and weak," and visits Julian during the physiologically liminal period when her own body must make the dramatic adjustments from internal to external nurture, from pregnancy to postpartum care for a new child (I:17, 73–74). Not surprisingly, Julian's words of comfort, as Margery records them, resonate with the conception and birth idioms of Julian's *Showings* discussed earlier. In language that strikingly echoes descriptions of the Annunciation, Julian assures Margery that "God wrought great grace in her" and encourages her "to bear" the slander of her enemies (I:18, 78–79). Here, as in other instances, the twofold message is clear. Even as Margery depicts Christ as insisting on leaving behind carnal motherhood, she finds in Julian an encouraging figure who creates a bridge between her present physical condition as newly delivered mother and her desired spiritual condition. Margery concludes the first book of her narrative with a marker of spiritual progress that reiterates the familiar theme of reconciling carnal maternity with spiritual motherhood. She discovers her most miraculous success as spiritual comforter to a woman living through an episode of postpartum psychosis like the one that initiates her own spiritual journey (I:75, 217–18).

Margery's behavior on pilgrimages suggests a similar focus on resolving the conflicts between earthly and spiritual motherhood. While sojourning in Rome, in a very domestic form of *imitatio Mariae*, she weeps prolifically at the sight of women carrying little boys who remind her of "Christ in his childhood" (I:35, 123). In fact, the birth and perhaps even death of her last child during this 1413 pilgrimage to Jerusalem is the event that initiates for Margery "the most intense phase of her mystical life as well as her notorious screaming fits."[30] Even beyond her reproductive years she makes plain her curiosity about instances in which physiological and spiritual motherhood are miraculously reconciled. On her last pilgrimage during her final continental stop at Aachen, of the four holy relics on exhibition the one that is of primary interest to her—the only one she mentions by name—is the birthing smock of the Blessed Virgin.[31]

All of this is to suggest that although Margery may invoke the rhetoric of child sacrifice, it is not necessarily in identification with the more self-alienating forms of continental mysticism's maternal martyrdom. Margery does not retreat from her role as earthly mother, rather she repeatedly engages metaphors of the maternal as well as concrete reminders of her own motherhood to mark her spiritual development and to underscore the difficulties of achieving spiritual growth while living in the world as a married woman. Margery's mysticism is, as Beckwith argues, "very often the site of self-making, rather than self-dissolution."[32] And although this self-making requires what David Aers has called "a rupture with the earthly family, an energetic struggle against the nuclear family, its bonds, its defences in the lay community, and its legitimating ideologies" (99), for Margery that rupture results paradoxically in the multiplication rather than the fragmentation of self. Through strategies of revoicing that range from self-abasement before authority to its parodic decrowning, Margery translates the miseries of reproduction into the powers of fictive self-engendering (Beckwith, "Problems with Authority," 189–99). Her literal experience of the maternal, with its prolific self-production, engenders in Margery the idea of voicing the self through a polyvalent "I."

Most telling is Margery's depiction of herself as a member of the extended holy family who finds herself playing out a spectrum of familial roles. Early in her narrative, when Margery momentarily doubts the holiness of her weeping, Christ clarifies for her the community of selves she creates through the faith that her weeping expresses:

> Although it may be that you do not always weep when you please, my grace is nevertheless in you. Therefore I prove that you are a *daughter* indeed to me, and a *mother* also, a *sister*, a *wife* and a *spouse* ... When you strive to please me, then you are a true *daughter*; when you weep and mourn for my pain and my Passion, then you are a true *mother* having compassion on her child; when you weep for other people's sins and adversities, then you are a true *sister*; and when you sorrow because you are kept so long from the bliss of heaven, then you are a true *spouse and wife*.... (I:15, 66–67; my emphases)

Regardless of the rejection she may experience when she fails to conform to her community's expectations about how to fulfill the various functions of womanhood appropriately, she can reproduce the dynamics of those traditional roles polyvalently through her spiritual relationship with Christ.

Margery's sense of herself as polyvalent "I" extends from her immediate domestic circle to the realm of biblical history. She presents her various visions of Christ's Passion with a kind of voyeuristic intensity that transforms contemplation into enactment and even results in a comic reengendering of biblical narrative. She supersedes her initial quite traditional figuration of herself as devout soul who mirrors Christ's agony (I:78, 226) with a more emphatic affiliation of herself with the quintessential mother. In her weeping at the foot of Christ's cross, Margery is the Virgin's "roaring" double (I:80, 234); in her role as comforter to the Virgin after Christ's death, her sole female companion while Christ harrows hell (I:81, 237), Margery even exceeds Mary (I:79, 228–29). In fact, to reestablish Mary's exclusive mourning rights as Christ's mother—a privilege that biblical narrative elides—and as a witty way of securing that privilege for herself, Margery renarrates Christ's resurrection. She includes an extrabiblical scene in which Christ after his harrowing appears to the Virgin and to her while they are praying together in a chapel *before* he meets Mary Magdalene at his tomb. It is a witty restoration of the Virgin's primary significance in this narrative: a redemptive reinclusion of her motherhood. Margery also subtly underscores her supercession of the Magdalene in this instance by describing her opportunity to watch Mary, in the ultimate expression of motherly love, "feeling and searching all over our Lord's body, and his hands and his feet, to see if there were any soreness or any pain" (I:81, 237).

After establishing this intimate connection between herself and Mary in her version of the Passion, Margery goes to great length to present herself in the final chapters of her book as the consummate mother: simultaneously an earthly mother valued by her own offspring and a spiritual mother sought out for the pious comfort she can provide. In a moment striking because of its retrospective quality, Margery narrates the episode of her earlier troubles with her irreverent son. By depicting him as prodigal son, she subtly revises the biblical narrative to emphasize the power with which she invests motherhood. Her son returns "to pray his mother for her blessing," not to ask his father's forgiveness, and to promise to be "obedient to God and to her" (II:1, 266).

In the closing chapter of her autobiography, Margery rounds out her self-portrait as mother who finally reconciles her carnal and spiritual selves. This final chapter consists largely of a model prayer to inspire readers to reproduce her distinctive spirituality, which she prefaces with a telling anecdote about subsequent generations moved by her devotion. She describes her encounter with a young man who, after watching her "abundant tears of compunction and compassion" during her devotion at the church in Sheen, is moved by the Holy Ghost to address her as "Mother" and to express his desire to understand the cause of her weeping (II:10, 290). Margery emphasizes that the incident takes place around Lammastide, a feast of harvest fruition used by at least one literary contemporary, the *Pearl*-poet, as the setting for a dream vision in which the dreamer's place in heaven is contingent upon reconciliation with the beloved earthly daughter he has lost. By constructing herself as a successful mother both to natural and to spiritual children, Margery projects a similar desire to achieve her ultimate union with Christ through a reconciliation of her carnal and spiritual maternal selves.

For Margery, as for Julian, even the process of producing her text takes on qualities of the maternal. If the 20 years that separate Julian's Long Text from her Short can be seen as an exceptionally long pregnancy, Margery's difficulties in securing an appropriate scribe for her text suggest the complications of a woman dissatisfied with the various midwives who assist at her birthing: a succession of clerics unfit to see her through the "labour" (I:Proem, 36) of transcribing her spiritual experiences.

Julian and Margery are bound together through the fundamental optimism of their mystical discourses—an optimism atypical of many of their contemporaries. Neither rejects the world out of hand. They circumvent the path of negative mysticism that, "by insisting on the unrepresentability of the Other (God) refuses the return to the social sphere."[33] Eschewing the extreme asceticism characteristic of continental mystics, they trope the maternal in more regenerative, even comic, ways. Julian, famous for her assuring refrain that "all manner of thing shall be well," laughs when Christ scorns the devil's malice at his Crucifixion (ST, 8; 138).[34] She finds her revelations of him both "matter for mirth and matter for mourning" (LT, 71; 320). Similarly, although most critics focus on Margery's "excessive weeping and emotional identifications with Christ" (Lochrie, 135–36), her narrative is replete with laughter as well. Her displacement of the biblical encounter between Christ and Mary Magdalene at Christ's tomb is an irreverent but divinely comic act of restoring what she understands as most significant: Christ's incomparable love for his mother. Through their laughter and their mystical joy, both Julian and Margery offer a dissolution of the self that reengenders the experience of abjection achieved through pain. Their mirthful abjection dissolves the individual as well as the social constraints associated with the female body and provides for a regenerative union with the Divine.

Mary of Burgundy prays from her *Book of Hours*, imagining herself in the presence of the Virgin Mary. The artist has depicted both Mary and her mental image as equally real, thereby illustrating the mutually constructing nature of medieval textual and social worlds. *Book of Hours of Mary of Burgundy.* Flemish, ca. 1470.
Bildarchiv der Oesterreichischen Nationalbibliothek, Vienna. Cod. 1857, fol. 14v.

Epilogue

Beyond the Middle Ages and Outside the Canon

The English Middle Ages are conventionally held to have ended in 1485. In that year the first English printer, William Caxton, published Malory's *Morte D'Arthur*, an early product of the printing press whose invention would change modes of literary production and so help to differentiate what we call Renaissance literature from the texts generated by medieval manuscript culture. Also in that year the future King Henry VII defeated Richard III, thereby ending the Plantagenet dynasty that had ruled England since 1154 and inaugurating the reign of the Tudors, who shaped the political, theological, and social face of Reformation England.

Looking back from the end of the fifteenth century, medieval texts, whether male- or female-authored, written either before or after the pivotal 1066 Norman Conquest of England, represent women in a manner that is simultaneously liberal (both artistically and politically) and conservative. On the one hand, medieval texts may challenge received orthodoxy about the feminine; they feature a variety of surprising strategies for reexamining culturally normative stereotypes of women. The ones explored in this volume only begin to suggest how variegated the tapestry is: the critique of male commerce and heroic diminishment of women in Anglo-Saxon literature; the inverse mirroring of courtly lyric and romance; the parodic repositioning of patristic typologies through the confluence of beguine mysticism and fabliaux in the drama; the rejection of the inherently antifeminist philosophical underpinnings of dream vision in Christine de Pizan; the ironic troping of rape in Chaucer; and the radical abjection essential to female mysticism. These literatures reconceive the virtually universal identification during the Middle Ages of women with the body and men with the mind. They consider the ways in which the carnal can be revalued, and they hold forth the possibility that woman's flesh is not irrevocably her soul's prison.

Most of the texts we have discussed in this volume are, as we emphasize in the introduction, in some way canonical. In spite of their rather orthodox function as touchstones for critics of English literature, they carve out imaginative spaces for "minding the body": for understanding women as endowed with powers of both mind and body and for seeing their bodies as constitutive both materially and spiritually of the social body. They are examples that catch our interest precisely because they call into question rather than reproduce the misogynic assumptions of the cultural mainstream in which they are produced.

Their innovative strategies, however, especially those of the post-Conquest texts, are admittedly extraordinary rather than ordinary—cultural exceptions rather than the rule. And although they offer ways of reimagining the status quo, they do not necessarily change prevailing social dynamics. Nor do they necessarily desire to. For no matter how radically medieval texts reevaluate the traditional identification of maleness with intellect, femaleness with body, they never question that fundamental identification. Nor do they question other essentializing attitudes toward women, attitudes that view them as secondary and subservient to men. In this respect, medieval texts are conservative, if not reactionary, repeating stereotypes that have their roots in classical and biblical works. The Wife of Bath, as we have seen, incarnates misogynist stereotypes of female carnality—the wandering, garrulous, lustful woman—dating back thousands of years to the ancient Near East.

Christine de Pizan offers an excellent example of the simultaneous progressivism and conservatism of medieval texts. In her *Book of the City of Ladies*, Christine describes the barriers to reform posed by the thoroughgoing misogyny she and other women faced. Her agenda is arguably protofeminist. Yet Christine's own politics are arguably conservative. In her "cautionary dossier on Christine," Sheila Delaney, although admiring Christine as a champion of women, asks us to consider the practical implications of some of Christine's ideas. For instance, her stance on the professional status of women encourages hierarchical rather than egalitarian relations between women and men, for she envisions women as virtuous helpmates to their husbands. Similarly, Christine eschews education as a tool for social reform. In spite of the uses she put her own education to, she recommends that women's learning be consonant with the social obligations they need to fulfill and not a pathway for self-advancement.[1] Christine is a contradictory figure who revealingly illustrates the compromises involved in negotiating the difficult terrain between the radical abjection of the female mystics and the constraining misogyny of clerical culture at the end of the Middle Ages. Not unlike many of the late-fourteenth- and early-fifteenth-century literary representations of the feminine we have explored—Cynewulf's Juliana, the Wife of Bath, the cycle drama's Blessed Virgin (and even its Christ)—she walks the line rather than assert a distinct protofeminist agenda. As a figure who blends the radical with the conservative, Christine is typically medieval.

Yet, writing in the early fourteenth century in a royal court already under the influence of Italian humanism, in a milieu Steven Ozment refers to as "the eve of the Reformation," Christine also anticipates the compromises of a subsequent age.[2] Her seemingly contradictory impulses—toward social reform for women on the one hand and political conservatism on the other—provide us with an intriguing preview of the increasingly compromised position of women after their late medieval flourish. Although the humanism stimulated in England by the Reformation may have celebrated the voices of its male religious and intellectuals, its impact on women, although initially favorable, ultimately resulted in a loss of intellectual, social, and religious autonomy.[3] Among Protestants as well as Catholics, male reformers eventually circumscribed the ministering and preaching functions of women—roles that historically affor ' not only female authors but also women from all classes greater socia quality. Renaissance authors who wished to challenge their age's restrictions on women, therefore, could not adopt a voice quite like Margery Kempe's, but one more like Christine's—mingling advocacy for women with reverence for religious and social traditions.

It lies outside the purview of this volume to detail the way Renaissance texts did or did not challenge restrictive stereotypes of women; still, even a brief overview reveals that those stereotypes are often inherited from the Middle Ages. Writers of sixteenth-century Petrarchan sonnets construct courtly ladies as narcissistic mirrors for their poetic personae; Sir Philip Sidney's Astrophel tells us that "Love gave me the wound" when he looked into the eyes of his beloved Stella.[4] Many of Shakespeare's women are modeled on medieval types. Hamlet (himself an echo of both the troubadour persona in search of a true identity and the romance hero who replaces his father) harbors incestuous feelings for his mother in a text concerned with lineage and inheritance, and he vilifies Ophelia as a painted whore. The Dark Lady of the Sonnets, "black as hell, dark as night" (Sonnet 147: 14) is one revision of the patristic female demonic tempting a male from the virtuous company of other men; the devil-conjured Helen of Troy who appears to Marlowe's Dr. Faustus is yet another. Renaissance women, like medieval virgin martyrs, need to be "unsexed," as Lady Macbeth puts it, to act in men's world—Spenser's Britomart in Book 3 of *The Faerie Queene* can take up armor and lance only because she is the "Knight of Chastity." It might be best to end with Milton's ever wandering Eve, whose "disheveled" and "wanton" locks represent the chaotic feminine's need for "subjection" to men (Book 4: 306–8)—except that medieval feminine stereotypes continue well past the Renaissance. Alexander Pope's Belinda is the object of a Chaucerian *Rape of the Lock*; his *Eloise to Abelard* moans, "How happy is the blameless vestal's lot!" (207); his "Epistle 2: To a Lady, Of the Characters of Women" repeats the misogynist stereotype of women's instability we saw, in the introduction, in *La Contenance des Fames*: Women are made of "matter too soft a lasting mark to bear" and can be depicted only with "wandering touches, some reflected light" (3, 153).

A remarkably unchanging image of women appearing and reappearing in texts through the eighteenth century and even beyond is due partly to how powerfully that image, created by men, worked to control women. The standard male view labeled women as irrational and chaotic, and thereby rationalized and worked to continue male control of economic and other resources. Most medieval (and later) literature, especially that in the traditional canon, tells us more about male views of women than about women themselves. As a result, scholars in the last 30 years or so wishing to reconstruct women's views of their experiences have turned to rediscovering, editing, translating, and interpreting texts by female authors.

Medievalists are limited in taking such an approach, however, by the scarceness of female voices extant from medieval times. The lack of women's voices is especially noticeable in medieval England, which has only a handful of woman authors. As far as we know, aside from the Anglo-Saxon nuns mentioned in chapter 2, some noblewomen and queens who wrote or dictated letters, and a certain Muriel of the nunnery at Wilton (ca. 1100), whose poems are lost, no English women wrote in Latin. This contrasts with the situation on the European continent, which had a strong tradition of women Latin writers, including some figures we have met: the Parisian Heloise, the Saxon dramatist Hrotsvitha, and the prolific Hildegard von Bingen.[5]

Anglo-Norman French was the language of the post-Conquest aristocracy, and we would expect educated Norman women to write in their vernacular. But there are few aside from the incomparable Marie de France. A certain twelfth-century Clemence at the convent of Barking wrote a verse life of Saint Catherine of Alexandria, freely adapting an earlier French version. Another Barking nun around 1165 anonymously translated Aelred of Rievaulx's Latin life of Saint Edward the Confessor. And as we have seen in chapter 5, a certain Marie from an unidentified convent, who may be Marie de France, translated into verse a Latin life of the Anglo-Saxon Saint Etheldreda (Saint Audrey).[6]

The situation is hardly better when we turn to the English language. Julian of Norwich and Margery Kempe are now, justly, canonical authors. Alexandra Barratt, in her *Women's Writing in Middle English*, recently provided a valuable service by publishing for the first time extracts from *The Feitis and the Passion of Our Lord Jhesu Crist*, a collection of meditative prayers written anonymously by a woman for a nun sometime after 1415.[7] She has also made more accessible a selection from another anonymous text, *A Revelation Showed to a Holy Woman*, a record of a series of dreams in which a nun, Margaret, guides the author through a tour of Purgatory.[8] Barratt also reminds us of three brief poems ascribed by manuscripts to female authors, and of the letters of the women of the Paston family, but otherwise there are no original compositions by women in English (232–62).[9]

We could increase the number of women writing in England if we wished to consider poems written anonymously but in a woman's voice. There are two fifteenth-century dream visions from a female point of view, *The Floure and the Leafe* and *The Assembly of Ladies*.[10] A number of lyrics have female personae as narrators, especially those contained in the Findern manuscript, a commonplace book in which women copied love poems, some of them perhaps their own compositions. The manuscript lists several women's names, but it is unclear whether they name themselves as authors or scribes. Even if the women were merely scribes, however, their choice of poems to record reveals much about a female view of conventional love poetry.[11]

The briefest overview of women's compositions in England, whatever the language, reveals that a sizable majority are religious texts, records of mystical experiences, devotional texts, and saints' lives. Although a modern reader might not immediately catalogue these texts as literature, medieval culture did not have any category comparable to what we think of as literature, texts produced and read for pleasure, especially aesthetic enjoyment. The Middle Ages believed that the primary purpose of serious books, fictive and otherwise, was to instruct; delight was merely a secondary consideration. Hence many works, particularly in England, were religious or didactic. However, if English medieval literary culture is religious, female literary culture is even more so. For although the church concurred with society's control of women, it provided, as we have noted, most women's access to education and authorship. And it also disseminated works by women, even of some of whom it did not approve. It burned the beguine Marguerite Porete in 1310, for example, because her book, *The Mirror of Simple Souls,* was heterodox, yet the work "continued to be read anonymously, in four languages, in the most impeccable monastic houses."[12] The church, too, could welcome women's influence in the shaping of religious sentiment. Some recent studies of women's literacy reveal that their demand for vernacular religious texts motivated the composition or translation of a great many books, thereby lending vitality to both late medieval religious culture and the English vernacular.[13]

To better listen to the voices of medieval women, then, we may need to expand our definition of literature to include religious tracts, and also to redefine our notion of authorship. The modern author whose work expresses his or her personal point of view is, like a primarily aesthetic literature, the invention of the Renaissance. The Middle Ages, as our introduction noted, did not view the author's intention as the only meaning of a work; Christine de Pizan and the other parties in the *Querelle* on the *Roman de la Rose,* in discussing author Jean de Meun's intention, are often cited as among the first readers to valorize authorial intention.

Many historians and literary critics who reconstruct medieval women's experiences, especially as those experiences are mediated through literature, therefore have returned to a more medieval notion of authorship. They consider women's contributions to the overall production of literature, with production broadly defined. We have seen that Anglo-Norman nuns translated or adapted saints' lives, and Barratt's anthology of *Women's Writings* prints selections from texts by continental women translated into English, as well as translations by English women of male-authored texts.[14] The women associated with the Findern manuscript, if they did not write their poems, at least compiled them, and other work has been done on women as compilers and scribes.[15] Susan Groag Bell initiated an important approach by considering women's influence as patrons and book owners.[16] Some scholars have concentrated on how texts attempt to construct their female readers and women's response to those attempts. Both Elizabeth Robertson and Anne Clark Bartlett have studied the female audiences of English devotional literature, and Roberta Krueger has investigated those of French romance.[17] There have been several studies of conduct or courtesy manuals aimed at a female audience.[18] Religious literature written for women has been made more accessible in editions or translations.[19] Since many medieval women could not write but authored texts nevertheless, attention has been drawn to women's relationship to their male amanuenses and to women's oral culture: Margery Kempe dictated her work, as did the continental Catherine of Siena and Bridget of Sweden, both of whom greatly influenced English spirituality. For dealing with all of these facets of literary production, P. J. P. Goldberg, in his book on women and work in York and Yorkshire, offers essential cautionary advice: Although "not invisible in medieval sources … [women] are often inconspicuous. [They] rarely speak for themselves through surviving records, but when they do it is filtered through male hands and according to formal conventions.... But these are not causes for despair; the medievalist is used to making a little evidence work very hard."[20]

The most recent work on women's literary activities, then, studies medieval women as translators and compilers, scribes and artists, patrons and readers. By concentrating on this broader range of roles, modern scholars have brought to light a fuller picture of medieval women's lives. One hopes this trend in scholarship will continue and produce a fuller picture of the manifold influence that literature had on women's lives, and that women's lives had on literature.

Chronology

(Many dates are approximate.)

203	d. Perpetua and Felicitas, martyrs, at Carthage
Late fourth century	Works of Augustine and Jerome
449	Anglo-Saxon tribes begin settlement in Britain
524	Boethius's *Consolation of Philosophy*
597	Augustine of Canterbury, first Roman Christian missionary, arrives in Kent
614–680	Life of Hild, Abbess of Whitby
731	Bede's *Ecclesiastical History*
ca. 750	*Beowulf* (estimates range from 8th to 11th century)
935–995	Life of dramatist Hrotsvitha of Gandersheim; Cynewulf writes *Elene* and *Juliana*
1066	Norman Conquest under William I
1066–1127	Reign of King William I ("the Conqueror")
1071–1127	Life of Guillaume IX, Duke of Aquitaine, first known troubadour
1087–1100	Reign of King William II
1089–1179	Life of Hildegard von Bingen
1090–1153	Life of Bernard of Clairvaux
1096–1160	Life of Christina of Markyate, English recluse, later Benedictine nun at Saint Albans and prioress of Markyate
1100–1135	Reign of King Henry I
1100–1163	Life of Heloise
1122–1204	Life of Eleanor of Aquitaine, Queen of France (1137–1152); Queen of England (1154–1204)
1135–1154	Reign of King Stephen
ca. 1140	b. Azalais de Porcairages and Countess of Dia, both trobairitz

mid-12th century	Life of William of Saint Thierry
1154–1189	Reign of King Henry II; marries Eleanor of Aquitaine (1152); around this time romance emerges as a popular form
ca. 1165	b. Maria de Ventadorn, trobairitz
1170	Andreas Capellanus's *De Amore*
1170–1260	Trobairitz compose
1173	d. Richard of Saint Victor
ca. 1180	Marie de France's *Lais*; Chrétien de Troyes writing at the court of Champagne; Béroul's *Tristan*
ca. 1182–1226	Life of Francis of Assisi
1189–1199	Reign of King Richard I
ca. 1190	b. Lombarda, trobairitz
1199–1216	Reign of King John
ca. 1200	b. Castelloza, trobairitz
ca. 1207–1282	Life of Mechtild of Magdeburg, beguine and mystic, later nun of Helfta
early 13th century	Life of Bieris de Roman, trobairitz
1215	Fourth Lateran Council held under Pope Innocent III: orders ghettoization of Jews, proclaims doctrine of transubstantiation, orders yearly confession
1216–1272	Reign of King Henry III
ca. 1220–1240	Life of Hadewijch, Flemish beguine and mystic
1221–1274	Life of Bonaventure
ca. 1224–1274	Life of Thomas Aquinas
ca. 1225	*Ancrene Wisse* and related texts
ca. 1235	Guillaume de Lorris begins *Roman de la Rose*
ca. 1240–1310	Marguerite of Oingt, Carthusian prioress and mystic
ca. 1248–1309	Angela of Foligno, Italian widow, Franciscan tertiary and mystic
mid-13th century	Gillelma de Rosers, trobairitz
1258	d. Juliana of Cornillon, mystic and Corpus Christi visionary
1264	Feast of Corpus Christi instituted on the continent
1272–1307	Reign of King Edward I
ca. 1275	Jean de Meun continues *Roman de la Rose*
1300–1349	Life of Richard Rolle, English mystic
ca. 1300–1361	Life of John Tauler, Rhineland mystic
1303–1373	Life of Birgitta of Sweden, noblewoman and mother of eight; visionary, prophet, activist
1304–1321	Dante's *Divine Comedy*
early 14th century	Rolle's *The Fire of Love*
1307–1327	Reign of King Edward II

1309–1377	Exile of the papacy ("the Babylonian Captivity") to Avignon
1310	Marguerite Porete executed as heretic
1318	Feast of Corpus Christi arrives in England
1327–1377	Reign of King Edward III
1338–1453	The Hundred Years' War
1347–1380	Life of Catherine of Siena, Italian mystic
ca. 1343	b. Julian of Norwich; b. Geoffrey Chaucer
1348–1349	Black Death
ca. 1364	b. Christine de Pizan
1368	d. Blanche, Duchess of Lancaster
ca. 1370	Chaucer's *Book of the Duchess* (in memorial to Blanche of Lancaster)
ca. 1373	Julian of Norwich's *Showings* (short version); b. Margery Kempe
1376	First record of York Corpus Christi plays
1377	Return of papacy under Pope Gregory XI to Rome, encouraged by Birgitta of Sweden and Catherine of Siena
1377–1399	Reign of King Richard II
1381	Peasants' Revolt
ca. 1382	Chaucer's *Parlement of Foules*
ca. 1382–1386	Chaucer's *Troilus and Criseyde*
ca. 1386–87	Chaucer's *Legend of Good Women*
ca. 1386	Gower begins *Confessio Amantis*
1388–1400	Chaucer's *Canterbury Tales*
1389–1418	Christine de Pizan writing at the French court
ca. 1390	B.M. MS Cotton Nero A.x.4, containing *Sir Gawain and the Green Knight, Pearl, Patience,* and *Cleanness*
1393	Julian of Norwich's *Showings* (long version)
1396	d. Walter Hilton
1399	d. John of Gaunt, Duke of Lancaster
1399–1413	Reign of King Henry IV
1400	d. Chaucer
1402–1404	The *Querelle* on the *Roman de la Rose*
1408	d. John Gower
1412–1431	Life of Joan of Arc
ca. 1413	d. Julian of Norwich
1413–1422	Reign of King Henry V
1422–1461	Reign of King Henry VI
1436–1438	*The Book of Margery Kempe*
ca. 1439	d. Margery Kempe
1450	First printed Bible, in Germany

1461–1483	Reign of King Edward IV
1476	Caxton introduces printing to England
1478	Caxton prints *Canterbury Tales*
1483	Reign of King Edward V
1483–1485	Reign of King Richard III
1485	King Henry VII accedes, ends Plantagenet dynasty and begins Tudor dynasty; Caxton's *Morte D'Arthur*
1555	The Reformation "officially" begins when the Peace of Augsburg makes legal the religious divisions formed during the previous century

Notes and References

Introduction

1. See the introduction by Sheila Fisher and Janet E. Halley, ed., *Seeking the Woman in Late Medieval and Renaissance Writings: Essays in Feminist Contextual Criticism* (Knoxville: University of Tennessee Press, 1989), 1–17.

2. An excellent introduction to medieval literacy is M. T. Clanchy, *From Memory to Written Record: England 1066–1307* (London: Edward Arnold, 1977).

3. David Herlihy, *Opera Muliebria: Women and Work in Medieval Europe* (New York: McGraw-Hill, 1990), xiii.

4. In *Three Medieval Views of Women*, ed. and trans. Gloria K. Fiero, Wendy Pfeffer, and Mathé Allain (New Haven: Yale University Press, 1989), lines 129–39; for a list of other Old French poems on women, see p. 2.

5. Theodore Mommsen, "Petrarch's Conception of the Dark Ages," *Speculum* 17 (1942): 226–42; Herbert Weisinger, "The Renaissance Theory of the Reaction against the Middle Ages as a Cause of the Renaissance," *Speculum* 20 (1945): 461–67.

6. Jacob Burckhardt, *The Civilization of the Renaissance in Italy*, 2 vols. (1867; rpt. New York: Harper & Row, 1975).

7. *The Norton Anthology of English Literature*, 5th ed., vol. 1. General ed. M. H. Abrams (New York: W. W. Norton, 1962, rpt. 1984), 8, 11.

8. Norman F. Cantor, *Inventing the Middle Ages* (New York: Wm. Morrow and Co., 1991), 181–86.

9. Andreas Capellanus, *The Art of Courtly Love*, trans. John J. Parry (New York: Columbia University Press, 1941; rpt. W. W. Norton, 1969), 3.

10. John F. Benton, "The Court of Champagne as Literary Center," *Speculum* 36 (1961): 551–91; "Clio and Venus: An Historical View of Medieval Love," in *The Meaning of Courtly Love*, ed. F. X. Newman (Albany: State University of New York Press, 1968), 19–42.

11. Joan Kelly-Gadol, "Did Women Have a Renaissance?" in *Becoming Visible: Women in European History*, ed. Renate Bridenthal and Claudia Koonz (Boston: Houghton Mifflin, 1977), 137–64.

12. Geoffrey Chaucer, General Prologue to the *Canterbury Tales* I (A): 725–42.

13. D. W. Robertson Jr., *Preface to Chaucer: Studies in Medieval Perspectives* (Princeton: Princeton University Press, 1962); and the essays reprinted in *Essays in Medieval Culture* (Princeton: Princeton University Press, 1980).

14. Although defining the context is problematic; see Gayle Margherita, "Historicity, Femininity, and Chaucer's *Troilus*," *Exemplaria* 6 (1994): 243–49.

15. For assessments of Robertson, see Lee Patterson, *Negotiating the Past: The Historical Understanding of Medieval Literature* (Madison: University of Wisconsin Press, 1987), 26–39; various essays in David Aers, ed., *Medieval Literature: Criticism, Ideology and History* (New York: St. Martin's Press, 1986); and Carolyn Dinshaw, *Chaucer's Sexual Poetics* (Madison: University of Wisconsin Press, 1989), 28–39.

16. Joan M. Ferrante, *Woman as Image in Medieval Literature* (New York: Columbia University Press, 1975), 1.

17. Mark Girouard, *The Return to Camelot: Chivalry and the English Gentleman* (New Haven: Yale University Press, 1981), 197–218.

18. Barrie Ruth Straus, "The Subversive Discourse of the Wife of Bath: Phallocentric Discourse and the Imprisonment of Criticism," *ELH* 55 (1988): 527–54; Thomas Hahn, "Teaching the Resistant Woman: The Wife of Bath and the Academy," *Exemplaria* 4 (1992): 431–40.

19. A. J. Minnis, *Medieval Theory of Authorship: Scholastic Literary Attitudes in the Later Middle Ages* (London: Scholar Press, 1984), 28–29; Judson Boyce Allen, *The Friar as Critic: Literary Attitudes in the Later Middle Ages* (Nashville: Vanderbilt University Press, 1971), 58–63.

20. Augustine, *Confessions*, 12.31, trans. R. S. Pine-Coffin (New York: Penguin Books, 1961), 308.

21. Marie de France, Prologue to *The Lais of Marie de France*, trans. Robert Hanning and Joan Ferrante (Durham, N.C.: Labyrinth Press, 1978), lines 1–16.

22. Margaret Schaus and Susan Mosher Stuard, "Citizens of No Mean City: Medieval Women's History," *Choice* (December 1992): 583–95.

Chapter One

1. Tertullian, *On the Apparel of Women* 1.1, trans. S. Thelwall, in *Ante-Nicene Fathers*, Vol. 4, ed. Alexander Roberts and James Donaldson (1885; rpt. Peabody, Mass.: Hendrickson Publishers, 1994), 14.

2. All biblical quotations are from the Douai-Rheims English translation of the Latin Vulgate; *The Holy Bible* (Baltimore: John Murphy Co., 1899; rpt. Rockford, Ill.: Tan Books, 1971).

3. 1 Peter, however, does put this neutral topos to antifeminist use, arguing that the proper adornment for women is "subjection to their own husbands," 1 Peter 3:5.

4. Most medieval theologians thought that Eve was more culpable in the Fall than Adam; a minority, but including the influential Augustine, thought them equally at fault. See Marie-Thérèse d'Alverny, "Comment les théologiens et les philosophes voient la femme," *Cahiers de civilisation médiévale* 20 (1977): 110–29, and the indispensable collection *Woman Defamed and Woman Defended: An Anthology of Medieval Texts*, ed. Alcuin Blamires (Oxford: Oxford University Press, 1992), passim.

5. Guillaume de Lorris and Jean de Meun, *The Romance of the Rose*, trans. Charles Dahlberg (Hanover, N.H.: University Press of New England, 1983), 135.

6. Augustine, *Two Books on Genesis against the Manichees* 2.11.15, in *St. Augustine on Genesis*, trans. Roland J. Teske, Fathers of the Church 84 (Washington, D.C.: Catholic University of America Press, 1991), 111–12.

7. Gratian, *Decretum* 2.33, quest. 5.13; quoted in Blamires, *Women Defamed*, 85.

8. Thomas Aquinas, *Summa Theologica* 1.92.1, trans. Fathers of the English Dominican Province, 5 vols. (London, 1911; rpt. Westminster, Md.: Christian Classics, 1981), I: 466–67.

9. John Chrysostom, *Homily 9 on the First Letter to Timothy*; quoted in Blamires, *Woman Defamed*, 59.

10. Jerome, *Commentary on Epistle to the Ephesians* 3:5, quoted by Katharina M. Wilson, ed. *Medieval Women Writers* (Athens: University of Georgia Press, 1984), xxiii, n.22. See Jo Ann McNamara, "Sexual Equality and the Cult of Virginity in Early Christian Thought," *Feminist Studies* 3 (1976): 145–58.

11. *St. Benedict's Rule for Monasteries*, Chapters 48 and 55, trans. Leonard J. Doyle (Collegeville, Minn: Liturgical Press, 1948), 67–70, 77.

12. Caesarius of Arles, "Rule for Nuns," in *Women's Lives in Medieval Europe: A Sourcebook*, ed. Emilie Amt (New York: Routledge, 1993), 224.

13. *The Letters of Abelard and Heloise*, ed. and trans. Betty Radice (New York: Penguin, 1974), 257–69.

14. Angela M. Lucas, *Women in the Middle Ages: Religion, Marriage, and Letters* (New York: St. Martin's, 1983), 137–56.

15. Margaret Wade Labarge, *A Small Sound of the Trumpet: Women in Medieval Life* (Boston: Beacon Press, 1986), 21–25.

16. *Holy Maidenhood*, ed. Anne Savage and Nicholas Watson, in *Anchoritic Spirituality: Ancrene Wisse and Associated Works* (New York: Paulist Press, 1991), 234–40.

17. Peter Brown, *The Body and Society: Men, Women, and Sexual Renunciation in Early Christianity* (New York: Columbia University Press, 1988).

18. *The Life of Christina of Markyate*, trans. C. H. Talbot (Oxford: Oxford University Press, 1959).

19. Gerald Constable, "Aelred of Rievaulx and the Nun of Watton," in *Medieval Women*, ed. Derek Baker, Studies in Church History: Subsidia I (Oxford: Basil Blackwell, 1978), 206–9.

20. Eileen E. Power, *Medieval English Nunneries, c. 1275 to 1535* (Cambridge: Cambridge University Press, 1922), 1.

21. Caroline Walker Bynum, *Fragmentation and Redemption: Essays on Gender and the Human Body in Medieval Religion* (New York: Zone, 1991), 53–78.

22. Peter Dronke, *Women Writers of the Middle Ages* (Cambridge: Cambridge University Press, 1986), 73–75.

23. Alexandra Barratt, ed., *Women's Writing in Middle English* (New York: Longman, 1992), 11–12.

24. There is ongoing controversy concerning whether Heloise wrote her letters or Abelard composed them; the debate is summarized by John F. Benton, "A Reconsideration of the Authenticity of the Correspondence of Abelard and Heloise," in *Petrus Abelardus*, ed. Rudolf Thomas (Trier: Trierer Theologische Studien 38, 1980), and further by Dronke, *Women Writers*, 140–43.

25. Glenda McLeod, "Wholly Guilty, Wholly Innocent: Self-Definition in Hélòise's Letters to Abélard," in *Dear Sister: Medieval Women and the Epistolary Genre*, ed. Karen Cherewatuk and Ulrike Wiethaus (Philadelphia: University of Pennsylvania Press, 1993), 64–86.
26. Barbara Newman, *Sister of Wisdom: St. Hildegard's Theology of the Feminine* (Berkeley: University of California Press, 1987), 42–88.
27. Christine de Pizan, *The Book of the City of Ladies*, trans. Earl Jeffrey Richards, 10; *A Medieval Woman's Mirror of Honor: The Treasury of the City of Ladies*, trans. Charity Cannon Willard, 69; both New York: Persea, 1982 and 1989, respectively.
28. Aristotle, *The Generation of Animals*, paragraph 738b; quoted in Blamires, *Women Defamed*, 40.
29. Marina Warner, *Alone of All Her Sex: The Myth and the Cult of the Virgin Mary* (1976; rpt. New York: Vintage, 1983), 50–67, summarizes the usual oppositions between Mary and Eve.
30. Roger S. Wieck, *Time Sanctified: The Book of Hours in Medieval Art and Life* (New York: George Braziller, 1988), 60–61, 159. On the iconography of Mary reading, see Susan Groag Bell, "Medieval Women Book Owners: Arbiters of Lay Piety and Ambassadors of Culture," in *Women and Power in the Middle Ages*, ed. Mary Erler and Maryanne Kowaleski (Athens: University of Georgia Press, 1988), 168–73.
31. Barbara Newman, "Divine Power Made Perfect in Weakness: St. Hildegard on the Frail Sex," in *Peace-Weavers*, ed. John A. Nichols and Lillian Thomas Shank, Medieval Religious Women, vol. 2 (Kalamazoo: Cistercian Press, 1987), 110–12.
32. Claudius of Turin, Preface to *Commentary on Leviticus*, quoted in Beryl Smalley, *The Study of the Bible in the Middle Ages* (1952; rpt. Notre Dame: Notre Dame University Press, 1964), 1.
33. R. Howard Bloch, *The Scandal of the Fabliaux* (Chicago: University of Chicago Press, 1986), 22–58.
34. David Herlihy, *Opera Muliebria: Women and Work in Medieval Europe* (New York: McGraw-Hill, 1990), 75–102; Elizabeth Wayland Barber, *Women's Work: The First 20,000 Years: Women, Cloth, and Society in Early Times* (New York: Norton, 1994).
35. *The Plays of Hrotsvit of Gandersheim*, trans. Katherina Wilson (New York: Garland, 1989), 5.
36. Gerda Lerner, *The Creation of Feminist Consciousness from the Middle Ages to Eighteen-Seventy* (Oxford: Oxford University Press, 1993), 51–52.
37. Chrétien de Troyes, *Arthurian Romances*, trans. William W. Kibler (New York: Penguin, 1991), 207.

Chapter Two

1. *Germania* 2–3, in *The Historical Works of Tacitus*, Vol. 2, trans. Arthur Murphy (New York: E. P. Dutton, 1908), 312–13.
2. On the lack of misogyny, see Christine Fell, *Women in Anglo-Saxon England* (London: British Museum Publications, 1984), 13–14; Janemarie Leucke, "The Unique Experience of Anglo-Saxon Nuns," in *Peace-Weavers*, ed. John A. Nichols and Lil-

lian Thomas Shank, Medieval Religions Women, vol. 2 (Kalamazoo: Cistercian Press, 1987), 55–6l.

3. Frances Gies and Joseph Gies, *Women in the Middle Ages* (New York: Harper and Row, 1978), 15–19, find Tacitus highly suspect; they argue that Germanic culture held women as chattel and that female status improved under Roman influence and Christianity.

4. *Maxims I*, lines 91b–92, in *The Exeter Book*, Vol. 3 of *The Anglo-Saxon Poetic Records*, 6 vols., ed. George Philip Krapp and Elliott Van Kirk Dobbie (New York: Columbia University Press, 1936). All citations of line numbers in Old English poetry, except *Beowulf*, will be to the poems as printed in the various volumes of ASPR. Translations are my own, in prose and literal, although I have sometimes preferred readability over fidelity to the letter.

5. Bede, *Ecclesiastical History of the English Nation* 4.23, trans. J. Stevens and J.A. Giles (New York: Dutton, 1965), 202.

6. Sheila C. Dietrich, "An Introduction to Women in Anglo-Saxon Society (ca. 600–1066)," in *The Women of England*, ed. Barbara Kanner (Hamden, Conn.: Archon Books, 1979), 32–56; Bernice Kliman, "Women in Early English Literature, 'Beowulf' to the 'Ancrene Wisse,'" *Nottingham Medieval Studies* 21 (1978): 32–49; Stephanie Hollis, *Anglo-Saxon Women and the Church: Sharing a Common Fate* (Rochester: Boydell Press, 1992).

7. R. Howard Bloch, *Medieval Misogyny and the Invention of Western Romantic Love* (Chicago: University of Chicago Press, 1991), 37–47.

8. Pat Belanoff, "The Fall (?) of the Old English Female Poetic Image," *PMLA* 104 (1989): 822.

9. Fred C. Robinson, "History, Religion, Culture," in *Approaches to Teaching Beowulf*, ed. Jess Bessinger Jr. and Robert F. Yeager (New York: Modern Language Association of America, 1984), 120–21.

10. *Beowulf*, lines 167, 715–16. *Beowulf and the Fight at Finnsburg*, ed. Frederic Klaeber, 3d ed. (Lexington, Mass.: D.C. Heath, 1922; rpt. 1950).

11. Alain Renoir, "Eve's I.Q. Rating: Two Sexist Views of *Genesis B*," in *New Readings on Women in Old English Literature*, ed. Helen Damico and Alexandra Hennessey Olsen (Bloomington: Indiana University Press, 1990), 262–72.

12. Helen Damico, *Beowulf's Wealhtheow and the Valkyrie Tradition* (Madison: University of Wisconsin Press, 1984).

13. F.T. Wainwright, "Aethelflaed, Lady of the Mercians," in *New Readings*, ed. Damico and Olsen, 44–55. For refutation of the argument that the widowed Aethelflaed was the model for Judith, see David Chamberlain, "A Fragmentary and Political Poem," in *Anglo-Saxon Poetry: Essays in Appreciation*, ed. Lewis E. Nicholson and Dolores Warwick Frese (Notre Dame: University of Notre Dame Press, 1975), 158–59.

14. Nicholas Howe, *Migration and Mythmaking in Anglo-Saxon England* (New Haven: Yale University Press, 1989).

15. Translations of some of the nun's letters and Huneburg's *Hodoeporicon* are in *The Anglo-Saxon Missionaries in Germany*, ed. C.H. Talbot (New York: Sheed and Ward, 1954). See Christine E. Fell, "Some Implications of the Boniface Correspondence," in *New Readings*, ed. Damico and Olsen, 29–43, and Peter Dronke, *Women Writers of the Middle Ages* (Cambridge: Cambridge University Press, 1986), 30–35.

16. Norman E. Eliason, "Healfdane's Daughter," in *Anglo-Saxon Poetry*, ed. Nicholson and Frese, 9–10.
17. L. John Sklute, "*Freothuwebbe* in Old English Poetry," in *New Readings*, ed. Damico and Olsen, 204–10, more positively imagines the peaceweaver as diplomat.
18. Gayle Rubin, "The Traffic in Women: Notes on the 'Political Economy' of Sex," in *Toward an Anthropology of Women*, ed. Rayna Reiter (New York: Monthly Review, 1975), 157–210.
19. Gillian Overing, *Language, Sign and Gender in* Beowulf (Carbondale: Southern Illinois University Press, 1990), 76.
20. E.g., John Leyerle, "The Interlace Structure of *Beowulf*" in *Interpretations of Beowulf: A Critical Anthology*, ed. R. D. Fulk (Bloomington: Indiana University Press, 1991), 155, sees both Grendel and his mother as allegories for "internecine strife."
21. Jane Chance, *Woman as Hero in Old English Literature* (Syracuse: Syracuse University Press, 1986), 95–108.

Chapter Three

1. Two anonymous lyrics, *The Wife's Lament* and *Wulf and Eadwacer*, do articulate women's desire; for commentary see Clifford Davidson, "Erotic Women's Songs in Anglo-Saxon England," *Neophilologus* 59 (1975): 451–62; Patricia A. Belanoff, "Women's Songs, Women's Language," in *New Readings on Women in Old English Literature*, ed. Helen Damico and Alexandra Hennessey Olsen (Bloomington: Indiana University Press, 1990), 193–203.
2. E.g., C. S. Lewis's outdated yet significant *Allegory of Love* (Oxford: Oxford University Press, 1936), 3–11.
3. Some argue that non-European traditions, especially Arabic, are the source of courtly love; see Roger Boase, *The Origin and Meaning of Courtly Love: A Critical Study of European Scholarship* (Totowa, N.J.: Rowman and Littlefield, 1977), 62–74; and Maria Menocal, *The Arabic Role in Medieval Literary History* (Philadelphia: University of Pennsylvania Press, 1987), especially 83–88, on the *kharjas*, Romance strophes in women's voices at the end of Arabic poems.
4. My sketch of the troubadours is indebted to two books by Frederick Goldin, *The Mirror of Narcissus in the Courtly Love Lyric* (Ithaca: Cornell University Press, 1967), and *Lyrics of the Troubadours and Trouvères: An Anthology and History* (Gloucester, Mass.: Peter Smith, 1983); to Sarah Kay, *Subjectivity in Troubadour Poetry* (Cambridge: Cambridge University Press, 1990); and to Stephen G. Nichols, "The Old Provençal Lyric," in *A New History of French Literature*, ed. Denis Hollier (Cambridge: Harvard University Press, 1989), 30–36.
5. Erich Köhler, "Observations historiques et sociologiques sur la poésie des troubadours," *Cahiers de Civilisation Médiévales* 7 (1964): 27–51. On male audiences, Simon Gaunt, "Poetry of Exclusion: A Feminist Reading of Some Troubadour Lyrics," *Modern Language Review* 85 (1990): 310–29.
6. Meg Bogin, *The Women Troubadours* (New York: Paddington, 1976), 50–51. Kay, *Subjectivity*, 86–93, argues that *midons* is grammatically both masculine and feminine, combining female desirability with a male mask for feminine inferiority.

7. Poem 18, lines 4, 25, 27, in Goldin's *Lyrics of the Troubadours and Trouvères*. All references to troubadour and trouvère lyrics unless noted otherwise will be to the poems as Goldin prints them; translations are my own.

8. Don A. Monson, "The Troubadour's Lady Reconsidered Again," *Speculum* 70 (1995): 265–67.

9. The more usual view is that the gaze "seems to fracture the boundaries of the private self"; Sarah Stanbury, "The Lover's Gaze in *Troilus and Criseyde*," in *Chaucer's Troilus and Criseyde: "Subgit to alle Poesye,"* ed. R. A. Shoaf (Binghamton, N.Y.: Medieval & Renaissance Texts & Studies, 1992), 227.

10. On the theory of Cathar origin, see Boase, *Origin and Meaning*, 77–81.

11. E. Jane Burns, "The Man Behind the Lady in Troubadour Lyric," *Romance Notes* 25 (1985): 239–53.

12. See evidence summarized by R. Howard Bloch, *Medieval Misogyny and the Invention of Western Romantic Love* (Chicago: University of Chicago Press, 1991), 186–97.

13. On the trobairitz canon, see Anne Callahan, "The Trobairitz," in *French Women Writers: A Bio-Bibliographical Source Book*, ed. Eva-Martin Sartori (New York: Greenwood, 1991), 495–502; François Zufferey, "Toward a Delimitation of the Trobairitz Corpus," and Frank M. Chambers, "Las trobairitz soiseubudas," both in *The Voice of the Trobairitz: Perspectives on the Women Troubadours*, ed. William D. Paden (Philadelphia: University of Pennsylvania Press, 1989).

14. Pierre Bec, "Trobairitz et chansons de femme: Contribution à la connaissance du lyrisme féminin au moyen âge," *Cahiers de civilisation médiévale* 22 (1979): 252–59.

15. Matilda Tomaryn Bruckner, "Fictions of the Female Voice: The Women Troubadours," *Speculum* 67 (1992): 865–91.

16. Joan Ferrante, "Male Fantasy and Female Reality in Courtly Literature," *Women's Studies* 11 (1984): 67–97.

17. Poem 10, line 33, in Angelica Rieger, *Trobairitz* (Tubingen: Max Niemeyer, 1991), who publishes 46 poems with German translations. All citations of trobairitz works are to this edition; translations are my own. Texts and English translations of 30 poems can be found in *The Songs of the Women Troubadours*, ed. Matilda Tomaryn Bruckner, Laurie Shepard, and Sarah White (New York: Garland, 1995).

18. Augustine, *Ennarationes in Psalmum* 103.4, in *Patrilogia Latina* 37:1338, ed. J. P. Migne (Paris, 1845).

19. For more on Lombarda's mirrors, see Sarah Kay, "Derivation, Derived Rhyme, and the Trobairitz," and Tilde Sankovitch, "Lombarda's Reluctant Mirror: Speculum of Another Poet," both in *Voice of the Trobairitz*, ed. Paden, 169–72 and 183–93.

20. Stephen G. Nichols, "Medieval Women Writers: *Aisthesis* and the Powers of Marginality," *Yale French Studies* 75 (1988): 89–91; and Bruckner, "Fictions of the Female Voice," 877–80.

21. Marianne Shapiro, "The Provençal Trobairitz and the Limits of Courtly Love," *Signs* 3 (1978): 564.

22. Angelica Rieger, "Was Bieris de Romans Lesbian?" in *Voice of the Trobairitz*, ed. Paden, 73–94.

23. I follow Rieger's translation, although this line might also be translated "every virtue a man or woman might seek"—suggesting that Maria is open to advances by both men and women.

24. As argued by William D. Paden Jr., et al., "The Poems of the *Trobairitz* Na Castelloza," *Romance Philology* 35 (1981): 165.

25. Peter Dronke, "The Provençal Trobairitz Castelloza," in *Medieval Women Writers*, ed. Katharina M. Wilson (Athens: University of Georgia Press, 1984), 137.

26. For what influence there was, see Henry John Chaytor, *The Troubadours and England* (Cambridge, 1923, rpt. Geneva: Slatkine, 1974).

27. Derek Pearsall, *Old English and Middle English Poetry* (Boston: Routledge, 1977), 127–28.

28. Poem 46, lines 6–7 in *Religious Lyrics of the XVth Century*, ed. Carleton Brown (Oxford: Oxford University Press, 1932). Citations of Middle English verse will be to this or to the two other volumes edited by Brown, *Religious Lyrics of the XIIIth Century* (Oxford, 1932) and *Religious Lyrics of the XIVth Century* (Oxford, 1924); I have modernized spelling and vocabulary.

29. Not in Brown, but in Maxwell S. Luria and Richard L. Hoffman, eds., *Middle English Lyrics* (New York: Norton, 1974), Poem 60, Stanza 2.

30. Rosemary Woolf, *The English Religious Lyric in the Middle Ages* (Oxford: Oxford University Press, 1968), 6. On Marian lyric, see 114–58, 239–308.

Chapter Four

1. Heldris de Cornuälle, *Silence: A Thirteenth-Century French Romance*, ed. and trans. Sarah Roche-Mahdi (East Lansing, Mich.: Colleagues Press, 1992).

2. R. Howard Bloch, "Silence and Holes: The *Roman de Silence* and the Art of the Trouvère," *Yale French Studies* 70 (1976): 81–99. On the work's feudal ideology, see Sharon Kinoshita, "Heldris de Cornuälle's *Roman de Silence* and the Feudal Politics of Lineage," *PMLA* 110 (1995): 397–409.

3. See Georges Duby, *The Knight, the Lady, and the Priest: The Making of Modern Marriage in Medieval France*, trans. Barbara Bray (New York: Pantheon, 1983).

4. E.g., Donald Maddox, "Specular Stories, Family Romance, and the Fictions of Courtly Culture," *Exemplaria* 3 (1991): 299–326, who specifically discusses Chrétien's *Perceval*.

5. *Sir Degaré*, line 26, in *The Breton Lays in Middle English*, ed. Thomas C. Rumble (Detroit: Wayne State University Press, 1965).

6. Jean D'Arras, *Roman de Melusine*, trans. Sara Sturm-Maddox and Donald Maddox (New York: Garland, 1995).

7. Stephen Knight, "The Social Function of the Middle English Romances," in *Medieval Literature: Criticism, Ideology, and History*, ed. David Aers (New York: St. Martin's Press, 1986), 99–122.

8. *Troilus and Criseyde* II.82–84; *Nun's Priest's Tale*, *Canterbury Tales* VII.3212–13.

9. On book ownership, Margaret Wade Labarge, *A Small Sound of the Trumpet: Women in Medieval Life* (Boston: Beacon Press, 1986), 234–35. On women's patronage, Angela M. Lucas, *Women in the Middle Ages: Religion, Marriage, and Letters* (New York: St. Martin's Press, 1983), 170–79; and Susan Groag Bell, "Medieval Women Book Owners," in *Women and Power in the Middle Ages*, ed. Mary Erler and Maryanne Kowaleski (Athens: University of Georgia Press, 1988), 168–73.

10. Roberta L. Krueger, *Women Readers and the Ideology of Gender in Old French Verse Romance* (Cambridge: Cambridge University Press, 1993), 39–51.

11. Chrétien de Troyes, *Arthurian Romances*, trans. William W. Kibler (New York: Penguin, 1991), 362–63. All citations to Chrétien's works will be to Kibler's translation.

12. Derek Brewer, *Symbolic Stories* (New York: Longman, 1988), 9–11.

13. For an introduction to the legend, see Joan Tasker Grimbert, ed., *Tristan and Isolde: A Casebook* (New York: Garland, 1995).

14. Béroul, *The Romance of Tristan*, trans. Alan S. Fedrick (New York: Penguin, 1970).

15. Peggy McCracken, "Women and Medicine in Medieval French Narrative," *Exemplaria* 5 (1993): 239–62.

16. On female virginity as a figure for integrity, see Bella Millett's introduction to *Hali Meithhad*, Early English Text Society 284 (London: Oxford University Press, 1982) xxiv–xliv.

17. On the histories of Arthurian characters see *The New Arthurian Encyclopedia*, ed. Norris J. Lacy (New York: Garland, 1991). For an overview of scholarship on Chrétien's *Lancelot*, see Matilda Tomaryn Bruckner, "*Le Chevalier de la Charrette (Lancelot),*" in *The Romances of Chrétien de Troyes: A Symposium*, ed. Douglas Kelly (Lexington: French Forum, 1985), 132–81; and "An Interpreter's Dilemma: Why Are There So Many Interpretations of Chrétien's *Chevalier de la Charrette?*" *Romance Philology* 40 (1986): 159–80.

18. *Le Chevalier de la Charrete*, ed. Mario Roques (Paris: Champion, 1975), line 26.

19. Lines 657, 660–61 in *Sir Gawain and the Green Knight*, in *The Complete Poems of the Pearl Poet*, ed. Malcolm Andrew, Ronald Waldron, and Clifford Peterson; trans. Casey Finch (Berkeley: University of California Press, 1993). Modernizations are my own.

20. Sheila Fisher, "Taken Men and Token Women in *SGGK*," in *Seeking the Woman in Late Medieval and Renaissance Writings*, ed. Sheila Fisher and Janet E. Halley (Knoxville: University of Tennessee Press, 1989), 71–105; Geraldine Heng, "Feminine Knots and the Other *SGGK*," *PMLA* 93 (1991): 500–514.

21. For a different view, see Maureen Fries, "Female Heroes, Heroines and Counter Heroes: Images of Women in Arthurian Tradition," in *Popular Arthurian Traditions*, ed. Salley K. Slocum (Bowling Green, Ohio: Popular Press, 1992), 5–17, who discusses Malory and Chrétien.

22. Sir Thomas Malory, *Le Morte D'Arthur*, ed. Janet Cowen, 2 vols. (New York: Penguin, 1969), Book 7, Chapter 1. All references to Malory will be to the book and chapter divisions made by William Caxton.

23. Richard Kieckhefer, *Magic in the Middle Ages* (Cambridge: Cambridge University Press, 1989), 176–201.

Chapter Five

1. E. Jane Burns, *Bodytalk: When Women Speak in Old French Literature* (Philadelphia: University of Pennsylvania Press, 1993), 13.

2. Roberta L. Krueger, *Women Readers and the Ideology of Gender in Old French Verse Romance* (Cambridge: Cambridge University Press, 1993), 3.

3. Heloise, Hildegard von Bingen, Eleanor of Aquitaine, and Marie de Champagne immediately spring to mind. This situation changes dramatically in the thirteenth century with the rise of beguine mysticism and its sophisticated fusion of monastic and courtly discourses on love. See Barbara Newman, *From Virile Woman to WomanChrist* (Philadelphia: University of Pennsylvania Press, 1995), 137–81.

4. Stephen G. Nichols, "Working Late: Marie de France and the Value of Poetry," *Women in French Literature*, ed. Michel Guggenheim (Stanford: Anma Libri, 1988), 8.

5. Claude Fauchet, in 1581, derives Marie's "de France" from her epilogue to the *Fables*. See Michael J. Curley, trans. and ed., "Introduction," *Saint Patrick's Purgatory: A Poem by Marie de France* (Binghamton, N.Y.: MRTS, 1993), 3.

6. See Glyn Burgess, *Marie de France: Text and Context* (Athens: University of Georgia Press, 1987), 17–19, for the relationship between chronology and geographical locations of individual lais.

7. *The Lais of Marie de France*, trans. Robert Hanning and Joan Ferrante (Durham, N.C.: Labyrinth Press, 1978), *Prologue*, ln. 43. For Marie's Old French text, see *Les Lais de Marie de France*, ed. Jean Rychner (Paris: Librarie Honoré Champion, 1968).

8. Curley, 5. Other candidates include Henri au Court Mantel, Henry II's eldest son, crowned king in 1170, and Louis VII of France (1137–1180).

9. *Marie de France: Fables*, ed. and trans. Harriet Spiegel (Toronto: University of Toronto Press, 1987), 256, ln. 9.

10. Curley, 5; these include William de Mandeville, earl of Essex, a patron of the arts and of various religious houses held in esteem by Henry II; William Longsword, earl of Salisbury, the natural son of Henry II and Rosamond Clifford; William Marshal, earl of Pembroke; William of Gloucester, son of Robert, earl of Gloucester, dedicatee of one of the versions of Geoffrey of Monmouth's *History of the Kings of Britain*.

11. *Fables*, 256–59, ll. 9–19. There are no surviving manuscripts of any Old English fables, so Marie's claim is somewhat problematic. At the very least, she establishes her own readerly connection with the native English tradition through Alfred the Great, well known to later generations for his translations and for his literary patronage.

12. The first 40 tales in her collection of 103 fables reveal a close correspondence with the *Romulus Nilantii*, the Latin prose branch of the fable tradition Marie was working from (Spiegel, 6–11). Her thorough knowledge of Latin is further underscored by her skillful translation of Henry of Saltrey's *Tractatus de Purgatorio Sancti Patricii* in *Saint Patrick's Purgatory*.

13. Curley, 5–6. Other possible candidates include Marie de Champagne (daughter of the French King Louis VII and Eleanor of Aquitaine); Marie de Boulogne (daughter of Stephen of Blois and Matilda, an abbess of the Benedictine monastery of Romsey in Hampshire); Marie de Meulan (daughter of Waleran II, count of Meulan, and Agnes de Montfort, married to the Englishman Hugh Talbot of Cleuville); and a nun at Reading Abbey named Marie. See Curley, 6–7, for the implications of parentage, patronage connections, and the importance of the various literary interests of the abbeys represented for the several candidates.

14. *Fables*, 1–8; *Guigemar*, 3–4; *Saint Patrick's Purgatory*, 2997–99 (although Curley's translation deemphasizes Marie's emphatic focus on memory, "memoire"). Marie

may also have translated a fourth work dating from the beginning of the thirteenth century, *The Life of Saint Audree*. It, too, closes with Marie's signature rhetorical trope of eponymic self-remembrance (Curley, 7, ll. 4618–20).

15. "The Prologue to the Lais of Marie de France and Medieval Poetics," *Modern Philology* 41 (1943): 102.

16. Beryl Smalley, *The Study of the Bible in the Middle Ages* (Notre Dame, Ind.: University of Notre Dame Press, 1978), 37–111.

17. Alexandre Leupin, "The Impossible Task of Manifesting 'Literature': On Marie de France's Obscurity," *Exemplaria* 3 (1991): 221–28.

18. My translation. Hanning and Ferrante's translation obscures slightly the sense of parallel agency that Marie crafts here. (Compare the Old French: "Ki Deus as duné escïence / E de parler bone eloquence / Ne s'en eit taisir ne celer, / Ainz se deit voluntiers mustrer. / Wuant uns granz biens est mult oïz, / Dunc a primes est il fluriz, / E quant loëz est de plusurs / Dunc ad espandues ses flurs.")

19. Ovid, *Metamorphoses*, trans. Mary M. Innes (1955; rpt. New York: Penguin Books, 1982), 83–87.

20. See Nichols, "Working Late," 7–16, and Tilde A. Sankovitch, "Marie de France: The Myth of the Wild," *French Women Writers and the Book* (Syracuse: Syracuse University Press, 1988), 15–41.

21. My translation. The connotative choices Hanning and Ferrante make in this section elide Marie's emphasis on "remembering" as an essential component of her poetic program.

22. See Mary Carruthers, *The Book of Memory: A Study of Memory in Medieval Culture* (Cambridge: Cambridge University Press, 1990), 48–52, 80–85, and 261–66. Medieval mnemonic treatises frequently cite the heart as the bodily locus of memory. In fact, they regularly pun on the Latin for heart (*cor*) in their discussions of remembering (*recordare*) as a process of re-hearting the self.

23. Stephen Nichols, "Medieval Women and the Politics of Poetry," *Displacements: Women, Tradition, and Literatures in French*, ed. Joan de Jean and Nancy K. Miller (Baltimore: Johns Hopkins University Press, 1991), 105.

24. On the complex relationship between oral and written cultures during this period, see M.T. Clanchy, *From Memory to Written Record: England, 1066–1307* (Cambridge: Harvard University Press, 1979), and Brian Stock, *The Implications of Literacy: Written Languages and Models of Interpretation in the Eleventh and Twelfth Centuries* (Princeton: Princeton University Press, 1983).

25. Jo Ann McNamara, "The Herrenfrage: The Restructuring of the Gender System, 1050–1150," in *Medieval Masculinities: Regarding Men in the Middle Ages*, ed. Clare A. Lees (Minneapolis: University of Minnesota Press, 1994), 3–29.

26. Jo Ann McNamara, "The Herrenfrage," 8. McNamara describes a gender system profoundly disturbed by the church's renewed insistence on clerical celibacy during the late eleventh and early twelfth centuries.

27. Louis Charbonneau-Lassay, *The Bestiary of Christ*, trans. and abridged D.M. Dooling (New York: Parabola, 1940), 118–19. For a rich discussion of how crucifixion iconography begins to register Christ's feminine self from the twelfth century on, see Caroline Walker Bynum, *Holy Feast and Holy Fast: The Religious Significance of Food to Medieval Women* (Berkeley: University of California Press, 1987).

28. See Bloch, *Medieval Misogyny*, 143–64, for the cultural assumptions that underpin the desire expressed in courtly literature for the unattainable or virginal lady.

29. On Marie's familiarity with the discourses of mysticism, see Denise Despres, "Redeeming the Flesh: Spiritual Transformation in Marie de France's *Yonec*," *Studia Mystica* 10 (1987): 26–39.

Chapter Six

1. Miri Rubin, *Corpus Christi: The Eucharist in Late Medieval Culture* (Cambridge: Cambridge University Press, 1991), 2.

2. For recent editions see: *The York Plays*, ed. Richard Beadle, York Medieval Texts (Baltimore: Arnold, 1982); *The Chester Mystery Cycle*, ed. Robert Lumiansky and David Mill, 2 vols., Early English Text Society SS 3, 9 (London: Oxford University Press, 1974–86); *The Wakefield Pageants in the Towneley Cycle*, ed. A. C. Cawley, Old and Middle English Texts (Manchester: Manchester University Press, 1958); *The Towneley Plays*, ed. George England and Alfred W. Pollard, Early English Text Society, e.s. 71 (London: Oxford University Press, 1897; rpt. 1966); *Ludus Coventriae, or The Plaie Called Corpus Christi*, ed. K. S. Block, Early English Text Society, e.s. 120 (London: Oxford University Press, 1922; rpt. 1960); *Non-Cycle Plays and Fragments*, ed. Norman Davis, Early English Text Society SS 1 (London: Oxford University Press, 1970).

3. Erich Auerbach, *"Figura,"* in *Scenes from the Drama of European Literature, Theory and History of Literature*, Vol. 9 (Minneapolis: University of Minnesota Press, 1984), 58.

4. V. A. Kolve, *The Play Called Corpus Christi* (Stanford: Stanford University Press, 1966), 99.

5. See Theresa Coletti, "A Feminist Approach to the Corpus Christi Cycles," *Approaches to Teaching Medieval English Drama*, ed. Richard K. Emmerson (New York: Modern Language Association of America, 1990), 79–89, on making the plays' representations of women focal, and "Purity and Danger: The Paradox of Mary's Body and the En-gendering of the Infancy Narrative in the English Mystery Cycles," *Feminist Approaches to the Body in Medieval Literature*, ed. Linda Lomperis and Sarah Stanbury (Philadelphia: University of Pennsylvania Press, 1993), 65–95, as an example of such a cultural study.

6. "Boundary and Transgression: Body, Text, Language," *Stanford French Review* 14 (1990): 10.

7. *Against Jovinian*, in *The Principal Works of Saint Jerome*, Select Library of Nicene and Post-Nicene Fathers, vi (New York: Christian Literature Co., 1893), 346–416.

8. For the function of women in fabliau, see E. Jane Burns, *Bodytalk: When Women Speak in Old French Literature* (Philadelphia: University of Pennsylvania Press, 1993), 31–70, especially 59.

9. Elizabeth Robertson, "Medieval Medical Views of Women," in *Feminist Approaches to the Body in Medieval Literature*, ed. Lomperis and Stanbury, 145.

10. Karma Lochrie, *Margery Kempe and Translations of the Flesh* (Philadelphia: University of Pennsylvania Press, 1991), 23–24.

11. Caroline Walker Bynum, *Fragmentation and Redemption: Essays on Gender and the Human Body in Medieval Religion* (New York: Zone, 1991), 187: Even female

mystics participate in this physiological model (although transgressively), with displays of unusual bodily "changes, closures, openings, or exudings."

12. *Sermo de conversione ad clericos*, in S. *Bernardi Opera*, vol. IV, ed. Jean Leclercq and H. M. Rochais (Rome: Editiones Cistercienses, 1957). See Lochrie's discussion of this sermon, 20–21.

13. A common alignment in fabliaux as well (Burns, 31–70, passim).

14. Bynum, *Fragmentation and Redemption*, chapters 1, 4, and 6.

15. Quoted in Rubin, *Corpus Christi*, 170.

16. See Alexander Schmemann, *Introduction to Liturgical Theology*, trans. Asheleigh E. Moorhouse (London: The Faith Press, Ltd., 1970), 72–115, on the chronological dualism of liturgical celebration.

17. On metaphor and metonymy, see Peter Brooks, "Freud's Masterplot: A Model for Narrative," in *Reading for the Plot: Design and Intention in Narrative* (New York: Alfred A. Knopf, 1984), 91.

18. The public processional modes that preceded the cycle drama during the first half of the fourteenth century in England provide a striking contrast. Rubin emphasizes that they characterized the feast's celebration of the Eucharist through a hierarchical display of the constituent factions of the social body, in effect speaking the society's "idiom of privilege and lordship" (240) rather than exploring, as I suggest the cycle plays do, its voiceless spaces.

19. Chaucer's *Miller's Tale* [*The Riverside Chaucer*, ed. Larry D. Benson (Boston: Houghton Mifflin Co., 1987), 66–77] serves as a splendid contemporary witness. His drunken Miller cries out "in Pilates voys," imitating one of the key characters from the Crucifixion sequences as he introduces his pilgrim audience to the fabliau he is preparing to tell. As Sandra Pierson Prior suggests ["Parodying Typology and the Mystery Plays in the *Miller's Tale*," *Journal of Medieval and Renaissance Studies* 16 (1986)], the tale shows "an appreciative awareness of the kinds of scatological humor, fabliau-like plots and parodic typology employed by the cycle drama" (70–71).

20. David Bevington, *Medieval Drama* (Boston: Houghton Mifflin Company, 1975), 258.

21. See especially in Bevington's *Medieval Drama*: from Wakefield, *The Creation and Fall of the Angels, The Killing of Abel, The Second Shepherds' Play*; from York, *The Fall of Man*.

22. R. Howard Bloch, *The Scandal of the Fabliaux* (Chicago: University of Chicago Press, 1986), 59–100, esp. 68–70.

23. *Medieval Drama*, 569–79 (hereafter cited by line number parenthetically).

24. So outlandish is the idea of a comic crucifixion that most critics overlook the dark humor of this play and the fabliau's influence on its portrait of Christ's death. For comparison see Paul Willis, "The Weight of Sin in the York *Crucifixion*," *Leeds Studies in English* 15 (1984): 109–16.

25. "Du Prestre crucefié," in *The French Fabliau, B.N. MS. 837*, ed. and trans. Raymond Eichmann and John DuVal, 2 vols. (New York: Garland Publishing, 1985), II: 62–67.

26. Barbara Newman, *From Virile Woman to WomanChrist* (Philadelphia: University of Pennsylvania Press, 1995), 24.

27. Lochrie, 17. Citing Danielle Jacquart and Claude Thomasset, *Sexuality and Medicine in the Middle Ages*, trans. Matthew Adamson (Princeton: Princeton University

Press, 1988), 36–37, Lochrie explains that female sexual anatomy was understood to mirror male anatomy inversely inside the body; "female 'testicles,' or ovaries, were judged to be smaller, less round, and less 'fertile' than men's." See also Thomas Laquer's recent discussion of the hierarchical model of medieval sexual physiology in *Making Sex: Body and Gender from the Greeks to Freud* (Cambridge: Cambridge University Press, 1990), 1–62.

28. "De Brunain, la vache au prestre," in *The French Fabliau*, B.N. MS. 837, ed. and trans. Eichmann and DuVal, II:122–25. In this fabliau, a peasant who has been encouraged by his local priest "to give for the sake of God, / Because God would return double to him / Who gave with his heart" (7–9) decides to give his old, barely productive milk cow to the priest. The priest, unaware of the cow's relative worthlessness, is of course delighted because he imagines himself enriched through the "freely given" gifts to God he encouraged in his sermon. Much to the surprise of the peasant, the priest's promise for doubled return on investments comes true materially. The peasant's cow, lonely and unhappy in her new home with the priest but fond of her new barnmate there, returns to the peasant's home leading the priest's cow. God is materially a good doubler because he doubles the peasant's livestock and metaphorically a good doubler because he turns the priest's doubly deceptive promise against itself. He is the ultimate trickster who tricks the initial trickster.

29. Bynum, "The Body of Christ in the Later Middle Ages: A Reply to Leo Steinberg," chapter 3 in *Fragmentation and Redemption*, 100. For further discussion of Christ's nurturing, Marian qualities, see Bynum's *Jesus as Mother: Studies in the Spirituality of the High Middle Ages* (Berkeley: University of California Press, 1982) and *Holy Feast and Holy Fast: The Religious Significance of Food to Medieval Women* (Berkeley: University of California Press, 1987).

30. Specifically, Julian of Norwich, whose *Showings* is contemporary with the English cycle drama ("The Body of Christ," 418).

31. See Peter Travis, "The Social Body of the Dramatic Christ in Medieval England," in *Early Drama to 1600*, ed. Albert H. Tricomi (Binghamton: Center for Medieval and Early Renaissance Studies, 1987), 29–32, for an intriguing discussion of how Christ's fragmented *corpus* graphically reflects the progressive urban decay and decimation of community in fifteenth-century York.

32. See Newman, *From Virile Woman*, 198–209, on the popularity of "Marian Trinities."

Chapter Seven

1. Toril Moi, "Desire in Language" in *Medieval Literature: Criticism, Ideology, and History*, ed. David Aers (New York: St. Martin's Press, 1986), 29. On the femaleness of language, see also Lee Patterson, "Feminine Rhetoric and the Politics of Subjectivity: La Vieille and the Wife of Bath," in *Rethinking the Romance of the Rose*, ed. Kevin Brownlee and Sylvia Huot (Philadelphia: University of Pennsylvania Press, 1992), 316–58.

2. See Howard R. Patch, *The Tradition of Boethius: A Study of His Importance in Medieval Culture* (Oxford University Press, 1935). On the epistemology of dream vision, Kathryn L. Lynch, *The High Medieval Dream Vision: Poetry, Philosophy and Literary Form* (Stanford: Stanford University Press, 1988).

3. Boethius, *Consolation of Philosophy*, Book I, Meter 5, trans. Richard Green (Indianapolis: Bobbs-Merrill, 1962), 15.

4. On Fortune as literary character, see Howard Patch, *The Goddess Fortuna in Medieval Literature* (Cambridge: Harvard University Press, 1927).

5. See the discussion in chapter 1 of Hrotsvitha. Susan Groag Bell's research indicates that women often owned copies of the *Consolation*; "Medieval Women Book Owners," in *Women and Power in the Middle Ages*, ed. Mary Erler and Maryanne Kowaleski (Athens: University of Georgia Press, 1986), 157–58.

6. On Nature's development as literary character, see George D. Economou, *The Goddess Natura in Medieval Literature* (Cambridge: Harvard University Press, 1972).

7. Alan of Lille, *The Plaint of Nature*, trans. James J. Sheridan (Toronto: Pontifical Institute of Medieval Studies, 1980), 133.

8. Compare Sheridan's commentary on the *Plaint* with Winthrop Wetherbee, *Platonism and Poetry in the Twelfth Century* (Princeton: Princeton University Press, 1972), 187–211. A good introduction to the poem's themes is R. H. Green, "Alan of Lille's *De planctu Naturae*," *Speculum* 31 (1956): 649–74.

9. Katharina M. Wilson and Elizabeth M. Makowski, *Wykked Wyves and the Woes of Marriage: Misogamous Literature from Juvenal to Chaucer* (Albany: State University of New York Press, 1990), 19.

10. Andreas Capellanus, *The Art of Courtly Love*, trans. John Jay Parry (New York: Columbia University Press, 1941), 35. For summaries of the chief schools of interpreting Andreas, see Moi, "Desire in Language," 1–20, and Don A. Monson, "Andreas Capellanus and the Problem of Irony," *Speculum* 63 (1988): 539–72.

11. A good introduction is Maxwell Luria, *A Reader's Guide to the* Roman de la Rose (New York: Archon Books, 1982).

12. Guillaume de Lorris and Jean de Meun, *The Romance of the Rose*, trans. Charles Dahlberg (Hanover, N. H.: University Press of New England, 1983), 113.

13. David Hult, "Language and Dismemberment: Abelard, Origen, and the *Romance of the Rose*," in *Rethinking the* Romance of the Rose, ed. Brownlee and Huot, 101–30. For a differing view of linguistics in this scene, see Maureen Quilligan, "Allegory, Allegoresis, and the Deallegorization of Language: The *Roman de la rose*, the *De planctu naturae*, and the *Parlement of Foules*," in *Allegory, Myth, and Symbol*, ed. Morton W. Bloomfield, Harvard English Studies 9 (Cambridge: Harvard University Press, 1981), 165–170; and John V. Fleming, *Reason and the Lover* (Princeton: Princeton University Press, 1984), 95–135.

14. Fleming, *Reason and the Lover*, 112; and *The Roman de la Rose: A Study in Allegory and Iconography* (Princeton: Princeton University Press, 1969), 135.

15. Letter of Jean de Montreuil, *La Querelle de la Rose: Letters and Documents*, trans. Joseph L. Baird and John R. Kane, North Carolina Studies in the Romance Languages and Literatures (Chapel Hill: University of North Carolina Press, 1978), 45, 154.

16. For details of Christine's life, see Charity Cannon Willard, *Christine de Pizan: Her Life and Works* (New York: Persea, 1984).

17. Christine de Pizan, *The Book of the City of Ladies*, trans. Earl Jeffrey Richards (New York: Persea, 1982), 10.

18. Maureen Quilligan, *The Allegory of Female Authority: Christine de Pizan's Cité des Dames* (Ithaca: Cornell University Press, 1991), thoroughly examines how Marie

reinvents literary tradition. On Christine as reader of the misogynous tradition, see Susan Schibanoff, "Taking the Gold Out of Egypt: The Art of Reading as a Woman," in *Gender and Reading: Essays on Readers, Texts, and Contexts*, ed. Elizabeth A. Flynn and Patrocinio P. Schweickart (Baltimore: Johns Hopkins University Press, 1986), 83–106.

19. Augustine, *The Trinity* 15.19; quoted by Maureen Quilligan, *The Language of Allegory: Defining the Genre* (Ithaca: Cornell University Press, 1979), 160–61.

20. V.A. Kolve, "The Annunciation to Christine: Authorial Empowerment in *The Book of the City of Ladies*," in *Iconography at the Crossroads*, ed. Brendan Cassidy (Princeton: Index of Christian Art, Princeton University, 1993), 171–96.

21. Aristotle, *Generation of Animals*, 775a; Galen, *On the Usefulness of the Parts of the Body*, II: 299. Both quoted by Alcuin Blamires, *Women Defamed and Women Defended* (New York: Oxford University Press, 1992), 41, 42.

22. That Genesis taught male and female equality is a commonplace theme made popular by dispersal through the sermons of Jacques de Vitry; see Blamires, *Women Defamed*, 145.

23. See Kevin Brownlee, "Martyrdom and the Female Voice: Saint Christine in the Cité de dames," in *Images of Sainthood in Medieval Europe*, ed. Renate Blumenfeld-Kosinski and Timea Szell (Ithaca: Cornell University Press, 1991), 115–35.

Chapter Eight

1. Chaucer's *Book of the Duchess* offers a fine dream vision example of this. Chaucer also uses this metaphor transparently in poems that are not dream visions: *Troilus and Criseyde*, *The Wife of Bath's Prologue and Tale*, *The Miller's Tale*, *The Franklin's Tale*, and *The Merchant's Tale*.

2. Groundbreaking studies include Carolyn Dinshaw, *Chaucer's Sexual Poetics* (Madison: University of Wisconsin Press, 1989); H. Marshall Leicester Jr., *The Disenchanted Self: Representing the Subject in the Canterbury Tales* (Berkeley: University of California Press, 1990); and Lee Patterson, *Chaucer and the Subject of History* (Madison: University of Wisconsin Press, 1991).

3. *Virgil's Aeneid, translated into Scottish Verse*, ed. David F.C. Coldwall, Scottish Text Society, 3rd series, nos. 25, 27, 28, 30, 4 vols. (Edinburgh: Blackwood, 1957–64), Vol. II (no. 25) (1957), 339, 410, 449.

4. On England's claim to be the new Troy, see C. David Benson, *The History of Troy in Middle English Literature* (Totowa, N.J.: Rowman and Littlefield, 1980).

5. Elaine Tuttle Hansen, *Chaucer and the Fictions of Gender* (Berkeley: University of California Press, 1992), 14.

6. R. Howard Bloch, *Medieval Misogyny and the Invention of Western Romantic Love* (Chicago: University of Chicago Press, 1991), 17–22.

7. The *Eneados* does double duty: first as a narrative of Scotland's entitlement to Aeneas's historical-mythic legacy, the legendary founding of Britain, and also as a narrative of Douglas's own entitlement to the Virgilian poetic laurels, which he implies Chaucer has betrayed. See Louise Fradenburg, *City, Marriage, and Tournament: Arts of Rule in Late Medieval Scotland* (Madison: University of Wisconsin Press, 1991), 91–93.

8. Gayle Margherita, "Historicity, Femininity, and Chaucer's *Troilus*," *Exemplaria* 6 (1994): 243–70.

9. Derek Pearsall, *The Life of Geoffrey Chaucer: A Critical Biography* (Oxford: Blackwell, 1992), 138.

10. The Wife is openly doubly self-commodifying: wife by profession and by private practice. May, *The Merchant's Tale*'s victim in effect of marital rape, brokers her husband's investment in the Genesis 2 creation narrative into a narrative of her own miraculous Marian conception. In *The Clerk's Tale*, Griselda, a peasant woman whom Walter, a local nobleman, acquires in marriage by striking an agreement with her father, responds to her husband's dehumanizing tests of her virtue (he punishes her with the fictions of having murdered their daughter and son) by publicly challenging Walter's private desecration of their marital trust. Criseyde, the archetype of mythic female fickleness and betrayal, explicitly articulates her culture's brokerage of women and her dual status as private and public object of rape.

11. See Bloch, *Medieval Misogyny*, 65–91, for a discussion of early Christianity's "both at once" construction of Woman simultaneously as "devil's gateway" and "bride of Christ."

12. Christopher Cannon, "*Raptus* in the Chaumpaigne Release and a Newly Discovered Document Concerning the Life of Geoffrey Chaucer," *Speculum* 68 (1993): 74. The translation is Cannon's; the Latin text reads "omnimodas acciones tam de raptu meo tam de aliqua re vel causa." For a full text of the release, see *Chaucer's Life-Records*, ed. Martin M. Crow and Clair C. Olson (Oxford, 1966), 343.

13. For discussion of the five witnesses and their connections with the English court, see Donald R. Howard, *Chaucer: His Life, His Works, His World* (New York: Fawcett Columbine, 1987), 317; and Derek Pearsall, *The Life of Geoffrey Chaucer*, 135.

14. For further details about the discovery of the release in 1873 and related documents in 1897, see Cannon, "*Raptus*," 74–75.

15. See Howard, *Chaucer*, 317–20, and Pearsall, *The Life of Geoffrey Chaucer*, 135–38.

16. "Medieval Medical View of Women," in *Feminist Approaches to the Body in Medieval Literature*, ed. Linda Lomperis and Sarah Stanbury (Philadelphia: University of Pennsylvania Press, 1993), 147.

17. See Pearsall, *The Life of Geoffrey Chaucer*, 135, and *The Chaucer Life-Records*, 3 and 375.

18. Groundbreaking works include Carolyn Dinshaw's *Chaucer's Sexual Poetics* and Elaine Hansen's *Chaucer and the Fictions of Gender* (cited earlier). For the suggestion that Chaucer's "personal experience with *raptus* in 1380 gave him a particular awareness of the subject," see Sheila Delaney, *The Naked Text: Chaucer's Legend of Good Women* (Berkeley: University of California Press, 1994), 77, and her earlier article on the Wife of Bath, "Strategies of Silence in the Wife of Bath's Recital," *Exemplaria* 2 (1990): 49–69.

19. Cannon, "*Raptus*," 89–91: "omnimodas acciones tam de feloniis transgressionibus compotis debitis quam aliis accionibus quibuscumque." This is the new record of the Chaumpaigne release that Cannon has recently uncovered.

20. I used the terms *private* and *public* advisedly. Both the close rolls release (which characterizes the crime as rape) and the *coram rege* rolls release (which character-

izes it as "felony, etc.") are public instruments. However, Cannon's distinction between their accessibility and the resulting frequency with which they were consulted tellingly suggests their different functions.

21. *The Riverside Chaucer*, ed. Larry D. Benson (New York: Houghton Mifflin Co., 1987), 650. I assign the authorship of "Adam Scriveyn" to Chaucer advisedly. Seth Lerer, *Chaucer and His Readers* (Princeton: Princeton University Press, 1993), 121, observes that many of Chaucer's shorter poems "appear as Chaucer's because of the efforts of one productive, highly influential scribe and bibliophile, John Shirley."

22. See the discussion of the famous "morning after" scene in *Troilus and Criseyde* in which, some critics suggest, Pandarus rapes his niece Criseyde, in Margaret Jennings's "To Pryke or to Prye: Scribal Delights in the *Troilus*, Book III," *Chaucer in the Eighties*, ed. Julian N. Wasserman and Robert J. Blanch (Syracuse, NY: Syracuse University Press, 1986), 121–33.

23. Marc Drogin, *Anathema! Medieval Scribes and the History of Book Curses* (Totowa/Montclair, N.J.: Allangheld and Schram, 1983), 46–111, passim.

24. *Middle English Dictionary*, vol. 10, S-SL, 250.

25. "Adam Scriveyn," ln. 6 footnote, *The Riverside Chaucer*, 650.

26. On the depiction of the fall from paradise as a fall into language, time, and sexuality, see Alexandre Leupin, *Barbarolexis: Medieval Writing and Sexuality*, trans. Kate M. Cooper (Cambridge, Mass.: Harvard University Press, 1989), 1–16.

27. Chaucer's "portrait gallery" includes Cleopatra, Thisbe, Dido, Hypsipyle and Medea, Lucrece, Ariadne, Philomela, Phyllis, and Hypermnestra.

28. Delaney, *The Naked Text*, 216–17. Whereas in Chaucer there is the barest mention of the tongue, in Ovid it virtually takes on a life of its own: It lies "pulsing and murmuring incoherently to the dark earth," writhes "convulsively, like a snake's tail when it has newly been cut off and, dying, trie[s] to reach its mistress' feet" [*Metamorphoses*, trans. Mary M. Innes (New York: Penguin Books, 1955), 149].

29. For comparison, see John Gower's treatment of this legend in Book Five of the *Confessio Amantis*, where "ravine" serves as one of the *exempla* for the sin of avarice. As Carolyn Dinshaw has observed in "Rivalry, Rape and Manhood: Gower and Chaucer," Gower's depiction of Tereus's behavior as mad, even bestial, paired with his inclusion of the cannibalism episode, paints a portrait of rape that is "spectacularly anomalous" (136). In *Chaucer and Gower: Difference, Mutuality, Exchange*, ed. R. F. Yeager (Victoria: University of Victoria English Literary Studies, 1991).

30. *Telling Classical Tales: Chaucer and the Legend of Good Women* (Ithaca: Cornell University Press, 1983), 112.

31. Hansen, *Chaucer and the Fictions of Gender*, 26–27.

32. In its divided sense of her voice, much of the criticism that explores the Wife's status as complex combination of verisimilar character and stereotype finds itself positioned within the very dichotomies the Wife's prologue unmasks. It is an easy kind of critical slippage, perhaps because the Mary-Eve dichotomy is still so pervasive in our own culture.

33. For the sources and analogues, see Helen Cooper, *Oxford Guides to Chaucer: The Canterbury Tales* (Oxford: Oxford University Press, 1989), 139–66. For a collection of contextual texts see *Chaucer: Sources and Backgrounds*, ed. Robert P. Miller (New York: Oxford University Press, 1977).

34. John Gower, *Confessio Amantis*, ed. Russell A. Peck (Toronto: University of Toronto Press, 1980), 58–72.

35. *Medieval English Literature*, ed. Thomas J. Garbaty (Toronto: D.C. Heath and Company, 1984), 418–39.

36. Geoffrey of Monmouth, *The History of the Kings of Britain*, trans. Lewis Thorpe (New York: Penguin Books, 1966), 208.

37. For a diametrically opposed reading, see Robert J. Blanch, "'Al was this land fulfild of fayerye': The Thematic Employment of Force, Willfulness, and Legal Conventions in Chaucer's *Wife of Bath's Tale*," *Studia Neophilologica* 57 (1985): 41–51.

38. *Chaucer and the Law* (Norman, Okla.: Pilgrim Books, 1988), 119.

39. Cannon, "*Raptus*," 82; see 79–84, passim. See as well Kathryn Gravdal's discussion of critics and historians who dispute the theory of victim-precipitated rape in *Ravishing Maidens: Writing Rape in Medieval French Literature and Law* (Philadelphia: University of Pennsylvania Press, 1991), 147.

40. The legal statutes on record at the end of the fourteenth century make rape punishable by death. In practice, however, a large percentage of the men who appealed for rape were not punished with the full force allowed by statute; rather, they were either merely fined or found not guilty (Hornsby, *Chaucer and the Law*, 119–20). As Cannon emphasizes, although intended to prosecute crimes that violated female consent, by the end of the fourteenth century rape law in practice "effectively transferred the concern of the law from the wrong done to the woman who had been 'ravished' to the rights of her family and its interests" (81).

41. Cannon, "*Raptus*," 81; J.A. Brundage, "Rape and Marriage in the Medieval Canon Law," *Revue de droit canonique* 28 (1978): 74.

42. Cannon, "*Raptus*," 89–90: "a principio mundi usque in diem confeccionis presencium."

Chapter Nine

1. Eugene TeSelle, "Augustine," in *An Introduction to the Medieval Mystics of Europe*, ed. Paul Szarmach (Albany: State University of New York Press, 1984), 19–35.

2. Caroline Walker Bynum, *Jesus as Mother* (Berkeley: University of California Press, 1982), 1–21.

3. Elizabeth Petroff, *Body and Soul* (Oxford: Oxford University Press, 1994), 7. For a broad range of primary texts complemented by useful critical introductions to the varieties of female religious experience in the Middle Ages, see Petroff's *Medieval Women's Visionary Literature* (New York: Oxford University Press, 1986). On the varieties of mysticism, see Szarmach's collection of essays (cited earlier).

4. Barbara Newman, *From Virile Woman to WomanChrist* (Philadelphia: University of Pennsylvania Press, 1995), 317–20.

5. Bynum, *Jesus as Mother*, 14–15; Petroff, *Medieval Women's Visionary Literature*, 171–78.

6. These include normal physical sight, bodily seeing, symbolic vision, and anagogic vision (Petroff, *Body and Soul*, 6).

7. Caroline Walker Bynum, *Fragmentation and Redemption: Essays on Gender and the Human Body in Medieval Religion* (New York: Zone, 1991), 194.

8. Bonaventure, *Itinerarium in Mentis Deum*, trans. Philotheus Boehner (Saint Bonaventure, N.Y.: Saint Bonaventure University Press, 1956).

9. Quoted in Newman, 22–23.

10. Elizabeth Robertson, "Medieval Medical Views of Women and Female Spirituality in the *Ancrene Wisse* and Julian of Norwich's *Showings*," *Feminist Approaches to the Body in Medieval Literature*, ed. Linda Lomperis and Sarah Stanbury (Philadelphia: University of Pennsylvania Press, 1994), 148.

11. Newman, 20–21: writings for "training professed religious in the spiritual life, practice of virtues, and communal and private discipline" that include "instruction for novices; commentaries on religious rules; works of guidance for solitaries; letters of direction to individual monks, nuns and recluses; and treatises dealing with aspects of spirituality and the common life."

12. On the paradoxes attending the Christian ideal of equality between the genders grounded in Saint Paul, Gal. 3:28, see R. Howard Bloch, *Medieval Misogyny and the Invention of Western Romantic Love* (Chicago: University of Chicago Press, 1991), 66–68.

13. Kathryn Gravdal, *Ravishing Maidens: Writing Rape in Medieval French Literature and Law* (Philadelphia: University of Pennsylvania Press, 1991), 5.

14. Quoted in Newman, 286, n. 20.

15. Paraphrase by Newman, 158, of Margret Bäurle and Luzia Braun, "'Ich bin heiser in der Kehle meiner Keuschheit': Über das Schreiben der Mystikerinnen," in *Frauen Literatur und Geschichte: Schreibende Frauen vom Mittelalter bis zur Gegenwart*, ed. Hiltrud Gnüg and Renate Möhrmann (Stuttgart, 1985), 1–15.

16. Julian of Norwich, *Showings*, trans. and ed. Edmund Colledge and James Walsh (New York: Paulist Press, 1978).

17. Colledge and Walsh, *Showings*, 17–118, passim. These include Augustine's *Confessions*; Boethius's *Consolation of Philosophy*; works on contemplative prayer by Gregory the Great, Bernard of Clairvaux, and William of Saint Thierry; and works on scholastic metaphysics, especially those of Thomas Aquinas.

18. Sarah Beckwith, "A Very Material Mysticism: The Medieval Mysticism of Margery Kempe" in *Medieval Literature: Criticism, Ideology and History*, ed. David Aers (New York: St. Martin's Press, 1986), 55, n. 4.

19. Petroff, *MWVL*, 299–301; Margery Kempe, *The Book of Margery Kempe*, trans. Barry Windeatt (New York: Penguin Books, 1985), 71–81.

20. For a discussion of medieval theories of moisture, including tears, as the primary female humor, see Elizabeth Robertson, "Medieval Medical Views of Women," 144–48.

21. "Medieval Medical Views of Women," 161. By "Irigarayan," Robertson has in mind the feminist Luce Irigaray's sense that difference can be reinvented, that women writing within a culture that constructs them as inferior can rework existing misogynic stereotypes.

22. Nancy Coiner, "'The Homely' and the *Heimliche*: The Hidden, Doubled Self in Julian of Norwich's *Showings*," *Exemplaria* 5 (1993): 319–20; Coiner's emphasis.

23. Robertson, "Medieval Medical Views of Women," 154; 145–48. For an edition of the handbook, see Beryl Rowland, *Medieval Woman's Guide to Health: The First English Gynecological Handbook* (Kent, Ohio: Kent State University Press, 1981).

24. Rowland, 61. Other symptoms that Julian echoes include heaviness of thighs, hips, hands, and legs as well as difficulty with vision.

25. ST, 13, 146. Although in the *Long Text* the merriment of the scene is more subdued, the joy is as intensely expressed. Christ actually invites Julian's "understanding into his side by the same wound … large enough for all mankind that will be saved and will rest in peace and love" (LT, 24, 220).

26. See Robertson, "Medieval Medical Views of Women," 144–46. For detailed discussion of Galenic theories, see Danielle Jacquart and Claude Thomasset, *Sexuality and Medicine in the Middle Ages*, trans. Matthew Adamson (Princeton: Princeton University Press, 1988), 12–80.

27. Barry Windeatt, "Introduction," *The Book of Margery Kempe* (cited above), 17–22, passim. Windeatt suggests that the illiterate Margery gains her detailed knowledge of the four devotional works that influence her narrative most (i.e., the *Stimulus Amoris* [the Middle English *Prick of Love*]. Walter Hilton's *The Scale of Perfection*; Richard Rolle's *Incendium Amoris*; Saint Bridget of Sweden's *Revelations*) by listening to others read. Her narrative includes a host of allusions to other female visionaries as well (Mary of Oignies, Elizabeth of Hungary, Mechthild of Hackeborn, Catherine of Siena, Elisabeth of Schönau, Angela of Foligno, and Dorothea of Montau), whom Margery hears of from those who read to her or discuss their religious reflections with her.

28. David Aers, *Community, Gender, and Individual Identity: English Writing, 1360–1430* (London: Routledge, 1988), 75. For Margery's description of her two business ventures, see I:2, 44–45.

29. Sheila Delaney, "Sexual Economics, Chaucer's Wife of Bath and *The Book of Margery Kempe*," *Writing Woman* (New York: Schocken, 1983), 86.

30. Newman, 91; Laura Howes, "On the Birth of Margery Kempe's Last Child," *Modern Philology* 90 (1992): 220–25.

31. II:7, 282; n. 7:1, 329. The other three relics are the swaddling clothes of Jesus, the cloth that received Saint John the Baptist's head, and the loin cloth Christ wore on the cross.

32. See "'A Very Material Mysticism'," as well as "Problems of Authority in Late Medieval English Mysticism: Language, Agency, and Authority in *The Book of Margery Kempe*," *Exemplaria* 4 (1992): 175.

33. Beckwith, "A Very Material Mysticism," 39–40. Beckwith would characterize Margery but not Julian in this way; she sees the kind of enclosure that Julian chooses as an acceptance of the traditional patriarchal hierarchies of her time. For an intriguing contrasting perspective, see Nancy Coiner, "'The Homely' and the *Heimliche*," 322–23.

34. Karma Lochrie, *Margery Kempe and Translations of the Flesh* (Philadelphia: University of Pennsylvania Press, 1991), 147. Lochrie compares her with the valiant woman from Proverbs 31:25 who laughs at the Last Judgment.

Epilogue

1. Sheila Delaney, "'Mothers to Think Back Through': Who Are They? The Ambiguous Example of Christine de Pizan," in *Medieval Texts and Contemporary Readers*, ed. Laurie A. Finke and Martin B. Schichtman (Ithaca: Cornell University Press, 1987), 187; 181; 177–97.

2. Steven Ozment, *The Age of Reform, 1250–1550: An Intellectual and Religious History of Late Medieval and Reformation Europe* (New Haven: Yale University Press, 1980).

3. Bonnie S. Anderson and Judith P. Zinsser, "Authority Given and Taken Away: The Protestant and Catholic Reformations," in *A History of Their Own*, Vol. I (New York: Harper & Row, 1988), 228–52.

4. Sir Philip Sidney, *Astrophel and Stella*, Sonnet 2:2, in *The Norton Anthology of English Literature*, Vol. 1, General ed. M. H. Abrams, 5th ed. (New York: Norton, 1962, rpt. 1986). All citations of postmedieval literature will be to the works as printed in the Norton.

5. David N. Bell, *What Nuns Read: Books and Libraries in Medieval English Nunneries* (Kalamazoo: Cistercian, 1995), 67, makes the comparison of England to the continent. On Muriel, see J. S. P. Tatlock, "Muriel: The Earliest English Poetess," *PMLA* 48 (1933): 317–21.

6. M. D. Legge, *Anglo-Norman Literature and Its Background* (Oxford: Oxford University Press, 1963), 60–72, 264–66.

7. Alexandra Barratt, ed., *Women's Writing in Middle English* (New York: Longman, 1992), 205–18.

8. Barratt, *Women's Writing*, 163–76. The full text of *A Revelation* is printed in *Yorkshire Writers: Richard Rolle of Hampole and his Followers*, ed. C. Horstmann, 2 vols. (London, 1895–96), I: 33–92.

9. More letters of the Paston men and women can be found in *The Paston Letters: A Selection in Modern Spelling*, ed. N. Davis (Oxford: Oxford University Press, 1963). For commentary on the Paston women, see Frances Gies and Joseph Gies, *Women in the Middle Ages* (New York: Harper and Row, 1978), 210–28; and Diane Watt, "No Writing for Writing's Sake: The Language of Service and Household Rhetoric in the Letters of the Paston Women," in *Dear Sister*, ed. Karen Cherewatuk and Ulrike Wiethus (Philadelphia: University of Pennsylvania Press, 1993), 122–38.

10. *The Floure and the Leafe, The Assembly of Ladies, and The Isle of Ladies*, ed. Derek Pearsall (Kalamazoo: Medieval Institute Publications, 1990). See Alexandra A. T. Barratt, " 'The Flower and the Leaf' and 'The Assembly of Ladies': Is There a (Sexual) Difference?" *Philological Quarterly* 66 (1987): 1–24; and Ann McMillan, " 'Fayre Sisters Al': *The Flower and the Leaf* and *The Assembly of Ladies*," *Tulsa Studies in Women's Literature* 1 (1982): 27–42.

11. For a checklist of female-voiced lyrics, see John Plummer, *Vox Feminae* (Kalamazoo: Medieval Institute Publications, 1981), 151–52. On the Findern manuscript: Elizabeth Hanson-Smith, "A Woman's View of Courtly Love: The Findern Anthology," *Journal of Women's Studies in Literature* 1 (1979): 179–94; Sarah McNamer, "Female Authors, Provincial Setting: The Re-Versing of Courtly Love in the Finden Manuscript," *Viator* 22 (1991): 279–310.

12. Gwendolyn Bryant, "The French Heretic Beguine: Marguerite Porete," in *Medieval Women Writers*, ed. Katharina M. Wilson (Athens: University of Georgia Press, 1984), 204–26.

13. See the essays by Bella Millett and Felicity Riddy in *Women and Literature in Britain, 1150–1500*, ed. Carol M. Meale (Cambridge: Cambridge University Press, 1993), 86–127. Also David Bell, *What Nuns Read*, 71–79.

14. The English women are Eleanor Hull (1394–1460), who translated *The Seven Psalms*, a thirteenth-century French commentary on the penitential psalms, and *Meditations upon the Seven Days of the Week* (219–31); and Margaret Beaufort (1443–1509), mother of Henry VII, who translated a portion of Thomas à Kempis's *Imitation of Christ* and a religious treatise, *The Mirror of Gold*, from French versions (301–10). The continental women's books translated into English are Gertrude the Great's record of Mechtild of Hackeborn's visions (ca. 1295) — in English called *The Book of Ghostly Grace*; *The Revelations of Saint Elizabeth of Hungary* (1294–1336); Marguerite Porete's *The Mirror of Simple Souls*; Catherine of Siena's *Dialogue* translated as *The Orchard of Syon*; and Bridget of Sweden's visionary *Liber Coelestis*.

15. Julia Boffey, "Women Authors and Women's Literature in Fourteenth- and Fifteenth-Century England," in *Women and Literature*, ed. Carol M. Meale (Cambridge: Cambridge University Press, 1993), 159–82.

16. Susan Groag Bell, "Medieval Woman Book Owners," in *Women and Power in the Middle Ages*, ed. Mary Erler and Maryanne Kowalewski (Athens: University of Georgia Press, 1986), 149–87; see also Carol M. Meale, "Laywomen and Their Books in Late Medieval England," in *Women and Literature*, ed. Meale, 128–58.

17. Elizabeth Robertson, *Early English Devotional Prose and the Female Audience* (Knoxville: University of Tennessee Press, 1990); Anne Clark Barlett, *Male Authors, Female Readers: Representation and Subjectivity in Middle English Devotional Literature* (Ithaca: Cornell University Press, 1995); Roberta L. Krueger, *Women Readers and the Ideology of Gender in Old French Verse Romance* (Cambridge: Cambridge University Press, 1993).

18. Alice Adèle Hentsch, *De la littérature didactique du moyen âge s'adressant spécialment aux femmes* (1903; rpt. Geneva: Slatkine, 1975); Diane Bornstein, *The Lady in the Tower: Medieval Courtesy Literature for Women* (Hamden, Conn.: Archon Books, 1983).

19. Lives of holy women were written especially to provide models of behavior. For the French tradition, see Bridgitte Cazelles, ed. and trans., *The Lady as Saint: A Collection of French Hagiographic Romances of the Thirteenth Century* (Philadelphia: University of Pennsylvania Press, 1991). In English, see the texts written for anchorites, *Anchoritic Spirituality*, ed. Anne Savage and Nicholas Watson (New York: Paulist Press, 1991) and *Heroic Women from the Old Testament in Middle English Verse*, ed. Russell A. Peck (Kalamazoo: Medieval Institute Publications, 1991).

20. P.J.P. Goldberg, *Women, Work, and the Life Cycle in a Medieval Economy: Women in York and Yorkshire c. 1300–1520* (Oxford: Oxford University Press, 1992), 26.

Selected Bibliography

Because complete bibliographic information is given in the notes to individual chapters, the entries here are not comprehensive; they represent, rather, those texts the authors thought readers would find most useful for future reading on medieval literary women and the Middle Ages in general.

Primary Sources

Amt, Emilie, ed. *Women's Lives in Medieval Europe: A Sourcebook*. New York: Routledge, 1993.

Anchoritic Spirituality: Ancrene Wisse and Associated Works. Ed. Anne Savage and Nicholas Watson. New York: Paulist Press, 1991.

Andreas Capellanus. *The Art of Courtly Love.*, Trans. John J. Parry, New York: Columbia University Press, 1941. Rpt. W. W. Norton, 1969.

The Anglo-Saxon Poetic Records: A Collective Edition. 6 volumes. Ed. George Philip Krapp and Elliott Van Kirk Dobbie. New York: Columbia University Press, 1931–53.

Barratt, Alexandra, ed. *Women's Writing in Middle English*. London and New York: Longman, 1992.

Beowulf. Ed. Frederic Klaeber. Lexington, Mass.: D. C. Heath, 1922.

Béroul. *The Romance of Tristan*. Trans. Alan S. Fedrick. New York: Penguin, 1970.

Blamires, Alcuin, ed. *Woman Defamed and Woman Defended: An Anthology of Medieval Texts*. New York: Oxford University Press, 1992.

Boethius. *Consolation of Philosophy*. Trans. Richard Green. Indianapolis: Bobbs-Merrill, 1962.

Bogin, Meg. *The Women Troubadours*. New York: Paddington, 1976.

Chaucer, Geoffrey. *The Riverside Chaucer*. Ed. Larry D. Benson. Boston: Houghton Mifflin Co., 1987.

The Chester Mystery Cycle. 2 volumes. Ed. Robert Lumiansky and David Mill. Early English Text Society SS 3 and 9. London: Oxford University Press, 1974–86.

Chrétien de Troyes. *Arthurian Romances*. Trans. William W. Kibler. New York: Penguin, 1991.

Christine de Pizan. *The Book of the City of Ladies*. Trans. Earl Jeffrey Richards. New York: Persea, 1982.

——. *A Medieval Woman's Mirror of Honor: The Treasury of the City of Ladies*. New York: Persea, 1989.

Eichmann, Raymond, and John DuVal, ed. and trans. *The French Fabliau, B.N. MS. 837*, 2 volumes. New York: Garland, 1985.

Goldin, Frederick. *Lyrics of the Troubadours and Trouvères: An Anthology and History*. Gloucester, Mass.: Peter Smith, 1983.

Guillaume de Lorris and Jean de Meun. *The Romance of the Rose*. Trans. Charles Dahlberg. Hanover, N.H.: University Press of New England, 1983.

Heldris de Cornuälle. *Silence: A Thirteenth-Century French Romance*. Ed. and trans. Sarah Roche-Mahdi. East Lansing, Mich.: Colleagues, 1992.

Heroic Women from the Old Testament in Middle English Verse. Ed. Russell A. Peck. Kalamazoo: Medieval Institute Publications for TEAMS, 1991.

Hrotsvithrot of Gandersheim. *The Plays of Hrotsvit of Gandersheim*. Trans. Katherina Wilson. New York: Garland, 1989.

Jean d'Arras. *Roman de Melusine*. Trans. Sara Sturm-Maddox and Donald Maddox. New York: Garland, 1995.

Julian of Norwich. *Showings*. Trans. Edmund Colledge and James Walsh. New York: Paulist Press, 1978.

Kempe, Margery. *The Book of Margery Kempe*. Trans. Barry Windeatt. New York: Penguin, 1985.

The Letters of Abelard and Heloise. Ed. and trans. Betty Radice. New York: Penguin, 1974.

Malory, Sir Thomas. *Le Morte D'Arthur*. 2 volumes. Ed. Janet Cowen. New York: Penguin, 1969.

Marie de France. *The Lais of Marie de France*. Trans. Robert Hanning and Joan Ferrante. Durham, N.C.: Labyrinth Press, 1978.

——. *Saint Patrick's Purgatory: A Poem by Marie de France*. Ed. and trans. Michael J. Curley. Binghamton: MRTS, 1993.

Medieval Drama. Ed. David Bevington. Boston: Houghton Mifflin Co., 1975.

Medieval Women's Guide to Health: The First English Gynecological Handbook. Ed. and trans. Beryl Rowland. Kent, Ohio: Kent State University Press, 1981.

Medieval Women's Visionary Literature. Ed. Elizabeth Petroff. New York: Oxford University Press, 1986.

Ovid. *Metamorphoses*. Trans. Mary M. Innes. New York: Penguin Books, 1955.

[Pearl Poet]. *The Complete Works of the Pearl Poet*. Ed. Malcolm Andrew, Ronald Waldron, and Clifford Peterson. Trans. Casey Finch. Berkeley: University of California Press, 1993.

La Querelle de la Rose: Letters and Documents. Trans. Joseph L. Baird and John R. Kane. North Carolina Studies in the Romance Languages and Literatures. Chapel Hill: University of North Carolina Press, 1978.

Religious Lyrics of the XIIIth Century. Ed. Carleton Brown. Oxford: Oxford University Press, 1932.

Religious Lyrics of the XIVth Century. Ed. Carleton Brown. Oxford: Oxford University Press, 1924. 2d ed. rev. G. V. Smithers. Oxford: Oxford University Press, 1956.

Religious Lyrics of the XVth Century. Ed. Carleton Brown. Oxford: Oxford University Press, 1939.

Rieger, Angelica, ed. *Trobairitz*. Tubingen: Max Niemeyer, 1991.

Rumble, Thomas C., ed. *The Breton Lays in Middle English*. Detroit: Wayne State University Press, 1965.

The Songs of the Women Troubadours. Ed. Matilda Tomaryn Bruckner, Laurie Shepard, and Sarah White. New York: Garland, 1995.

Three Medieval Views of Women. Ed. and trans. Gloria K. Fiero, Wendy Pfeffer, and Mathé Allain. New Haven: Yale University Press, 1989.

The Towneley Plays. Ed. George England and Alfred W. Pollard. Early English Text Society ES 71. London: Oxford University Press, 1897. Rpt. 1966.

Wilson, Katharina M., ed. *Medieval Women Writers*. Athens: University of Georgia Press, 1984.

The York Plays. Ed. Richard Beadle. York Medieval Texts. Baltimore: Arnold, 1982.

Secondary Sources

Aers, David. *Community, Gender, and Individual Identity: English Writing, 1360–1430*. New York: Routledge, 1988.

———, ed. *Medieval Literature: Criticism, Ideology and History*. New York: St. Martin's Press, 1986.

Anderson, Bonnie S., and Judith P. Zinsser. *A History of Their Own*, Vol. I. New York: Harper and Row, 1988.

Baker, Derek, ed. *Medieval Women*. Studies in Church History: Subsidia I. Oxford: Basil Blackwell, 1978.

Bal, Mieke. "Sexuality, Sin and Sorrow: The Emergence of Female Character (A Reading of Genesis 1–3)." *Poetics Today* 6 (1985): 21–42.

Bell, David N. *What Nuns Read: Books and Libraries in Medieval English Nunneries*. Cistercian Studies Series #158. Kalamazoo: Cistercian Publications, 1995.

Bell, Susan Groag. "Medieval Women Book Owners: Arbiters of Lay Piety and Ambassadors of Culture." In *Women and Power in the Middle Ages*. Ed. Mary Erler and Maryanne Kowaleski. Athens: University of Georgia Press, 1988.

Bloch, R. Howard. *The Scandal of the Fabliaux*. Chicago: University of Chicago Press, 1986.

———. *Medieval Misogyny and the Invention of Western Romantic Love*. Chicago: University of Chicago Press, 1991.

Boase, Roger. *The Origin and Meaning of Courtly Love: A Critical Study of European Scholarship*. Totowa, N. J.: Rowan and Littlefield, 1977.

Bridenthal, Renate, and Claudia Koontz, eds. *Becoming Visible: Women in European History*. Boston: Houghton Mifflin, 1977.

Brown, Peter. *The Body and Society: Men, Women and Sexual Renunciation in Early Christianity*. New York: Columbia University Press, 1988.

Brownlee, Kevin, and Sylvia Huot, eds. *Rethinking the Romance of the Rose: Text, Image, Reception*. Philadelphia: University of Pennsylvania Press, 1992.

Brundage, J. A. *Law, Sex, and Christian Society in Medieval Europe*. Chicago: University of Chicago Press, 1987.

Burns, E. Jane. *Bodytalk: When Women Speak in Old French Literature*. Philadelphia: University of Pennsylvania Press, 1993.

Bynum, Caroline Walker. *Jesus as Mother: Studies in the Spirituality of the High Middle Ages*. Berkeley: University of California Press, 1982.

———. *Holy Feast and Holy Fast: The Religious Significance of Food to Medieval Women*. Berkeley: University of California Press, 1987.

———. *Fragmentation and Redemption: Essays on Gender and the Human Body in Medieval Religion*. New York: Zone, 1991.

Camille, Michael. *The Gothic Image*. Chicago: University of Chicago Press, 1989.

Cannon, Christopher. "*Raptus* in the Chaumpaigne Release and a Newly Discovered Document Concerning the Life of Geoffrey Chaucer." *Speculum* 68 (1993): 74–94.

Chance, Jane. *Woman as Hero in Old English Literature*. Syracuse: Syracuse University Press, 1986.

Cherewatok, Karen, and Ulrike Wiethaus, eds. *Dear Sister: Medieval Women and the Epistolary Genre*. Philadelphia: University of Pennsylvania Press, 1993.

Coiner, Nancy. "The 'Homely' and the *Heimliche*: The Hidden, Doubled Self in Julian of Norwich's *Showings*." *Exemplaria* 5 (1993): 305–24.

Coletti, Theresa. "Purity and Danger: The Paradox of Mary's Body and the En-gendering of the Infancy Narrative in the English Mystery Cycles," in *Feminist Approaches to the Body in Medieval Literature*. Ed. Linda Lomperis and Sarah Stanbury. Philadelphia: University of Pennsylvania Press, 1993.

Damico, Helen, and Alexandra Hennessey Olsen, eds. *New Readings on Women in Old English Literature*. Bloomington: Indiana University Press, 1990.

Delaney, Sheila. " 'Mothers to Think Back Through': Who are They? The Ambiguous Example of Christine de Pizan." In *Medieval Texts and Contemporary Readers*. Ed. Laurie A. Finke and Martin B. Schichtman. Ithaca: Cornell University Press, 1987, 177–97.

———. *The Naked Text: Chaucer's Legend of Good Women*. Berkeley: University of California Press, 1994.

Dinshaw, Carolyn. *Chaucer's Sexual Poetics*. Madison: University of Wisconsin Press, 1989.

Dronke, Peter. *Women Writers of the Middle Ages*. Cambridge: Cambridge University Press, 1986.

Duby, George. *The Knight, the Lady, and the Priest: The Making of Modern Marriage in Medieval France*. Trans. Barbara Bray. New York: Pantheon Books, 1983.

Erler, Mary, and Maryanne Kowaleski, eds. *Women and Power in the Middle Ages*. Athens: University of Georgia Press, 1986.

Fell, Christine. *Women in Anglo-Saxon England*. London: British Museum Publications, 1984.

Ferrante, Joan. *Woman as Image in Medieval Literature*. New York: Columbia University Press, 1975.

Fisher, Sheila, and Janet E. Halley. *Seeking the Woman in Late Medieval and Renaissance Writings: Essays in Feminist Contextual Criticism*. Knoxville: University of Tennessee Press, 1989.

Frantzen, Allen J., ed. *Speaking Two Languages: Traditional Disciplines and Contemporary Theory in Medieval Studies*. Binghamton: State University of New York Press, 1991.

Gies, Frances, and Joseph Gies. *Women in the Middle Ages*. New York: Harper and Row, 1978.

Goldin, Frederick. *The Mirror of Narcissus in the Courtly Love Lyric*. Ithaca: Cornell University Press, 1967.

Gravdal, Kathryn. *Ravishing Maidens: Writing Rape in Medieval French Literature and Law*. Philadelphia: University of Pennsylvania Press, 1991.

Hanawalt, Barbara, ed. *Chaucer's England: Literature in Historical Context*. Minneapolis: University of Minnesota Press, 1992.

Hansen, Elaine Tuttle. *Chaucer and the Fictions of Gender*. Berkeley: University of California Press, 1992.

Herlihy, David. *Opera Muliebria: Women and Work in Medieval Europe*. New York: McGraw-Hill, 1990.

Hollier, Denis, ed. *A New History of French Literature*. Cambridge, Mass.: Harvard University Press, 1989.

Howard, Donald R. *Chaucer: His Life, His Works, His World*. New York: Fawcett Columbine, 1987.

Howell, Martha C. *Women, Production, and Patriarchy in Late Medieval Cities*. Chicago: University of Chicago Press, 1986.

Jacquart, Danielle, and Claude Thomasset. *Sexuality and Medicine in the Middle Ages*. Trans. Matthew Adamson. Princeton: Princeton University Press, 1988.

Jean, Joan de, and Nancy K. Miller, eds. *Displacements: Women, Tradition, and Literatures in French*. Baltimore: Johns Hopkins University Press, 1991.

Kanner, Barbara, ed. *The Women of England*. Hamden, Conn.: Archon Books, 1979.

Kay, Sarah. *Subjectivity in Troubadour Poetry*. Cambridge: Cambridge University Press, 1990.

Kolve, V. A. *The Play Called Corpus Christi*. Stanford: Stanford University Press, 1966.

Krueger, Roberta L. *Women Readers and the Ideology of Gender in Old French Verse Romance*. Cambridge: Cambridge University Press, 1993.

Labarge, Margaret Wade. *A Small Sound of the Trumpet: Women in Medieval Life*. Boston: Beacon Press, 1986.

Laquer, Thomas. *Making Sex: Body and Gender from the Greeks to Freud*. Cambridge: Cambridge University Press, 1990.

Lees, Clare A., ed. *Medieval Masculinities: Regarding Men in the Middle Ages*. Minneapolis: University of Minnesota Press, 1994.

Leicester Jr., H. Marshall. *The Disenchanted Self: Representing the Subject in the Canterbury Tales*. Berkeley: University of California Press, 1990.

Lerer, Seth. *Chaucer and His Readers*. Princeton: Princeton University Press, 1993.

Leupin, Alexandre. *Barbarolexis: Medieval Writing and Sexuality*. Trans. Kate M. Cooper. Cambridge: Harvard University Press, 1989.

Lewis, C. S. *Allegory of Love*. Oxford: Oxford University Press, 1936.

Lochrie, Karma. *Margery Kempe and Translations of the Flesh*. Philadelphia: University of Pennsylvania Press, 1991.

Lomperis, Linda, and Sarah Stanbury, eds. *Feminist Approaches to the Body in Medieval Literature*. Philadelphia: University of Pennsylvania Press, 1993.

Lucas, Angela M. *Women in the Middle Ages: Religion, Marriage, and Letters*. New York: St. Martin's, 1983.

Meale, Carol M., ed. *Women and Literature in Britain, 1150–1500*. Cambridge, England: Cambridge University Press, 1993.

Moi, Toril. "Desire In Language." In *Medieval Literature: Criticism, Ideology and History*, ed. David Aers. Brighton, Sussex: Harvester Press, 1986.

Mickel, Emanuel J. *Marie de France*. New York: Twayne, 1974.

Monson, Don A. "Andreas Capellanus and the Problem of Irony." *Speculum* 63 (1988): 539–72.

Newman, Barbara. *From Virile Woman to WomanChrist: Studies in Medieval Religion and Literature*. Philadelphia: University of Pennsylvania Press, 1995.

Newman, F.X., ed. *The Meaning of Courtly Love*. Albany: State University of New York Press, 1968.

Nichols, John A., and Lillian Thomas Shank, eds. *Distant Echoes*. Medieval Religious Women, Vol. 1. Kalamazoo: Cistercian, 1984.

———. *Peace-Weavers: Medieval Religious Women*, Vol. 2. Kalamazoo: Cistercian, 1987.

Nicholson, Lewis E., and Dolores Warwick Frese, eds. *Anglo-Saxon Poetry: Essays in Appreciation*. Notre Dame: University of Notre Dame Press, 1975.

Overing, Gillian. *Language, Sign and Gender in* Beowulf. Carbondale: Southern Illinois University Press, 1990.

Ozment, Steven. *The Age of Reform, 1250–1550: An Intellectual and Religious History of Late Medieval and Reformation Europe*. New Haven: Yale University Press, 1980.

Paden, William D., ed. *The Voice of the Trobairitz: Perspectives on the Women Troubadors*. Philadelphia: University of Pennsylvania Press, 1989.

Partner, Nancy F., ed. "Studying Medieval Women: Sex, Gender, Feminism." Special issue of *Speculum* 68 (April 1993).

Patterson, Lee. *Negotiating the Past: The Historical Understanding of Medieval Literature*. Madison: University of Wisconsin Press, 1987.

———. *Chaucer and the Subject of History*. Madison: University of Wisconsin Press, 1989.

Pearsall, Derek. *Old English and Middle English Poetry*. Boston: Routledge, 1977.

———. *The Life of Geoffrey Chaucer: A Critical Biography*. Oxford: Blackwell, 1992.

Petroff, Elizabeth Avilda. *Body and Soul: Essays on Medieval Women and Mysticism*. Oxford: Oxford University Press, 1994.

———, ed. *Medieval Women's Visionary Literature*. Oxford: Oxford University Press, 1986.

Plummer, John F., ed. *Vox Feminae: Studies in Medieval Woman's Song*. Studies in Medieval Culture, XV. Kalamazoo: Medieval Institute Publications, 1981.

Quilligan, Maureen. *The Allegory of Female Authority: Christine de Pizan's Cité des Dames*. Ithaca: Cornell University Press, 1991.

Reiter, Rayna, ed. *Towards an Anthropology of Women*. New York: Monthly Review, 1975.

Robertson, D.W. Jr. *Preface to Chaucer: Studies in Medieval Perspectives*. Princeton: Princeton University Press, 1962.

———. *Essays in Medieval Culture*. Princeton: Princeton University Press, 1980.

Robertson, Elizabeth. *Early English Devotional Prose and the Female Audience*. Knoxville: University of Tennessee Press, 1990.

———. "Medieval Medical View of Women." In *Feminist Approaches to the Body in Medieval Literature*. Ed. Linda Lomperis and Sarah Stanbury. Philadelphia: University of Philadelphia Press, 1993, 142–67.

Rose, Mary Beth, ed. *Women in the Middle Ages and the Renaissance: Literary and Historical Perspectives*. Syracuse: Syracuse University Press, 1986.

Rubin, Miri. *Corpus Christi: The Eucharist in Late Medieval Culture*. Cambridge: Cambridge University Press, 1991.

Sartori, Eva Martin, ed. *French Women Writers: A Bio-Bibliographical Source Book*. New York: Greenwood, 1991.

Schaus, Margaret, and Susan Mosher Stuard. "Citizens of No Mean City: Medieval Women's History." *Choice* (December 1992): 583–95.

Shahar, Shulamith. *The Fourth Estate: A History of Women in the Middle Ages*. Trans. Chaya Galai. London and New York: Methuen, 1983. Rpt. Routledge, 1990.

Smalley, Beryl. *The Study of the Bible in the Middle Ages*. Notre Dame: University of Notre Dame Press, 1978.

Southern, R. W. *Western Society and the Church in the Middle Ages*. New York: Penguin, 1970.

Stallybrass, Peter, ed. "Boundary and Transgression in Medieval Culture." *Stanford French Review* (Special Issue) 14 (1990).

Stallybrass, Peter, and Allon White. *The Politics and Poetics of Transgression*. Ithaca: Cornell University Press, 1986.

Szarmach, Paul E. *An Introduction to the Medieval Mystics of Europe*. Albany: State University of New York Press, 1984.

Tricomi, Albert H. *Early Drama to 1600*. Binghamton: Center for Medieval and Early Renaissance Studies, 1987.

Warner, Marina. *Alone of All Her Sex: The Myth and the Cult of the Virgin Mary*. New York: Knopf, 1976. Rpt. New York: Vintage, 1983.

Wiethaus, Ulrike, ed. *Maps of Flesh and Light: The Religious Experience of Medieval Women Mystics*. Syracuse: Syracuse University Press, 1993.

Willard, Charity Cannon. *Christine de Pizan: Her Life and Works*. New York: Persea Books, 1984.

Wilson, Katharina M. *Medieval Women Writers*. Athens: University of Georgia Press, 1984.

Wilson, Katharina M., and Elizabeth M. Makowski. *Wykked Wyves and the Woes of Marriage: Misogamous Literature from Juvenal to Chaucer*. Albany: State University of New York Press, 1990.

Windeatt, Barry, ed. *English Mystics of the Middle Ages*. Cambridge: Cambridge University Press, 1994.

Woolf, Rosemary. *The English Religious Lyric in the Middle Ages*. Oxford: Oxford University Press, 1968.

Index

Abelard, Peter, 20, 27
Adam, 71, 84, 128, 149; in *Genesis B*, 34–35. *See also* Eve
adultery, 3, 65; Mary suspected of, 107–8
Advent Lyrics, 32, 33
Aers, David, 184
Alan of Lille, *Plaint of Nature*, 126, 128, 130–32, 135
allegorical reading, 128, 131–33, 135; Pauline, 25; D. W. Robertson Jr. on, 5–6, 8
allegories, women as, 127–30, 139
anchorites, 21–22, 24,167, 178–79, 223
Andreas Capellanus, *De Amore*, 3, 6–7, 126, 129–30, 131–32
Angela of Foligno, 175, 221
Annunciation, 26–27, 136, 180, 183
antifeminism. *See* misogynist stereotypes; misogyny
Aquinas, Thomas, 19
Aristotle, 26, 28, 37, 71, 108, 117, 134, 136, 170
Arthur, 73–75, 92, 157–58
Assembly of Ladies, 193
audience: as active collaborators, 8; of drama, 105–6; of dream vision, 128–29; for *Legend of Good Women*, 150; in Marian lyric, 60–62; Marie de France as, 11, 79; Marie de France's, 81; for romance, 67–69, 76, 78–79, 83,

99, 95; for troubadours, 49–50; women as, 8, 11, 67–68, 78–79, 83, 99, 194–95
Augustine, 8, 18–19, 57, 69, 118, 135, 172, 202
authors, women, 1, 10, 13, 15, 39, 55–60, 79, 84–85, 192–93; as "men," 19–20, 81; self-image of, 23–29. *See also names of individuals*
Avalon, 67, 74, 95–98
Azalais d'Altier, 58

Barratt, Alexandra, 193–94
Beaufort, Margaret, 223
beauty: conventional, 51, 94–95, 98; demonic, 33–34; divine, 34, 36, 40; otherworldly, 97–98
Bec, Pierre, 55
Beckwith, Sarah, 178, 184
Bede, 32
beguines, 22, 109, 167–68, 174–76, 210. *See also* "mystique courtoise"
Belanoff, Pat, 35
Benedict, 20
Benton, John F., 3
Beowulf, 33, 40–46
Bernard of Clairvaux, 24, 108, 118
Bernart de Ventadorn, 51, 52, 54
Béroul, 69–70
Bertran de Born, 51, 53
Bell, Susan Groag, 194